MW01097333

Risk Management

Concepts and Guidance

Fifth Edition

Risk Management

Concepts and Guidance

Fifth Edition

Carl L. Pritchard
PMP, PMI-RMP, EVP

CRC Press
Taylor & Francis Group
Boca Raton London New York

CRC Press is an imprint of the
Taylor & Francis Group, an **informa** business
AN AUERBACH BOOK

CRC Press
Taylor & Francis Group
6000 Broken Sound Parkway NW, Suite 300
Boca Raton, FL 33487-2742

© 2015 by Taylor & Francis Group, LLC
CRC Press is an imprint of Taylor & Francis Group, an Informa business

No claim to original U.S. Government works

Printed on acid-free paper
Version Date: 20140722

International Standard Book Number-13: 978-1-4822-5845-5 (Hardback)

Visit the Taylor & Francis Web site at
http://www.taylorandfrancis.com

and the CRC Press Web site at
http://www.crcpress.com

Contents

PART II RISK MANAGEMENT TECHNIQUES

List of Figures

List of Tables

Preface

Welcome to the future. What we thought might be here tomorrow is now a reality. The challenge for most of us is trying to predict what's coming tomorrow and how we'll deal with it. Risk, as a future phenomenon, is the focus of many business and personal discussions and is perennially part of our decision making. The challenges come when I'm creating a degree of consistency in risk management and risk process. It is part of the eternal quest to control some small component of the future. The latest steps in that quest are reflected in two significant project management documents—*A Guide to the Project Management Body of Knowledge (PMBOK® Guide),* Fifth Edition, and the project management guidance of ISO 21500. These latest guides take into account fresh concepts in risk management, including risk attitudes, risk appetites and futures thinking. They also remain firmly rooted in risk management tradition, dating back half a century. The first edition of this book was in part edited from the publication of the same title by the Defense Systems Management College. Over time, as project risk philosophy has evolved away somewhat from U.S. Department of Defense (DoD) practice, this book has evolved as well.

With the perspectives of the latest project management guidance, the effort here is to keep the focus of this book on the pragmatic orientation of its predecessors. With an emphasis on the need to deploy tools consistently, and affirm a common risk language, there is an opportunity for organizations to use this text to draw out their tools of choice and evolve a risk culture that mirrors their organizational and individual needs. Project management and risk management go hand in hand to ensure that organizations can build in more consistent outcomes, more consistent approaches and more effective responses to the vagaries of life in an uncertain world.

As I teach risk management around the globe, I listen time and again as organizations affirm that their environment is "special." They're right. Each organizational environment is a culture unto itself. As risk managers, our challenge and our objective is to minimize (to the degree practicable) the uncertainty that such unique environments create. This book is structured as a reference guide to serve that objective.

My hope is that it will also serve the objective of providing support for those studying for the PMI-RMP® Risk Management Professional Certification Exam. The book has been modified in this latest edition to ensure the language of the text mirrors the language of that exam.

In keeping with *Risk Management*'s DoD roots, I have retained the format the tables and the matrixes that allow for quick analysis and cross-reference of the contents herein. References to specific analyses still hark back to the 380 surveys initially done for this work, but the original caveat holds true. The risk techniques resulting from this effort have not been evaluated for all circumstances: therefore, you must determine the validity and appropriateness of a particular technique for your own organization and applications. The appendixes have been largely untouched, as most of their content is rooted in history and accepted practice.

My sincere thanks go out to those who have provided invaluable risk insight over the past few years. Most recently, working with Karen Tate, Bruce Falk, LeRoy Ward, Lisa Hammer, David Newman, John Kos, Eric Perlstein and Fran Martin, I have explored risk avenues that might otherwise have gone uncultivated.

I also wish to extend my thanks to the team at my new publisher, Taylor and Francis, for their unwavering support of the book, and for shepherding it (and me) through their publication process. Without the guidance of John Wyzalek, Kat Everett and Amy Blalock, this fifth edition would never have become reality. My thanks also go to Elise Weinger Halprin, graphic designer, for the cover art that gives the book a distinctive flavor all its own.

Author

Carl L. Pritchard is the principal of Pritchard Management Associates and is a widely recognized risk management authority and lecturer. He was the lead chapter author for the risk management chapter of *A Guide to the Project Management Body of Knowledge (PMBOK® Guide)*, Fourth Edition. Mr. Pritchard's publications include courses in risk management, *The Risk Management Memory Jogger* (GOAL/QPC, 2012), as well as *Project Management: Lessons from the Field* (iUniverse, 2009), *The Project Management Communications Toolkit, Second Edition* (Artech House, 2012), *How to Build a Work Breakdown Structure*, and *Precedence Diagramming: Successful Scheduling in the Team Environment*. He co-produced (with ESI's LeRoy Ward) the landmark 9-CD audio collection *The Portable PMP® Exam Prep: Conversations on Passing the PMP® Exam* (Fourth Edition). He is the U.S. correspondent for *Project Manager Today*, a project management journal published in the United Kingdom.

Mr. Pritchard also designs and develops project management programs and was the original architect of ESI International's landmark offerings in project management in a distance-learning format. He is a trainer both online and in the classroom.

In his role as lecturer, Mr. Pritchard speaks regularly at national symposia on project management and serves as the "speaker's coach" for several national conferences, providing guidance on how most effectively to share the project management gospel.

He is active in professional project management associations and is a certified Project Management Professional (PMP), a certified Risk Management Professional (PMI-RMP®), and an Earned Value Professional (EVP), as certified by the Association for the Advancement of Cost Engineering (AACE) International. Mr. Pritchard earned a B.A. degree in journalism from The Ohio State University.

Mr. Pritchard lives with his wife and best friend, Nancy, in Frederick, Maryland, and has two sons, Adam and James. He can be reached via e-mail at carl@carlpritchard.com.

Introduction

This latest edition of *Risk Management: Concepts and Guidance* is designed to provide a look at risk in light of the current information and yet remains grounded in the history of risk practice. As a reference volume, it provides a fundamental introduction on the basics associated with particular techniques; as an educational tool, it clarifies the concepts of risk and how they apply in projects. For those immersed in project management culture, it is now compliant with the Project Management Institute, Inc. publication, *A Guide to the Project Management Body of Knowledge* (*PMBOK® Guide*), Fourth Edition.

When originally published, this material was geared toward the government environment. In the first edition, the effort was to reorient and edit the government material toward a more general business audience. In the second edition, the content was redesigned to align with day-to-day project management practice and the application of risk management in the field coupled, with the latest cutting-edge risk practices.

In the second and third editions, this book aligned with the *PMBOK® Guides* of the respective times (*PMBOK® Guide* 2000 and *PMBOK® Guide*, Third Edition). In this latest edition, very few of the tools have been altered, but the processes have indeed changed. In their fourth and fifth editions of the *PMBOK® Guide*, the Project

Management Institute redefined some of the risk management process terms and slightly modified their practice and interpretation. This volume reflects those changes.

Scope

Risk management is a "method of managing that concentrates on identifying and controlling the areas or events that have a potential of causing unwanted change… it is no more and no less than informed management" (Caver 1985). In keeping with this definition, this book addresses project risk management from the project manager's perspective. It does not cover insurance risk, safety risk, or accident risk outside the project context. *Risk Management* does, however, adopt PMI®'s perspective that risk is both threat *and* opportunity, and it acknowledges that any effective risk management practice must look at the potential positive events that may befall a project, as well as the negatives. Risk management remains an integral part of project management and should be considered a component of any project management methodology rather than an independent function distinct from other project management functions.

Approach

Risk Management uses a holistic approach to risk. That is, risk is examined as a blend of environmental, programmatic, and situational concerns. Although technical issues are a primary source of risk and figure prominently throughout the book, they must be balanced with managing other aspects of the project.

Throughout the text, risk is considered exclusively as a future phenomenon. Risks are events that *may* happen to a project; they are not events that have already occurred. It is vital to consider risk in that context because otherwise, every negative issue or change in plans may potentially be mislabeled as a risk event.

Using This Book

When using *Risk Management*, remember that risk is a complex concept subject to individual perception. Some people take risks, whereas others are more risk averse. Hence, it is difficult to develop universal rules for dealing with risk. Nevertheless, this book includes substantial guidance, structure, and sample handling techniques that follow sound management practice. Although the principles, practices, and theories presented hold true in nearly all situations, yet under certain circumstances, the rules by which risk is evaluated may change drastically. For example, when confronted by an extreme threat, people can do extraordinary things. They will take risks that under ordinary circumstances would be deemed unacceptable. As a result, high-risk projects are not always bad and should not necessarily be avoided. Rather, if risks are accepted, they should be rigorously monitored and controlled, and others should be made aware that those significant risks exist.

Risk Management is structured in a tutorial fashion and is presented in two parts. Part I begins in Chapter 1 by analyzing the systems that can be used to apply risk management. The next chapter defines risk in terms relevant to project management and establishes the basic concepts necessary to understand the nature of risk. Chapter 3 defines the risk management structure and processes that can be applied to all project phases, with an emphasis on risk management planning.

Part II presents specific techniques necessary to successfully implement the processes described in Part I. Using these techniques, the project manager can gain some of the insights essential to proceed with risk management. The techniques evaluated include

Expert interviews
Planning meetings
Risk practice methodology
Documentation reviews
Analogy comparisons
Plan evaluation
Delphi technique
Brainstorming
Crawford Slip Method (CSM)
SWOT analysis
Checklists
Risk breakdown structure
Root cause identification and analysis

Risk registers/tables
Project templates
Assumptions analysis
Decision analysis—expected monetary value
Estimating relationships
Network analysis (excluding PERT)
Program Evaluation and Review Technique (PERT)
Other diagramming techniques
Rating schemes
Urgency assessment
Data quality assessment
Risk modeling
Sensitivity analysis
Monte Carlo simulations (including merge bias and path convergence)
Risk factors
Risk response matrix
Performance tracking and technical performance measurement
Risk reviews and audits
Other common techniques

The appendixes serve as reference materials and provide supporting detail for some of the concepts presented in the text:

Appendix A, Contractor Risk Management: A review of some standard clauses and language incorporated to address contractor risk issues.

Appendix B, An Abbreviated List of Risk Sources: A compilation that serves as an initial risk checklist.

Appendix C, Basic Probability Concepts: A refresher and basic primer for the material in the text.

Appendix D, Quantifying Expert Judgment: A deeper exploration of how to transform qualitative information into quantitative information during expert interviews.

Appendix E, Special Notes on Software Risk: A series of tables designed to support probability and impact analysis in software projects.

Risk Management also provides a glossary, bibliography, and index.

As you work through all this material, remember that risk is a highly personal and unique experience. No two projects will share exactly the same risks. No two project managers will seize the same set of opportunities. As such, the ultimate authority on risk is not any tool or technique addressed between these covers. Rather, the ultimate authority on your project's risk is the project manager: you!

PART I
RISK
PROCESSES AND
PRACTICES
Why Risk Management?

The first part of *Risk Management: Concepts and Guidance* reviews the basic processes and practices associated with risk management in the project environment. It does so in depth, assessing the "rules of the road" in planning for, identifying, assessing, developing responses to, and controlling risk. It is a conceptual overview of how risk should be addressed.

In institutionalizing risk management in an organization, there is inevitably a dread of "analysis paralysis," the fear that so much time will be spent examining concerns and potential problems that none of them is ever resolved. There is also anxiety with regard to administrative overburden. Project managers are frequently among the busiest people in an organization. They are apprehensive that they will have to do even more, and risk management is just one more administrative function they don't have time for.

As a result, risk sometimes becomes a secondary issue. In organizations where success is the norm and failure is a rarity, risk management is relegated to obscurity in the hope that project managers will be able to handle project issues and problems as they occur. Nevertheless, these organizations *should* embrace risk management. Risk remains a secondary issue only as long as an organization's luck holds out or until a grand opportunity is missed. Sooner or later, bad things happen to good projects, and a project manager without a clear strategy will eventually pay a price. Regardless of whether calculated in terms of lost resources, a blown schedule, or a budget overrun, the repercussions of such failure fall directly on the project manager.

Needless to say, there is also a stigma associated with risk management. It is perceived as the "dark side" of a project, and the project manager becomes the prophet of doom and gloom. When applied inconsistently, risk management makes good risk managers appear to be pessimists and naysayers, whereas those who take no proactive posture on risk are regarded as team players. Therefore, the only time a project manager can really succeed as a risk manager, both individually and organizationally, is when that manager has the support of the organization and its practices. That is why a clear, well-developed set of risk practices and protocols is vital to the long-term survival of any project organization.

1

RISK MANAGEMENT PRACTICES

Even the simplest business decision involves some risk. Since every project involves some measure of risk, it is the project's success criteria that often serve as the determining factors for which risks are worth taking and which risks are not. Consider, for example, the decision to drive or fly on a business trip. If cost is the success criterion, then risk determination is simple: compare the costs of flying and driving (compounded by potential inflationary factors). However, another success criterion might be safety, and thus statistics concerning accidents should be evaluated. If punctual arrival is added as a third criterion, then airline on-time statistics, automobile dependability, and road conditions should be evaluated. As other success criteria are added, decision making becomes more complicated and involves more judgment. In the business trip example, increased cost is perhaps an acceptable risk, being late may be unacceptable, and not arriving safely is certainly unacceptable. If project managers do not know what success criteria are driving the project, then they cannot hope to identify the risks that may impede their road to success.

Increasing technical complexity, in turn, increases risk. Every new generation of technology is layered on the old. Nevertheless, most organizations tend to weight decisions heavily toward cost and schedule goals because they are easy to understand. But the effect of cost and schedule decisions related to technical performance risk frequently is unclear. Thus, a formal methodology for evaluating the effects of decision making and foreseeable problems is indispensable and should also help to identify practical and effective workarounds for achieving project goals.

A Systematic Process

Not all projects require a formal risk management approach, but to get the maximum benefit, risk management must become a systematic process applied in a disciplined manner. Put more simply, not every project has to follow every step, but implementing the basic practices should be rote.

Many project managers use intuitive reasoning (guessing) as the starting point in the decision-making process. That's not a bad place to start. However, truly effective managers will look beyond simple reasoning and experience in making decisions that involve significant risk. Even the most experienced project managers have not encountered every risk. There are some risks that they cannot imagine or that do not match their paradigm; and there are still others they just cannot predict. Some risks are so far outside any individual's expectations or experience that those risks cannot possibly be considered without any external inputs.

Numerous inhibitions restrain implementing risk management as a standard project practice. It's unpopular. It points out the negative. It primarily focuses on potentially bad news.

The Project Management Institute, Inc. (PMI®)* has established a six-step set of processes and practices. The PMI approach to risk comprises:

- Plan risk management. In this area, we establish project risk infrastructure and a project-specific risk management plan. This includes creating risk language, tolerances, and thresholds.
- Identify risks. We describe events that will have potentially negative or positive impacts on projects, with descriptions that include the event that may happen and its specific impact.
- Qualify risks. We evaluate risk according to nonnumeric assessment protocols.
- Quantify risks. We evaluate the most significant risks and/or the project as a whole according to their numeric probability and impact.

---

* "PMI" is a service and trademark of the Project Management Institute, Inc., which is registered in the United States and other nations.

- Plan risk responses. We determine, evaluate, and communicate strategies to deal with or preclude risks.
- Monitor and control risks. We put risk management and response plans into action.

The six-step process is not in lockstep with every other process in every other organization. But for the most part, the differences are semantic in nature. In earlier editions of PMI's A *Guide to the Project Management Body of Knowledge* (*PMBOK® Guide*, second edition)[*], risk management was a four-step process. The U.S. military's Defense Acquisition University applies a six-step process that includes planning, identification, analysis, handling, monitoring, and implementation.[†] The Australian government's Department of Commerce applies a six-step process involving establishing context, identifying and defining risks, conducting analysis, conducting evaluations, developing and implementing treatments, and monitoring, reporting, updating, and managing risks.[‡] Regardless of the labels applied, all the processes designed seem to encourage more flexible, adaptive approaches within an organization's project methodology and to facilitate risk management implementation.

All project managers should perform some documented risk management activity, either qualitative or quantitative. All significant projects should include formal, intense risk management activities; smaller, less critical projects may require only a scaled-down risk effort. Thus, the ultimate authority on risk is the project manager, who must make determinations based on the project's cost, schedule, and performance challenges.

Summary

- Risk management is essential for every project.
- Risk management should be a systematic process.
- All projects should have some documented risk management activity.

---

[*] "PMBOK" is a trademark of the PMI, which is registered in the United States and other nations.

[†] https://acc.dau.mil/CommunityBrowser.aspx?id=17607

[‡] http://infostore.saiglobal.com/store/Details.aspx? ProductID=1378670

2
RISK CONCEPTS

Although the terms risk and uncertainty are often used interchangeably, they are not the same. Risk is defined as the "cumulative effect of the probability of uncertain occurrences that may positively or negatively affect project objectives" (Ward 2008, 353). This is unlike uncertainty, which considers only the event and where the probability is completely unknown. The traditional view says that risk is a situation where an event may happen and the frequency of occurrence can be evaluated based on a probability distribution of past occurrences or environmental considerations. Although that observation has limited utility in project management, it does distinguish between risk and uncertainty. With risk, there is a sense of the relative level of event probability. With uncertainty, however, that probability is completely unknown.

To understand whether an event is truly "risky," the project manager must understand the potential effects resulting from its occurrence or nonoccurrence. Determining risk in this manner requires judgment. For example, although an event may have a low likelihood of occurring, the consequences, if it does occur, can be catastrophic. A commercial airline flight illustrates this type of situation: Although the probability of a crash is low, the consequences are generally grave. Although many people feel uncomfortable about flying because of the consequences of failure, most people do not consider flying a high risk. This example also emphasizes the principle that risk greatly depends on individual perception.

The nature of any given risk is composed of three fundamental elements: the event, the probability, and the severity (or impact) (see Figure 2.1). The event is the description of the risk as it may occur. Event descriptions are crucial. The probability and impact of a plane crash at the gate are far different from the probability and impact of a plane crash from an altitude of 30,000 feet. Thus, risk managers

7

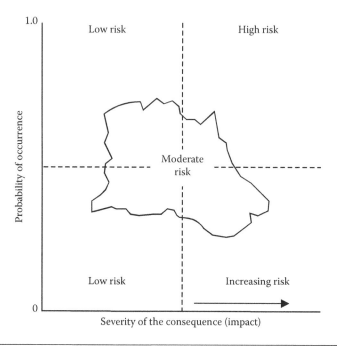

Figure 2.1   Concept of risk.

must explore the nature of the risk event itself before they can begin to examine risk probability and impact. Without a clear definition of the risk event, ascertaining probability and impact become far more difficult. As a rule, risk events should be described in full sentences. A template for such a sentence can be as simple as: (Event) may happen to the project, causing (impact to the project objectives). Such a consistent approach to the risk definition affords a much easier journey through the remainder of the risk process.

After the risk event has been defined, we must establish the potential severity of its impact. How badly could it hurt the objective? Only when we have a sense of the degree of impact under consideration can probability be assessed. Statistical data and probability theory play important roles in determining this variable. However, because projects in the traditional project environment are unique, it is sometimes difficult to ascertain whether an applicable historical record for comparison exists.

In most organizations and for most projects, there is little disagreement about the level of risk if the variables are classified as follows:

- Low probability and low impact equal low risk
- High probability and high impact equal high risk
- High probability and low impact equal low risk (to the project's overall success)

However, as you move toward the low probability/high- impact quadrant of the figure, determining the risk level becomes more subjective and requires guidelines. A project with many moderate-risk items may be considered high risk, whereas a project with a few high-risk items may have a lower overall risk rating. These situations usually require some type of modeling to ascertain the project risk level. Consequently, many attempts have been made to model this subjective evaluation of risk mathematically. Some statisticians and project managers may apply probability distributions (see Appendix C), whereas others may not.

As stakeholders rate risks, disagreements can occur. Although project managers must sometimes rely on technical experts in the risk management process, they must also be prepared to make the final judgment themselves. Some guidelines on rating risks are included in Chapter 3 under "Risk Quantification." And whereas it is important to examine the quantifiable probabilities for loss, an additional item to consider is opportunity. If no real opportunity exists, then there is no reason to pursue a risky activity. However, as the potential gain increases, so does the threshold for accepting risk.

Risk Attitudes and Appetites

In the past few years, risk attitude and appetite have moved to the fore in many project discussions. Stakeholder risk ratings and evaluations are in many ways based on these two considerations. Risk appetite reflects the environmental willingness to face certain risks (or not face them). Appetite is the degree to which organizations, project teams, and individuals can "stomach" or tolerate certain types or degrees of risk.

While appetite can be a driving force in terms of organizational behavior and overall willingness to take on certain risks, the ultimate determinant is risk attitude. Every individual has risk attitude. Some people would never dream of skydiving. Others embrace it as a thrilling opportunity. No matter the pressures from outside or the appetites of those around them, attitude prevails. Ideally, some alignment between organizational risk appetites and individual risk attitudes should exist.

Classifying Risk

To the project manager, risks are primarily rooted in the process to deliver a specified product or service at a specified time for a specified cost. A properly planned project will provide the project manager with some reserve funds and slack time to work around unanticipated problems and still meet the original cost, schedule, and performance goals. But a wide variety of problems can keep the manager from meeting project objectives: the product may not attain the performance level specified, the actual costs may be too high, or delivery may be too late. (There is, of course, a risk that the original cost, schedule, and performance goals were unattainable, unrealistic, or conflicting.)

To make it manageable, risk must be classified. The fifth edition of the *PMBOK® Guide* incorporates a risk breakdown structure to draw emphasis toward such classification (*PMBOK® Guide* 2013, 317). The Software Engineering Institute, in its *Taxonomy-Based Risk Identification* (Carr et al. 1993), also broke down risk into classes and subclasses. Moreover, the original edition of this book, created by the Defense Systems Management College (DSMC), emphasized five primary facets of risk. What is important, however, is not to select one particular scheme, but rather to choose approaches that mirror an organization's risk needs.

Risk Breakdown Structure

The fifth edition of the *PMBOK® Guide* (2013) not only examines the importance of categorizing risk but also explores the notion that risks are both organization- and project specific, based on the environment and culture. In earlier editions, this risk text examined breaking down risks by facets (characterizing the U.S. Department of Defense environment and culture) and using tools such as the affinity diagram (discussed in Chapter 15) to identify the environment and culture of a specific project. Although the risk breakdown structure is dealt with in much greater depth later (see Chapter 15), its existence is important to note here, because it reflects a shift in risk management practice from generic categories (as were found in the original *PMBOK®Guide*) to a set of categories that are more germane to a given project. These categories become crucial to effective risk management, as ultimately, they reflect the sources of risk on a project or in a project organization.

Risk Taxonomy

In their groundbreaking *Taxonomy-Based Risk Identification*, Carr et al. generated a risk hierarchy for the software development industry that remains peerless. The beauty of their analysis is invaluable. Not only does their discussion list the categories of risk that they identified across myriad software projects, but it also provides in-depth explanations of what the categories mean and the environmental considerations inherent in organizations plagued by problems in a specific category.

Project managers seeking to build a more comprehensive understanding of the nature of risk in their organizations and to generate categories that are helpful and supportive of risk identification and qualification efforts can regard this work as a benchmark of how these goals can be achieved most effectively. In addition to classifying the risk categories, their subsets, and sub-subsets, the taxonomy even catalogs specific binary (yes/no) questions to help project managers determine the likelihood that a given area, subset, or category is endemic in their projects. Again, project managers who generate their own risk breakdowns or taxonomies would be prudent to consider the potential efficacy of such an effort.

Risk Facets

The original *Risk Management: Concepts and Guidance* (Defense Systems Management College 1986) classified risk into five facets:

- Technical (performance related): Appendix B contains an abbreviated list of technical risk areas. It does not list the types of risks by processes, components, parts, subassemblies,

assemblies, subsystems, and systems for all the many associated integration design tasks. Nor does it address all possible aspects of performance, which vary widely from project to project. As the design architecture, performance, other requirements, and project constraints become known on a given project, a more detailed list of risks should be prepared based on project-specific information.

- Programmatic (performance related): Programmatic risk is the risk associated with obtaining and using applicable resources and activities that can affect project direction, but that may be outside the project manager's control. Generally, programmatic risks are not directly related to improving the state of the art. Programmatic risks are grouped into categories based on the nature and source of factors that have the potential to disrupt the project's implementation plan. They include disruptions caused
  - By decisions made at higher levels of authority directly relative to the project
  - By events or actions that affect the project but are not directed specifically toward it
  - Primarily by a failure to foresee production-related problems
  - By imperfect capabilities
  - Primarily by a failure to foresee problems other than those included in the first four categories
- Supportability (environment related): Supportability risk is the risk associated with fielding and maintaining systems or processes that are currently being developed or that have been developed and are being deployed. Supportability risk comprises both technical and programmatic aspects.
- Cost
- Schedule

Since cost and schedule risks frequently serve as indicators of project status, they are treated somewhat differently from the others. That's also because they tend to be *impacts* of other risks, in addition to being risk sources themselves.

There are few risks that can be labeled true cost or schedule risks. But more often than not, cost or schedule uncertainty reflects technical, programmatic, and supportability risk. Some of the truest schedule risks are those that are driven by dependencies (relationships with other activities). It is noteworthy that in many instances, it is not a single risk event but rather a series of dependent risk events that generate the greatest pain in a project scenario. This ties to the old axiom that "when it rains, it pours," inasmuch as a single schedule delay may drive another and another and so on; and in the haste to rectify earlier delays, even greater schedule risks can evolve. Similarly, in the cost environment, relationships may again spawn greater risk as efforts to perform with increasingly meager cost margins (caused by earlier dependent risks) thus create cost behaviors that otherwise would have been deemed unacceptable.

With cost and schedule indicators, at some juncture, there is a need to identify the specific triggers that will cause changes in a project organization's behavior. Triggers are those conditions that indicate that a risk event is either about to come to pass or has come to pass. For example, a budget overrun of 0.05% may not be the cause for concern in the organization and may not be indicative of problems in the offing. A budget overrun of 5%, however, may be wholly unacceptable. At some point, triggers are established to set off alarms that risk is imminent.

In situations where risks seem insurmountable, alternatives can sometimes be found in examining the outcomes rather than the sources of risk. Still, having an understanding of both is crucial.

Other Risk Categories

There are yet other ways to examine the sources and categories of risk. In the 1987 *PMBOK® Guide*, risk categories included

- External unpredictable: Issues that loom at the doorstep of any given project are the classic "act of God" risks. Natural disasters, capricious acts of the government, societal upheaval, or environmental change can happen without warning, thus changing the entire tenor of a project.

  In recent years, an emphasis on continuity of operations plans (COOPs) has highlighted a shift in cultural concerns about the external unpredictable. Such plans detail how an

organization will deal with major crises that cannot be foreseen, but which are sufficiently cataclysmic to sever ties to
existing structures and systems.

- External predictable: External predictable risks are those
externally driven problems that can be foreseen. Although
the total impact may be difficult or impossible to discern, it
is possible to work through the issue in depth and examine
potential outcomes and potential time frames.

- Internal (nontechnical): By virtue of their existence, organizations generate risk. Levels of bureaucracy, staffing policies, administrative procedures, and basic internal procedures
drive certain risks.

- Technical: As the name implies, technical performance drives
technical risks. Given the current marketplace of ideas and
approaches, technical risks increase dramatically as new technologies are brought to bear in any environment or industry.

- Legal: When the earliest version of the *PMBOK® Guide*
(1987) was published, legal risks were regarded as having
sufficient weight to merit their own category—and with
good reason. Within projects, legal risks are legion because
many are contractually based and all serve a body of widely
varied stakeholders. Together with the societal propensity
for lawsuits (particularly in the United States), the unique
nature of projects makes them an open and ready target for
the litigious.

Sample risks or risk sources from each category are shown in
Table 2.1.

These categories shifted slightly in the 2000 edition of the *PMBOK® Guide* thus becoming

- Technical, quality, and performance: The categories of technical, quality, and performance mirror the category designated
"technical" in the earlier *PMBOK® Guide* (1987) and the
original DSMC text. However, with our increasing emphasis on quality and performance, there is recognition that the
level of quality requested and the capabilities of the system
can drive additional risks.

Table 2.1   Risk Categories and Sources Based on *PMBOK® Guide* 1987

RISK CATEGORY	SAMPLE RISKS/RISK SOURCES	
External Unpredictable	Unplanned regulatory change	Site zoning or access denied
	Flood	Earthquake
	Sabotage	Vandalism
	Social upheaval	Environmental catastrophe
	Political unrest	Unpredictable financial collapse
External Predictable	Financial market fluctuation	Raw materials demand
	Competitive shifts	Product/service value
	Inflation	Taxation
	Safety	Health regulation
Internal (Nontechnical)	Procurement process delays	Team member inexperience
	Senior staff changes	Integration mistakes
	Poor human resources coordination	Access limitations
		Late deliveries
	Cash flow concerns	
Technical	Technology shifts	Design imprecision
	Quality demand changes	Requirement changes
	Productivity limitations	Improper implementation
	Operational demand changes	Reliability challenges
Legal	License challenges	Contract failures
	Patent litigation	Staff lawsuits
	Customer lawsuits	Government action

- Project management: Project managers are not solely responsible for project management, but they must take responsibility for its outcomes. Project management risks include the risks of poor project plans, poor resource allocation, poor budget planning, and poor schedules—all of which lead to varying levels of stakeholder dissatisfaction. The creation of this category places the onus on project managers to bring together disparate stakeholders in the process and to unite them behind a single vision as to what the plan(s) should be.
- Organizational: Project management's classic dilemma is that project managers are burdened with extensive responsibility but have no authority to carry it out. Organizational risks directly point to that issue because they are primarily bureaucratic in nature. They are borne both out of organizations' inability to support projects and their excessive zeal in dictating how projects should be carried out.

Table 2.2   Risk Categories and Sources Based on *PMBOK® Guide* 2000

RISK CATEGORY	SAMPLE RISKS/RISK SOURCES	
Technical, quality, and performance	Higher performance goals	New industry standards
	Technology shifts	Complex technology
	Platform changes	Unproven technology
Project management	Poor time allocation	Poor resource allocation
	Poor budget planning	Poor project planning
Organizational	Weak infrastructure	Intraorganizational resource conflict
	Unclear organizational objectives	Shifting funding availability
External	Legal challenges	Natural disasters
	Shifting customer goals	Regulatory shifts

- External: Discussed earlier in both of their forms (predictable and unpredictable), while external risks are always a component of the discussion, they are not a risk type where the project manager has direct influence on either the likelihood of their occurrence or their impact.

Sample risks and sources of risk are shown in Table 2.2.

In the latest *PMBOK® Guide* (2013), there are no preordained categories. These were superseded by the introduction of the risk breakdown structure. Although PMI® has chosen to eliminate prescribed categories, organizations that wrestle with "where to start" on risk should not. A prescribed set of categories can frequently open the discussion as to what concerns may potentially plague projects based on organizational culture and environment. Preordained categories may also help to emphasize the risk drivers rather than the risk indicators.

Taxonomically Developed Risks

Organizations and individuals have their own tendencies when it comes to risk. Some organizations, types of projects, and even individuals seem to attract risk like a magnet. Normally, it's not due to an individual or project but rather the environment. Since environmental conditions are somewhat predictable, so too are the categories of risk common to a given environment. The advantage of decomposing risks into a hierarchy to support a given environment is that the risk categories then help establish the nature of risks common to the project. This is discussed in greater depth in Chapter 15.

In later discussions, it will become more evident why the varied (and perhaps seemingly arbitrary) categories and facets of risk are critical to effective risk management organizations. For now, suffice it to say that these categories provide a sound context in which risk management can be framed. By applying these categories, managers can ensure a level of consistency for identifying and reviewing the breadth of risks that their organizations face. Without them, it becomes increasingly likely for one particular risk category to be favored to the exclusion of the others.

Other Relevant Considerations

There are two other areas worthy of mention when discussing risk concepts in terms of projects. Both deal with organizational management structure.

Risk Management Perspectives

Project risk management must be viewed from two vantage points:

- Short-term perspective: Dealing with the current project phase and the immediate future
- Long-term perspective: Dealing with anything beyond the short term

Like many other aspects of risk management, the distinction between the two perspectives is somewhat unclear, and further explanation is needed to define and justify the separation. The short-term perspective normally refers to managing risk related to satisfying the immediate needs of the project, such as "This is the performance level I need to achieve today, and how are my contractors managing to achieve this?" On the other hand, the long-term perspective deals with "What can I do today to ensure that the project, in the end, will be a success?" This perspective might include, among other things, introducing engineering issues related to project support and production into the design process earlier in the project.

Short- and long-term perspectives are closely linked in achieving the desired performance level in the short term, but the project manager may be forced to sacrifice long-term capability. Projects that require new approaches or new tools may suffer in the short term yet may have higher productivity and performance levels in the long term. Nevertheless, as with any good management decisions, short- and long-term implications must be well understood. The project manager can provide a risk response early only if these implications are known.

Another look at the two perspectives is illustrated in Figure 2.2, which depicts an overall design selected for a project having certain risk elements. This was a decision that obviously had long-term implications. The current task for the project manager is to complete this

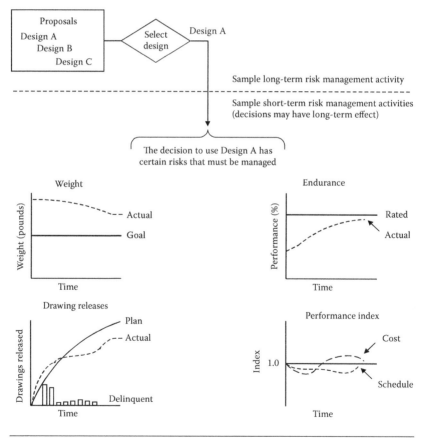

Figure 2.2   Short-term and long-term risk perspectives.

design within the existing resource constraints. The project manager has selected some technical, cost, and schedule parameters to manage risk on an operational, day-to-day basis (short-term risk management). While focusing on the short term, the project manager must also keep an eye on long-term implications.

Computer buyers face this same quandary on a daily basis. A low-cost option is attractive for its price but may not have the support of a more expensive unit. A midrange computer may have the support but not the technical capability to handle newly released versions of software. An expensive unit may have all the features and support desired but may not have the management's endorsement for the long term. Thus, achieving a balance between short- and long-term perspectives is indeed a daunting task.

Realities of Project Management

Ideally, the same management team will stay with a project from the earliest phases through closeout. However, because ideal conditions rarely exist, a given project will likely employ several management and staff teams. As a result, the transition in project management personnel often creates voids in the risk management process. These voids, in turn, create knowledge gaps, whence valuable information collected earlier in the project is lost. Precious time must therefore be spent becoming familiar with the project, often at the sacrifice of long-term planning and risk management. A formal system for recording, analyzing, and acting on project risk facilitates the transition process, and when done properly, forces long-term risk management. The formal risk management approach is covered in Chapter 3.

Although it is desirable to make decisions based on long-term implications, it is not always feasible. The project manager is often forced to act on short-term considerations. One reason for this—a change in personnel—has already been mentioned. Another reason is project advocacy. Sudden shifts in organizational priorities can wreak havoc on long-term plans (which is a risk area in itself). This results in short-term actions to adjust to new priorities. Often, these decisions are made before long-term effects can be thoroughly evaluated. And finally, in some instances, long-term effects are not always apparent at the time a decision must be made.

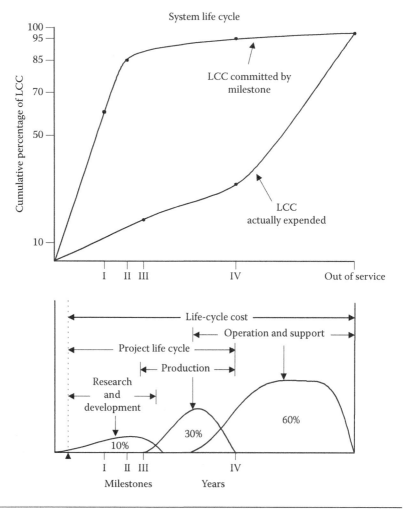

Figure 2.3 Life-cycle cost.

Day-to-day operational risks must be addressed to complete any given phase of a project. As much as possible, the solutions developed to handle these risks must be examined from a long-term viewpoint and must provide the project manager with a strong, structured argument to defend his or her position. As many studies have pointed out, actions taken early in a project's development have a major effect on the overall performance and cost over the life of the project. One example is illustrated in Figure 2.3 (DSMC 1985).

Summary

- Risk considers both probability and impact as aspects of the risk event.
- Rating risk is a subjective process requiring strict guidelines.
- There are multiple ways to categorize risk, but regardless of the scheme, the categories will be strongly interrelated.
- Risk has both long-term and short-term perspectives.

3

THE RISK MANAGEMENT STRUCTURE

This chapter focuses on defining and explaining the elements of risk management and presents the recommended overall structure for implementing risk management. In the past, several different structures and definitions have been used for basically the same concept, which has been a source of continuing confusion. Figure 3.1 reflects a structure that mirrors the perspective of the Project Management Institute's *PMBOK® Guide* (2013) within the organizational environmental context.

Risk Management Planning

Risk—present in some form and to some degree in most human activity—is characterized by the following principles:

- Risk is usually (at least) partially unknown.
- Risk changes with time.
- Risk is manageable in the sense that the application of human action may change its form and degree of effect.

The purpose of risk management planning is simply to compel project managers to devote organized, purposeful thought to project risk management and to provide organizational infrastructure to aid them as they attempt to

- Determine which risks are worth an investment of time and energy
- Isolate and optimize risk
- Eliminate negative risk and enhance positive risk where possible and practical
- Develop alternative courses of action

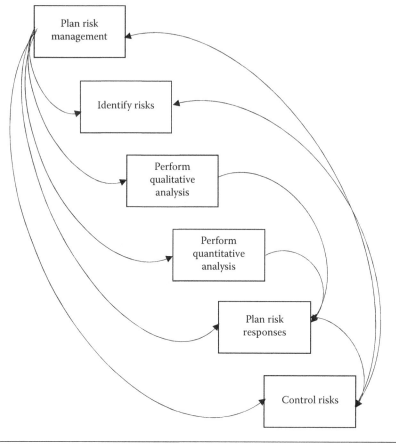

Figure 3.1   Risk management processes (updated).

- Establish time and money reserves to cover threats that cannot be mitigated
- Ensure that organizational and project cultural risk boundaries are not breached

As an integral part of normal project planning and management, risk planning is sensibly done and repeated and should occur at regular intervals. Some of the more obvious times for evaluating the risk management plan include

- In preparation for major decision points and changes
- In preparation for and immediately following evaluations
- As significant unplanned change occurs that influences the project

Most major projects are guided by a series of plans that provide the rationale and intended processes through which projects will be executed. A risk management plan is recommended as part of this suite of guiding documents. Such a plan would publish the results or the latest status of the risk management planning process.

Compared to some other plans, risk planning has not been developed as much in terms of content and format, which allows project managers some latitude to establish documents that suit their situation. One approach to the content of a risk management plan is illustrated in Table 3.1, the highlights of which are described in the following paragraphs.

Description and Project Summary

This material should be the same in all the project's supporting plans. Together, they should provide a frame of reference for understanding the operational need, the mission, and the major functions of

Table 3.1   Sample Risk Management Plan Outline

Part 1, Description	4.3 Timing
1.1 Objective (from charter)	4.4 Metrics
1.2 Project	4.5 Thresholds
1.2.1 Project description (from work breakdown structure or WBS)	4.6 Implementation
	4.6.1 Evaluation
1.2.2 Key functions (from charter and WBS)	4.6.2 Tracking
1.3 Required operational characteristics	4.6.3 Roles/responsibilities
1.4 Required technical characteristics	
1.5 Required support (roles/responsibilities)	Part 5, Process approaches
	5.1 Identify risks
Part 2, Project summary	5.2 Qualify risks
2.1 Summary requirements	5.3 Quantify risks
2.2 Management	5.4 Plan risk responses
2.3 Integrated schedule	5.5 Control risks
Part 3, Risk environment	Part 6, Other relevant plans
3.1 Organizational risk management policy	Part 7, Risk governance
3.1.1 Internal	
3.1.2 Client organization	Part 8, Approach summary
3.2 Stakeholder risk tolerances	
3.3 Organizational risk management plan template(s)	Part 9, Bibliography
	Part 10, Approvals
Part 4, Approach to risk management	
4.1 Definitions	
4.2 Practices	

the project. They should include the basic inputs to risk management planning, some of which are common to many other processes of project management. Specifically, the charter, the project roles and responsibilities, and the work breakdown structure (WBS) are crucial to establish the terms of the project, as well as the potential parameters of project risk. They should also include the key operational and technical characteristics of the project deliverables.

The conventional elements of the charter and the WBS afford clear descriptions of the project and the nature of the deliverables. Such clarity of description will prove invaluable in ascertaining the relative magnitude of the project risk management effort. On smaller projects, sometimes, the temptation exists to completely circumvent the risk management process. Although the process should be scaled back to reflect the level of project effort, risk management can never be completely ignored. A well-crafted project charter and WBS will provide information on the scope essential for determining how much risk management will be sufficient and how much risk management effort constitutes "too much."

The roles and responsibilities information is also essential. Skilled, savvy, and well-practiced team members can frequently remove significant levels of risk from the project. They can render the need for intense project monitoring virtually moot. In contrast, less skilled team members may have neither the background, understanding, nor appreciation of potential concerns and may, as a result, increase the requirement for intensely procedural risk management.

Risk Environment

In every project, there is a risk environment. There are threats that must be faced and opportunities that may present themselves, and there are myriad different ways to deal with them. Risk management planning is the effort, organizationally, to draw together the risk policies, practices, and procedures of the organization into a cohesive whole that will address the nature of risk peculiar to the project. In addition to the inputs of the WBS, project summary, and roles and responsibilities, there are inputs specific to risk planning. According to the Project Management Institute, they are the scope statement, the cost, schedule and communications management plans, organizational process assets, and environmental factors. The process assets can be reduced to the organizational risk management policy, stakeholder risk tolerances, and a template for the organization's risk management plan. In many organizations, these conventions simply do not exist. Nevertheless, they are essential to risk management success.

Not only must the environment for the producing organization be considered, the client organization and their environment must also be taken into account. Their risk culture may, in some situations, supersede that of the producing organization.

The levels of depth and detail and their effect on the project risk management effort should be communicated in the organizational risk management policies. In some organizations, such policies are scant, if they exist at all. Risk management policies will offer insight into the amount of information and risk reporting that is required on projects, as well as general guidance on risk qualification, quantification, and response development. That guidance may include, but is not limited to, organizational definitions and descriptions of approaches to the risk procedure, guidance on risk reserve allocation, explanations of risk probability and impact descriptions, and clarification on proper application of risk response strategies.

Stakeholder risk tolerances are a vital input because different members of the customer, project, and management teams may have different perspectives on what constitutes "acceptable" risk. This is rarely preordained or predetermined. Project managers must gather this information by vigorously pursuing the key stakeholders to identify what they are and are not willing to accept. This extends beyond simple thresholds for cost and schedule. Some stakeholders have passionate perspectives on project visibility. Some want to ensure the project is regularly in the public eye and consistently in the best possible light. Others, by contrast, want to ensure that project publicity is kept to an absolute minimum and consider any public disclosure to be "bad exposure." Thresholds can be established for a variety of issues, ranging from satisfaction survey responses to team attrition to technology exposure. Failure to develop an acute awareness of the stakeholders' tolerances may lead to unidentified risks or improperly assigned impact levels.

In some organizations, risk management is sufficiently well entrenched that there are standard forms and formats for risk management plans. This is more common in organizations where there is a project management office (PMO) or project support office (PSO). These formats encourage consistency and knowledge transfer as risk management history is conveyed continually from project to project and from team to team.

These inputs may take some time to amass. Gathering these data is frequently done in concurrence with other project efforts, such as budget estimating and high-level scheduling. Ideally, these efforts would be done in concurrence with the planning steps as the insights from risk management planning may have a significant impact on the outcomes.

Approach to Risk Management

This section is actually developed during planning meetings with the project team. This plan may be both specific to the project risks and the framework in which these risks will be addressed. (Project risks are addressed more thoroughly in the subsequent steps in this process.) During these meetings, team members should work to build documentation that will encourage consistent adherence to the risk management policy and procedure within the organization and to ensure that there is an unchanging vision as to the levels of risk that are deemed tolerable. Participants should review all available inputs and acknowledge (and document) any deviation from organizational practices.

The meeting (and subsequent research and analysis efforts) should produce an overall risk management plan—that is, a risk approach within which the project will function. This framework includes oversight on the definitions, practices, risk categories, timing, metrics, risk thresholds, evaluation, tracking, and roles and responsibilities associated with the risk management effort. The structure for the risk register is another vital component of this plan, and should be established or affirmed at this stage of the process. A preliminary risk budget may also be developed, although more in-depth documentation and budget support is frequently developed during or after risk quantification.

Definition of terms is crucial. People differ in their interpretations of terms such as risk, probability, workaround, contingency, and most risk language. Thus, creating a common lexicon and how it will be applied will ensure that risk processes are managed consistently.

Organizational risk practices should be distilled to a methodology specific to the project. Such a methodology may include a variety of types of information, but at a minimum, should include the frequency of risk reviews, tools to be deployed, and a list of valid resources for project risk data. Methodologies for risk management will not be identical from project to project, but there should be some similarities within an organization. Organizations should strive to use tools consistently and ensure that their outputs are recorded in common repositories. Such effective storage of project risk information leads to more effective knowledge transfer over the long term and across projects.

Risk categories common to the organization are identified to provide a sense of the prevalent areas of concern and prevalent sources of risk. These categories may take the form of a hierarchical decomposition known as a risk breakdown structure or RBS (see Figure 3.2). The RBS allows for a common understanding of the risk endemic to an organization and how risks can be categorized. All RBSs are project specific. But because risk is frequently common within an organization, the RBS from one project in an organization may frequently appear very similar when compared to that of other projects within the same organization. Even so, the RBS may vary from project to

Figure 3.2   Risk breakdown structure.

project as each project can have risk areas specific to the nature of the work being performed.

Risk timing is the effort to establish consistency in the frequency of risk reporting, reevaluation, and review throughout the project life cycle. In some cases, short-term projects may require a risk review only at the beginning and end of the project. However, more involved or longer-term efforts may require risk reviews at a variety of interim points. The frequency of these points varies according to project complexity.

Optimally, risk metrics are an organizational phenomenon. Risk metrics relate to the specific organizational interpretations of issues such as risk probability, risk impact, and related qualitative and quantitative measures. These metrics address how project team members will determine the threshold for high probability and what rate of occurrence denotes low probability. Similarly, these scoring practices set down the differences among low, moderate, and high impacts on issues that include budget, cost, requirements, organizational politics, and customer relations. This ensures that team members share the same point of view on levels of risk acceptability.

The interplay among these high, medium, and low metrics can be displayed in a probability-impact matrix (see Table 3.2). Such a chart can highlight the relative weights of those risks that are high probability, high impact and those that are low probability, high impact. It allows for the comparison of weights to determine which areas will

Table 3.2 Probability-Impact Matrix

	Relative Weight = Probability Times Impact		
High probability (more likely than not)	High–low (later response)	High–medium (third response)	High–high (first response)
Moderate probability (above low, but not high)	Moderate–low (later response)	Moderate–medium (later response)	Moderate–high (second response)
Low probability (seen it happen once)	Low–low (later response)	Low–medium (later response)	Low–high (second response)
Remote probability (never seen it, but it could happen)	Remote–low (later response)	Remote–medium (later response)	Remote–high (third response)
	Low impact (as defined in the qualitative analysis)	Medium impact (as defined in the qualitative analysis)	High impact (as defined in the qualitative analysis)

be dealt with first after qualitative risk analysis has been conducted. Such matrices can be established qualitatively or quantitatively, but the emphasis is on building the information so that there is a shared understanding of which risks will be addressed first and which, based on their relative probability and impact, will be dealt with next in the order.

In addition to the probability and impact of individual risk events, risk thresholds must be considered. Thresholds are those barriers that, when crossed, trigger specific action by the management or the project team. By setting thresholds in advance of the project, team members can share an understanding of when certain actions are required.

Risk budgets are those funds allocated to deal with risk either proactively or reactively. Risk budgets may take the form of contingency reserve funds set aside to deal with risks after they have occurred. In some organizations, the risk budget may also be deployed to fund mitigation strategies or to generate a richer documentation set related to the risks. However, the key to effective risk budgeting is that the use of any funds drawn from the risk budget must be recorded to build the lessons-learned database for the project.

Any discussion of risk evaluations in the plan will establish the format, level, and frequency of risk reassessments. Establishing such formats again ensures consistency in terms of data depth, data retention, and understanding of critical risk information on the project.

Application Issues and Problems

This section includes the procedures for the following processes (at the project level):

- Identify risks
- Perform qualitative analysis
- Perform quantitative analysis
- Plan risk responses
- Monitor and control risks

Other Relevant Plans

Every major project should be governed by a set of plans, including the project plan. Other plans may include quality, communications, contracting, testing, and training (to mention only a few). Typically, these plans are not written from a risk viewpoint. But when read with risk in mind, they provide valuable information and may suggest considerations for risk. These plans should be reviewed before, during, and after preparing the risk management plan. Moreover, the risk management plan may also suggest items to be addressed in the other plans. Although the risk management plan deals with analyzing and managing risk, risk should be identified and highlighted in any plan.

Risk Governance

In many ways, the elements of oversight and control that dictate project risk governance have been addressed by the paragraphs above. But there are other considerations that may be included here as well. Escalation protocols are often overlooked as a component of risk management plans, but can provide clear direction on how and when different organizational echelons should be drawn into the risk process. Continuity of operations plans (COOPs), an organizational "must-have" since 9/11, need to be integrated into the risk processes, and may be seen as a core component of governance. Since COOPs address the organizational need to have plans for *any* eventuality, there is an inextricable link between them and the project risk management plans. In many ways, the risk management plan can be seen as an extension of the COOP, in that the COOP cannot address the unique nature of individual projects, while the risk management plan (RMP) can. Risk governance, as the name implies, is the process(es) by which risk practices are applied, uniformly, from a managerial level. The key in this component of the risk management plan is to address any managerial actions, interfaces, and relationships that are not otherwise addressed in the risk management plan as a whole.

Approach Summary

In developing the risk management plan, there may be global concepts and principles that will be applied. However, such thinking may not be self-evident in the supporting documentation. Any overarching goals or driving objectives should be clearly identified as a summary statement. Summary statements should not provide any new information but should instead capture the essence of the strategies reflected in the information already provided.

Bibliography

Perhaps, the most important aspect of any plan bibliography is the location and identification of any supporting documentation. If such information is retained electronically, then the bibliography should include the file names and server locations. Because of the ever-fluctuating nature of data storage, a schedule should be set for regular bibliography reviews to ensure the integrity of the information package.

Approvals

Approvals for all risk documentation should be identified here. These approvals should include, but not be limited to, the sanctioning authority for the risk management plan, as well as a list of names and titles for those individuals responsible for authorizing updates to the plan and its supporting documentation.

Identify Risks

A critical step in the risk management process, risk identification is an organized, thorough approach to finding real risks associated with a project. It is not, however, a process of inventing highly improbable scenarios in an effort to cover every conceivable possibility. Risks cannot be assessed or managed until realistic possibilities are identified and described in an understandable way.

Perhaps, the key failing of project managers in risk identification is the actual description of risk events. Many project managers attempt to identify risks simply as "schedule" or "cost." (The schedule in and of itself is not a risk.) A risk event is something that may happen to the benefit or detriment of the project. (If it happens in favor of the project, some describe it as an "opportunity event.") Risk events are most effective when they are described clearly and in depth. A high-quality risk event description will describe the potential occurrence and how it would influence the project. On a construction project, the risk that a "wall will collapse, causing a delay" is different from the risk that a "wall will collapse, killing someone."

To carry out risk identification effectively, basic project documentation must be in place. The project charter, scope statement, and project management plan (including the WBS) need to be available to build a thorough list of risks. Without these elements as a frame of reference, it's impossible to effectively evaluate the risks on a project. The risk management plan and the organizational environment also must be clearly understood to conduct risk identification. These establish the environment in which the risks will be evaluated. The risk management plan may also identify specific risk identification practices that are either preferred or rejected by the organization as part of their risk culture. All this information can spur thinking about different risk issues and concerns when evaluated using the tools and techniques of risk identification.

The tools and techniques that are applied in risk identification are as varied as the projects they serve. However, some groups of tool and technique types are most commonly applied. According to PMI®, they include documentation reviews, information-gathering techniques (including SWOT analysis), checklists, assumptions analysis, and diagramming techniques.

Documentation Reviews

On the surface, this would seem to be an easy task. However, because different stakeholders have different perspectives, it becomes a thought-provoking and controversial process. For example, a comparison of the requirements and the WBS will often provide a gap analysis, identifying risks that requirements will not be met. A study of the high-level schedule may point to unrealistic deadlines or potential performance gaps. A review of the procurement plan or resource plan may highlight shortcomings in organizational or project capability or capacity. Reviews of organizational or project strategy documentation may illustrate potential disconnects between the project's and the organization's purpose.

Information-Gathering Techniques

Expert interviews, analogy comparisons, the Delphi technique, brainstorming, the Crawford slip method, and root cause identification analysis are especially useful techniques in risk identification. The objective is to obtain straightforward, clear narrative statements describing project risks. Mathematic techniques are inappropriate here because the objective is to gather data about what might happen rather than the degrees of probability and impact. While more of a presentation technique than an information-gathering technique, SWOT (strengths, weaknesses, opportunities, and threats) analysis is a powerful interpretive tool for sharing information about the risk information gathered.

Checklists

The purpose of any project is to achieve a specified set of goals. The project must be scrutinized systematically to identify those events that may reasonably occur and threaten project goals. The search should emphasize showstoppers—that is, those events that will have a major effect on the project. Checklists frequently reflect the organization's risk history and those risks that have had a sufficiently pervasive effect to be included as part of this regular review.

The top-level risk matrix (see Table 3.3) is a tool designed to organize this process. It can be developed by using any of the sets of risk

Table 3.3 Top-Level Risk Matrix

	PROJECT PHASE			
RISK CATEGORY	CONCEPT	DEVELOPMENT	IMPLEMENTATION	TERMINATION
Technical				
Goals				
Strategies				
Risks				
Cost				
Goals				
Strategies				
Risks				
Schedule				
Goals				
Strategies				
Risks				
Customer relationship				
Goals				
Strategies				
Risks				
Politics				
Goals				
Strategies				
Risks				

categories (or the risk breakdown structure) and is applied at the total project level as a starting point. The concept can be refined and carried out to a greater detail as needed. In an organization with well-developed risk practices, specific questions will be developed to reflect organizational propensities for risk as they relate to the risk category's goals and strategies. The top-level risk matrix can also be used as a starting point to identify positive risks (or opportunities). In organizations where opportunities are identified, they may be identified at a higher level than threats, inasmuch as some organizations are willing only to pursue opportunities that have broad implications for organizational or project influence.

Assumptions Analysis

The mere documentation of assumptions often drives project teams to a clearer sense of the risks that may befall a project. Assumptions are the environmental hypotheses or scenarios that are established for planning purposes and are assumed to be real or valid. The validity of the assumptions may determine the validity of the project itself. Assumptions analysis involves listing the assumptions under which the project plan is evolving and then validating these assumptions through research.

Assumptions analysis clarifies where information on risk analysis will be valid and where it will be based on uncertainty. Uncertainty exists when the project team can never reasonably establish the probability of possible outcomes.

Diagramming Techniques

Because of the nature of relationships in projects and their effects on risks, diagramming techniques will sometimes provide insights that are not available from raw project data. Network diagrams, cause-and-effect diagrams, flowcharts, influence diagrams, and force field charts can all provide insight based on relationships that are not otherwise readily evident. Application of the techniques is discussed in Part II.

Risk identification is an iterative process. At the end of any risk identification cycle, risk events will be identified and logged in a risk register or database. Ideally, some of the triggers or symptoms that warn of risk will also be flagged. Although response development is not an objective, it is possible during this process that some participants will identify solutions to some risks. These solutions should be captured so that they are not forgotten as the process progresses. Moreover, if clear root causes of risk become evident, then they should be cataloged as well.

Perform Qualitative Analysis

The identification process produces a well-documented description of project risks. As analysis begins, it helps to organize and stratify the identified risks. By using the information for conducting risk identification plus the outputs from risk identification, it's possible to begin a basic analysis of the risks identified.

Baselining Risk

Risk exists only in relation to the two absolute states of uncertainty: total uncertainty (usually expressed as 0 percent probability) and total certainty (usually expressed as 100 percent probability). Risk will always fall somewhere within this range. Risk qualification is a first, best effort to sort risk in relation to its probabilities and impacts. The process is simplified significantly by defining the total failure and total success so that the full range of possibilities can be understood. Defining one or both of the performance measurement baselines (cost and schedule) helps set a benchmark on the curves (see Figure 3.3).

It is certainly desirable (but difficult) to describe the technical content as an absolute percentage of either 0 percent or 100 percent. Few organizations have the rigor to apply those values to technical performance. Those that do may apply them through a technique known as technical performance measurement (TPM). But in most organizations, the technical issues are tied closely to cost and schedule; so, those values are applied with the assumption that technical content has been addressed. After defining a baseline position, it becomes easier to qualify and quantify the degree of risk for each impact area.

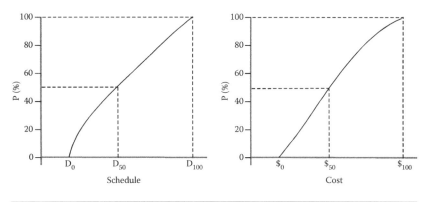

Figure 3.3   Risk baselines.

Rating Schemes and Definitions

The degree of risk assigned in a given situation reflects the personality of the risk analyst. Twenty people can look at the same situation, and each would come up with a different risk value. Consequently, a risk-rating scheme built against an agreed-to set of criteria helps minimize discrepancies.

The scales of probability and impact can (and probably should) be simple—such as high, medium, and low—applying the notion that the degree of risk is a consideration of probability of occurrence and severity of impact. Figure 3.4 is a diagram for a risk-rating mechanism. Defining a risk becomes a matter of identifying impacts, deciding on a scale, and then shaping the boundaries. With a defined risk-rating scheme in place (at least tentatively), the task of evaluating and quali-fying each identified risk may be accomplished using this structure.

Organizations need to establish consistent terms and terminology for probability because impact levels vary radically from project to project. For example, one project's two-week delay may be a minor issue, whereas another project's two-week delay is a showstopper. The same cannot be said of probability. Organizations need consistent val-ues for probability to support congruent applications of the principles. Thus, if terms and values statements can be established for probability, then it will facilitate project managers' efforts to qualify their risks consistently.

A high probability can be expressed as a percentage (80%), as a values statement (extremely likely), as a comparison (as often as the Bay Bridge

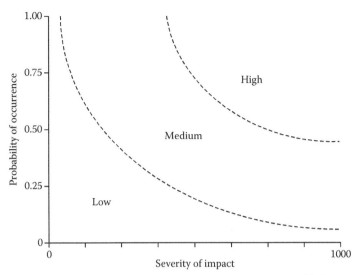

Figure 3.4   Risk rating.

is backed up at rush hour), or as a frequency level (in at least four out of five instances). The same can be done for low probability. Moderate probabilities are frequently described most simply as the range between the high and low values statements. Many organizations also accommodate extremely remote risks (acts of God, civil unrest, as examples) with a supplemental probability value for improbable or abnormal risk. These probability values are assigned at well below 1 percent to account for those issues that are remarkably rare but which potentially pose a dramatic risk to the project or organization as a whole.

Impact weights are conventionally established on a project-by-project basis as different projects have significantly different effects on the organization. Impact may be established for cost and schedule as percentages, as absolute values, or as values relative to specific tasks or functions. Impact may also be established for other cultural issues within the organization. In some organizations, political, socioeconomic, customer relationship, or image risks may weigh just as heavily as cost and schedule. As such, the more that can be done to establish high, medium, and low values for such risks, then the easier it will be to ascertain the relative levels of risk on a given project and the more effectively the risk qualification practice will reflect strategic organizational interests.

Probability and impact do not necessarily share the same weight in a probability/impact risk-rating matrix. When using this tool, probability may be weighted less heavily than impact (or consequence) to allow the organization to acknowledge its concern for those risks that, while unlikely, can cause significant detriment to the project. On such a scale, probability values may be incremental, whereas impact values may be subjectively weighted, as shown in Figure 3.5.

This type of scale allows for the qualitative evaluation and comparison of seemingly similar risks. If both scales use equal increments, then a risk having a high probability of occurrence but a low impact is weighted identically to a risk with a low probability of occurrence but a high impact. In some organizations, that's acceptable; but in most organizations, the greater concern is for impact; so, the scale in Figure 3.5 may be more appropriate.

Rating schemes are discussed in greater depth in Chapter 25.

Assumptions Testing

During risk identification, assumptions are identified and validated. During qualification, assumptions are tested. Such testing is performed not to establish the validity of the assumption; presumably, that has already been done. Rather, the assumption tests evaluate stability and consequences.

- Stability—This is the evaluation of the potential for change in a given assumption. Some assumptions, by their very nature, will change; they will not remain stable. This assessment should be used to determine the degree of stability for a given assumption.
- Consequences—This is the evaluation of the potential impact to the project if the assumption proves invalid.

Risk Modeling

In some instances, project risk will be qualified using risk models. Generally, such models are organizationally specific and are applied consistently to all projects during risk qualification. Risk model development and application is discussed in Chapter 28. Risk models and

Probability / Impact	Low probability (1)	Moderate probability (2)	High probability (3)
Low impact (1)	Low probability, low impact (1x1=1)	Moderate probability, low impact (2x1=2)	High probability, low impact (3x1=3)
Moderate impact (3)	Low probability, moderate impact (1x3=3)	Moderate probability, moderate impact (2x3=6)	High probability, moderate impact (3x3=9)
High impact (6)	Low probability, high impact (1x6=6)	Moderate probability, high impact (2x6=12)	High probability, high impact (3x6=18)

Figure 3.5   Probability/impact risk-rating matrix.

the other risk qualification practices support development of an over-all risk ranking, one of the critical outputs from this stage in the process. This allows the project to be compared to other similar efforts in terms of risk. It also supports other comparative analyses for project prioritization, contingency-funding support, or basic go/no-go decision making.

Using Analogies

Analogy comparison is an attempt to learn from other projects or situations and is used for many actions, such as cost estimating and scheduling. It is important to distinguish between analogous projects and projects with analogous risks. Analogy comparison is discussed in detail in Chapter 8.

Conducting Data Quality Assessments

Data quality assessments need to be done at some point during this process to ensure that the sources of data are sufficiently valid to warrant inclusion of the data in the process. Bad data quality means weak qualification; good data quality improves the chances that the risk qualification will be valid.

Risk Categorization

In the *PMBOK® Guide* (2013), the risk breakdown structure is identified as a categorization tool (see Chapter 15). Other tools, such as the affinity diagram (see Chapter 15) or the work breakdown structure, can also serve as structures against which to sort project risks. Sorting and categorizing risks during risk qualification can provide a sense of which areas of risk are driving the greatest concern and which (by sheer volume) warrant greater attention.

Risk Urgency Assessment

When qualifying risks, there is sometimes sufficient volume of risk to create the quandary of "which of the 'high' risks should be dealt with first?" When such uncertainty exists, determining which risks will have an impact on the organization first is a valid concern. Urgency assessment, as discussed in Chapter 26, adds a new dimension to risk qualification by addressing which risks are imminent and which would not have an impact until much later in the project. Urgency assessment may also relate to which risks need to be addressed in the near term (for efficacy's sake) and which may not require mitigation or response until later in the project life cycle.

Risk qualification sets the stage for significant risks to be quantitatively evaluated. It also affords project managers a tool to evaluate those risks that do not lend themselves to more quantitative analysis.

Perform Quantitative Analysis

Quantitative risk analysis is the effort to examine risk and assign hard metric values to both the project risk as a whole and to the most significant risks (as established through risk qualification). Project managers conduct risk quantification to establish the odds of achieving project goals, to justify contingency reserves, to validate targets associated with the triple constraint, and to conduct in-depth "what-if" analyses.

In a perfect world, the pool from which quantitative risk information is drawn is deep and rich with data. It includes information from the previous processes discussed here as well as any statistical data repositories existing within the organization. To augment those data, project managers use a variety of tools, including expert interviews, expected monetary value, decision tree analyses, program evaluation and review technique (PERT) assessments, sensitivity analysis, and simulations.

Expert Interviews

The technique for interviewing technical experts to rate risk quantitatively is discussed in detail in Chapter 4.

Expected Monetary Value (EMV)

Expected monetary value is a statistical concept that takes into account the probability and impact of risks by multiplying those values together to generate a numeric value to be applied in risk decision making. Decision analysis is discussed in depth in Chapter 20.

Decision Tree Analysis

Decision trees are classic project risk tools that provide a wealth of information in an easy-to-interpret format. They are particularly helpful in risk quantification as they provide information on the options, the probabilities of events associated with those options, the expected value of those options, and the potential impacts of all possible outcomes. Decision trees are discussed in greater depth in Appendix C.

Program Evaluation and Review Technique

The program evaluation and review technique takes the network analyses (briefly mentioned under risk identification) a step further by embedding multi-data-point duration estimates to establish risk values for schedules. This concept is addressed further in Chapter 23.

Sensitivity Analysis

Sensitivity analysis examines risk from a one-at-a-time perspective. In a sensitivity analysis, individual variables are modified one by one to assess their relative impact on the project's outcomes. Sensitivity analyses are normally conducted in the context of a risk simulation.

Simulations

Both cost and schedule risks can be evaluated using risk simulation tools, the most popular of which is the Monte Carlo analysis. These tools provide ranges of possible outcomes and the likelihood of achieving these outcomes. Cost and schedule risk simulations are explored in Chapter 30.

Risk quantification provides project managers with both a sense of the overall level of risk in the project and a value (in terms of cost or duration) for that risk. Often, that value becomes the contingency reserve or a component of the contingency reserve. The quantification process can also provide probability assessments that manifest themselves as "confidence levels." A confidence level is a measure of the likelihood or percent probability that the project organization will be able to achieve a given target.

One of the most useful outputs of the analysis process is the watch list or the prioritized risk listing. The watch list can serve as the worksheet that managers use for recording the risk management progress (Caver 1985). An example of a watch list is shown in Table 3.4. This prioritized risk list provides a convenient means to track and document outputs from the risk analysis process. It can be generated either by conducting pairwise comparisons of qualified risks or by comparing values generated in risk quantification. In risk qualification and quantification, as the watch list is being built, only the risk item and impact area are listed. After responses are developed, they are incorporated here as well.

Note that a watch list will include all risks identified and not just the high risks. The watch list serves as an ongoing point of reference

Table 3.4 Sample Watch List

EVENT ITEM	AREA OF IMPACT	RISK RESPONSE
Loss of vendor	Production cost	Qualify second vendor
		Obtain technical data as a deliverable
Incomplete logistic support analysis	Support cost	Contractor support for 2 to 3 years
		Warranty on high-risk items
		Emphasis on contractor reviews
		Logistics reviews
Immature technical data package with many engineering changes for design fixes	Production cost with high first-unit cost	Production engineers on contractor design team
		Fixed-price contract
		Competition
		Producibility engineering planning
		Production readiness reviews
Long lead-time items delayed	Production schedule	Early identification of long lead-time items
		Emphasis on early delivery
		Transfer or leveling from less urgent programs

Table 3.5   Risk Register in Software

WBS #	TASK NAME	TEXT 12	NUMBER 13	NUMBER 14	NUMBER 15	NUMBER 16

for reviews to determine whether the status of the risks has changed relative to the other project risks.

Some project managers will generate this information and store the identified risks, their probabilities, impacts, overall risk levels, and priorities in the same database as their work breakdown structure. This can be accomplished in most of the project management software packages by using some of the available spare text or number fields that frequently go unused. If, however, these fields are used, then a central authority (such as the project office) should coordinate their use to ensure that they are used consistently from project to project and from functional organization to functional organization. In most tools, the underlying information will look similar to this (Table 3.5).

When renamed, the fields take on a different look and now support the project (Table 3.6).

The *PMBOK® Guide* (2013) refers to this alignment of information as the "risk register." The risk register, as per the *PMBOK® Guide*, may include the risks, their description, category, cause, probability, impact, responses, owners, and status. This element of the project plan is the ultimate repository for risk insights that the project manager and the team have garnered.

Cumulative probability distribution, another useful product of risk analysis, is illustrated in Figure 3.6. The cumulative probability distribution curve is a common, conventional method that depicts cost, schedule, and performance risk. Project managers can use cumulative probability distributions by determining an appropriate risk level (threshold) for the item and then by determining from the curve the corresponding target cost, schedule, or performance. Project managers may also alter variables to determine sensitivities of the project to those variables. These are typical outputs of many automated risk tools

Table 3.6   Risk Register Updated in Software

WBS #	TASK NAME	RISK EVENT	PROBABILITY	IMPACT	OVERALL RISK	PRIORITY

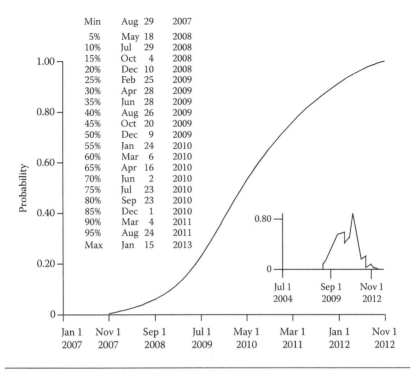

Figure 3.6 Sample cumulative probability distribution.

that are discussed in Chapter 30. Appendix C explains probability curves in more detail.

Risk quantification, which generally provides an in-depth understanding of the sources and degree of risk, can be portrayed quickly in a few charts. This generates an effective communication of project status to decision makers. Chapters 32 and 34 have suggestions for communicating risk information.

Risk quantification provides extensive information on which risks are the most important and which pose the greatest potential threats to the project. Ideally, the outputs from qualification and quantification will include a comprehensive, prioritized risk listing. Even then, there will be those team members who challenge such a list, arguing that it represents either individual or organizational bias. Because of that possibility and because of the reality that all the risks involve at least some degree of uncertainty, final determinations must reside with the project manager. When it comes to prioritization, the project manager should be the ultimate decision maker in establishing which risks are the most worrisome.

Plan Risk Responses

Risk response development is a critical element in the risk management process that determines what action (if any) will be taken to address risk issues evaluated in the identification, qualification, and quantification efforts. All information generated to date becomes crucial in determining what the organization will do that is in keeping with the risks, the organization's tolerance, the project tolerances, and the customer culture.

To some measure, risk is a cultural phenomenon. Different countries, regions, and organizations have different cultural tolerances for risk and risk responses. Determining what limits exist early in the risk response planning process is important to ensure that time is not wasted on approaches that are intolerable. Risk thresholds frequently are as significant here as they are in establishing basic probability and impact for the risks. These risk thresholds should become a component of the risk management plan.

All risks have causes; sometimes, multiple risks within a given project arise from a common cause. In developing risk responses, the project team should work to identify any common causes, as these causes may have common risk responses.

As mentioned earlier, in some project communities, risk is split into two very distinct, polar groups—threat and opportunity. Since some risk events have potentially positive outcomes, the belief is that there should be responses outlined for both threat and opportunity. Generally, response strategies for threats fall into one of the following categories:

- Avoidance
- Transference
- Mitigation
- Acceptance

For opportunities, the strategies fall into these categories:

- Exploitation
- Sharing
- Enhancement
- Acceptance

Risk Avoidance

The fundamental premise of risk avoidance (as the name implies) is the removal of the possibility that the risk event can influence the project objectives. Classic risk avoidance includes the options of eliminating the project or completely changing the approach to the work. In many situations, a lower risk choice is available from a range of risk alternatives. Selecting a lower risk option or alternative approach represents a risk avoidance decision. For example, "I accept this other option because of less potentially unfavorable results." Certainly, not all risk can or should be avoided.

Communication is critical to risk avoidance. Eliminating an approach or requirement will be in vain if the rationale for the action is not clearly documented because others may augment the project with approaches that reintroduce the risk.

Risk Transference

Also known as "deflection," risk transference is the effort to shift responsibility or consequence for a given risk to a third party. Transference rarely serves to eliminate the risk. Instead, it creates an obligation for mitigation, acceptance, or avoidance on another individual or organization. Risks can be transferred to a variety of organizations and individuals outside the project, including

- Insurers (including warranty firms, guarantors, and bondsmen)
- Subcontractors
- Vendors
- Partners
- Customers

Surprisingly, project managers frequently overlook the customer as a potential party to risk transference. Nonetheless, the customer is one of the few recipients of a transferred risk who can completely assume the risk from the project organization.

Risk deflection often benefits the project as well as the customer. The type of contract, performance incentives, and warranties may be structured to share risk with others and in part, deflect risk.

Risk Mitigation

Risk mitigation is the most common of all risk-handling strategies. It is the process of taking specific courses of action to reduce the probability and/or reduce the impact of risks. This often involves using reviews, risk reduction milestones, novel work approaches, and alternative management actions. The project manager must develop risk mitigation plans and then track activities based on these plans. All these actions are built into the risk register, the project plan (cost plans, schedule plans), and ultimately into the work breakdown structure.

Through risk mitigation, the project manager may emphasize minimizing the probability that the risk will occur or minimizing the impact if the risk occurs. Depending on the specific risk, either approach may be effective. Note that risk mitigation, though popular, is also time consuming and potentially expensive. Yet, it remains popular primarily because it conveys that clear action is being taken as opposed to a sense that the risk is simply lying dormant.

Risk Acceptance

Acceptance, also known as retention, is the decision to acknowledge and endure the consequences if a risk event occurs. It is broken down into two basic types of acceptance, passive and active.

Passive acceptance is the acceptance of risk without taking any action to resolve it, cope with it, or otherwise manage it. The only actions required in passive acceptance are documentation of the risk, as well as acknowledgment by the management and the team (and the customer, if appropriate) that the risk exists and that the organization is willing to endure its consequences should the risk occur.

Active acceptance acknowledges the risk as well but calls for the development of contingency plans, and in some cases, fallback plans. Contingency plans are implemented to deal with risks only when the risk events come to pass. This may include detailed instructions on how to manage risks retroactively or may be as simple as a contingency reserve budget of time or cost established for the project.

Contingency reserves are frequently the fodder for discussion because some view them as project panaceas and others see them as a crutch for those who cannot manage effectively. These reserves are sometimes referred to as contingency allowances. Organizations should not establish universal rules for applying contingency, such as flat percentages or fixed monetary (or schedule) amounts. Instead, contingency reserves should reflect the degree of risk acceptance in a project, as well as the overall levels of risk associated with the project. Organizations may set contingency values by applying culturally acceptable metrics to the risk models (discussed in Chapter 28). They may also set contingency reserves through negotiation with the project manager or by using the expected values of the project's quantified risks as analyzed earlier. Nonetheless, if contingency reserves are to be applied, they must reflect the realities of the project as a unique effort toward a specific objective, thus requiring a specific level of risk support.

Fallback plans are implemented in active acceptance to deal with managing accepted risks if the contingency plans are insufficient. They are, in essence, the contingency plans should the original contingency plans fail. They are sometimes referred to as the contingency plans for the contingency plans. Fallback plans represent the safety net that ensures the entire project will not collapse in failure.

Opportunity Exploitation

In some instances, opportunities identified as a result of a risk analysis are too positive to ignore. Organizations realize that opportunities represent significant occasions to improve their organizational or project position in the marketplace (or the marketplace of ideas) and must be pursued. Exploitation is that pursuit, which strives to ensure that the opportunity actually comes to pass and is fully realized. Exploitation leaves nothing to chance. If the opportunity is there, then an exploitation strategy ensures that the organization can take full advantage.

Opportunity Sharing

In some instances, partners can improve the chance that an opportunity will be realized. An organization may not be able to pursue the opportunity on its own or may run the risk of losing the opportunity without support. In such cases, sharing partnerships (such as joint ventures, teaming, or other documented relationships) can help optimize both the probability and impact of the opportunity (as well as the management thereof). Because of the nature of sharing, the impact of the opportunity to each sharing party will ultimately be less than if they had pursued the opportunity alone.

Opportunity Enhancement

While risk mitigation minimizes probability and impact of threats, opportunity enhancement increases the probability and/or impact of opportunities. Pursuing the causes of opportunities, the environments in which they exist, and the culture in which they evolve opens the door either to enhance the chances they will occur or to increase their relative magnitude.

Opportunity Acceptance

Acceptance, also known as retention, is the decision to acknowledge and accept the consequences if an opportunity event occurs. As with threat events, opportunity acceptance takes the form of passive acceptance (where no action is required) or active acceptance (where stakeholders identify the intent and series of actions that will take place should the opportunity be realized).

For both threat and opportunity, selecting the proper strategy may require project managers to identify specific strategies for each risk. It may also require that managers identify single strategies that may be applicable to a broader subset of risks or to common causes. A popular tool for identifying such opportunities is the risk response strategy matrix. This matrix encourages the examination of risk responses both in the context of other risks in the project and in the context of the other risk responses. The risk response strategy matrix is examined in Chapter 32.

Ideally, the project team that has completed risk response planning will have established a contingency reserve for the necessary funds and time to deal with project risk. They will have an adjusted WBS that reflects issues that surfaced during risk response analysis and incorporates any new activity that the strategies require. They also will have communicated the risks, risk strategies, and any residual risks to the management team to ensure there is buy-in on the approach. (The response information will be captured in the risk register for the project and for posterity.) Moreover, they will have contractual agreements to support any deflection or transference. As a by-product, there is also the possibility that new risks will arise as a result of the new strategies. These new risks should be examined using the same process as the earlier risks—identification, qualification, quantification, and response planning—as appropriate.

Monitor and Control Risks

After risks have been identified, qualified, and quantified, and clear responses have been developed, these findings must be put into action. Risk monitoring and control involves implementing the risk management plan and risk responses, which should be an integral part of the project plan. Two key challenges are associated with monitoring and control. The first is putting the risk plans into action and ensuring that the plans are still valid. The second is generating meaningful documentation to support the process.

Implementing the risk plans should be a function of putting the project plan into action. If the project plan is in place and the risk strategies have been integrated, then the risk plans should be self-fulfilling. Ensuring that the plans are still valid, however, is not as simple. Risk monitoring involves inquiry and extensive tracking of the risks and their environment. Have the plans been implemented as proposed? Were the responses as effective as anticipated? Did the project team follow organizational policy and procedure? Are the project assumptions still valid? Have risk triggers occurred? Have new external influences changed the organization's risk exposure? Have new risks surfaced?

Answers to these questions may drive radically different approaches to the project and to its risks. Alternative strategy development, reassessments, reviewing contingency plan implementation, or replanning may be essential to project survival or success.

Different tools serve the evaluation requirements of risk monitoring and control. Basic project management tools, such as earned value analysis, provide insight on the relative levels of variance and the tasks that drive the variance. Technical performance measurement (TPM) is a quality management tool that examines the performance of the organization in terms of each individual work package objective. Dubbed by some as the "earned value of quality," TPM affords insight on performance variance and the potential influences of risks that have occurred.

As the project progresses, there are risk-specific evaluations to facilitate risk control. Formal risk audits examine the project team's success at identifying risks, assessing probability, and developing appropriate strategies. The frequency of risk audits is largely determined by the duration of the project and the criticality of the deliverables involved. A project with mission-critical deliverables will, by its very nature, undergo more frequent audits than a project developed for a support mission.

Risk reviews, though less formal than risk audits, are vital nonetheless. Risk reviews allow for an examination of the risks, probabilities, impacts, and strategies, largely to determine whether supplemental action or review will be required. As with audits, the criticality of the project and its duration determine in large part the frequency of such reviews.

The challenge is dealing with risk events as they occur. Flaws in carefully structured plans become evident when these plans are implemented. Some strategies work very effectively; others prove to be far less effective. Thus, it often becomes necessary to begin the cycle anew, which involves either reconsidering risk responses or probing even further back in the process to reevaluate identified risks.

However, the process cannot possibly manage all risks. Some risks will occur without having been preemptively identified. Those that do will be managed "on the fly" without careful consideration and review. Such impromptu approaches are called workarounds. They are unplanned responses to negative risk events. These actions are often the project teams' last chance to deal with problems. Workarounds are reactive rather than proactive and rarely have the level of support that well-considered risk responses do. Thus, because workarounds are developed without a long-term planning window, they are also frequently more costly or time consuming. In essence, workarounds are contingency plans without the planning.

As risk control and monitoring are applied, data are generated. Responses succeed and fail. Some risks materialize and some do not. Probabilities shift and time alters impact values. These changes may

Table 3.7   Risk Register in Software

WBS #	TASK NAME	TEXT 12	NUMBER 13	NUMBER 14	NUMBER 15	NUMBER 16

Table 3.8   Risk Register Updated in Software

WBS #	TASK NAME	RISK EVENT	PROBABILITY	IMPACT	OVERALL RISK	PRIORITY

drive changes in the organization's existing risk identification checklists and should also be captured in a risk database along with any new information. Such a database need not rely exclusively on database tools such as Microsoft Access® but may be cataloged in the project management software with the project plan. As discussed earlier, text and number fields in the project management software can be used to support risk identification as follows (Table 3.7).

Renamed, the fields take on a different look and now support the project (Table 3.8).

This same approach can also augment risk response information and the effectiveness of the strategies deployed (Table 3.9).

Renamed, the fields take on a different look and now support the project (Table 3.10).

As with the earlier example, retention of this information with the project plan significantly increases the probability that others will reuse this information as the project plan is appropriated for use on other, similar efforts. Without this documentation, the corrective and preventive actions that are recommended may not be carried out or may be lost for future projects. Risk strategies and their outcomes are critical elements of an organization's intellectual property. Failure to properly

Table 3.9   Risk Register in Software

WBS #	TASK NAME	TEXT 12	TEXT 13	TEXT 14	TEXT 15	TEXT 16

Table 3.10   Risk Register Updated in Software

WBS #	TASK NAME	RISK EVENT	STRATEGY	OWNER	OUTCOME	LOG DATE

store them in an accessible manner is to diminish the value of the project and the project team in their contributions to technical capital.

Summary

- Plan risk management is the development of organizational and project-specific infrastructure to support all the other risk processes.
- Identify risks is the process of identifying (and in many cases, categorizing) project risks.
- Perform qualitative analysis is the process of sorting risks by general probability and impact terms to facilitate analysis of the most critical risks.
- Perform quantitative analysis is the process of quantifying risks and honing that quantification to assess the impact to the cost, schedule, and quality of specific project areas, as well as to assess the overall project impact.
- Plan risk responses involves evaluating and refining risk mitigation strategies.
- Monitor and control risks involves the implementation of risk mitigation strategies and their evaluation and recording.
- Risk management is a continual process throughout any project.

PART II
RISK MANAGEMENT TECHNIQUES

The second part of this book introduces specific techniques that have proved useful to both customers and project managers in carrying out the risk management process.

Each chapter describes techniques for accomplishing the basic steps of the risk management process: risk management planning, risk identification, risk qualification, risk quantification, risk response development, and risk monitoring and control. Many of these techniques can serve more than one step of the process. For example, an in-depth evaluation of a critical path network is useful in initial overview evaluations, risk identification, and risk response development. The resource requirements, applications, and output capabilities of each technique are summarized in Table II.1. Multiple-technique applications are distinguished in Table II.2 between predominant and secondary use.

Moreover, each technique must be evaluated in context using consistent criteria to determine whether or not it is the most effective technique to apply. These criteria include—

- Technique description
- When applicable
- Inputs and outputs
- Major steps in applying the technique
- Use of results

Table II.1   Risk Analysis Technique Selection Matrix

TECHNIQUE	RESOURCE REQUIREMENTS					APPLICATIONS							OUTPUTS		
	COST (RESOURCE MONTHS)*	PROPER FACILITIES AND EQUIPMENT	IMPLEMENTATION TIME (MONTHS)*	EASE OF USE	TIME COMMITMENT	PROJECT STATUS REPORTING	MAJOR PLANNING DECISIONS	CONTRACT STRATEGY SELECTION	MILESTONE PREPARATION	DESIGN GUIDANCE	SOURCE SELECTION	BUDGET SUBMITTAL	ACCURACY	LEVEL OF DETAIL	UTILITY
Expert interviews	0.1–3	Y	0.1–3	E	S	H	H	M	H	M	H	L	L–H	L–H	H
Planning meetings	0.1–1	Y	0.1	E	S	H	H	L	L	H	L	M	M	M	H
Risk practice methodology	0.1–3	N	0.1–3	M	M	H	M	L	L	NA	NA	M	H	H	H
Documentation reviews	0.1	Y	0.1	H	S–M	H	H	L	L	H	M	H	L–H	H	H
Analogy comparisons	0.2–2	Y	0.2–2	M	S	L	H	H	L–M	M	H	L–M	L–M	L–H	M
Plan evaluation	1–1.5	Y	0.2–1.5	M	H	M	H	NA	L	M	L	L	H	L–H	M–H
Delphi technique	0.2–0.5	Y	1–2	H	S	L	L	H	NA	H	L–M	L	H	H	H
Brainstorming	0.1	Y	0.1	H	S	L	L	NA	NA	M	NA	NA	L	H	H
Crawford slip method (CSM)	0.1	Y	0.1	H	S	NA	M	NA	NA	L	NA	NA	L	L–H	H
SWOT analysis	0.1	Y	0.1	H	S	M–H	L	NA	L	NA	NA	NA	L	L	H
Checklists	0.1	Y	0.1	H	S	H	M	L	NA	M	M	NA	H	H	H
Risk breakdown structure	0.1–0.5	Y	0.1–0.5	M	M	H	M	NA	NA	M	H	NA	M–H	M	H
Root cause identification and analysis	0.1	Y	0.1	H	S–H	H	M	L	L	M	M	NA	M–H	H	H

Technique															
Risk registers/tables	0.1–0.5	Y	0.1–3	H	S	M	M	M	M	NA	L	L	L	H	H	H
Project templates	0.5	Y	0.5	E	M	H	H	H	L	H	H	M–H	L	M	L–H	H
Assumptions analysis	0.1	Y	0.1	H	M	H	H	H	H	H	M	M	H	M–H	L–H	H
Decision analysis– Expected monetary value	0.5–1	Y	0.2–0.6	M	S–M	M	H	H	M	M–H	M	M	M	L–H	L–H	M
Estimating relationships	0.1–3	Y	0.1–3	E	M	H	L	L	L	NA	NA	NA	H	L	L	L
Network analysis	0.1–3	Y	0.1–3	H	S–M	H	M	H	M	M	M	H	L	H	L–H	H
Program evaluation and review technique (PERT)	0.1–3	Y	0.1–3	H	S–M	H	L	H	H	L	L	NA	NA	H	L	H
Other diagramming techniques	0.1–3	N	0.1–3	E–H	M	M	NA	M	NA	NA	H	L	L	M	H	H
Rating schemes	0.1–1	Y	0.1–0.2	H	S	L	L	M	L	NA	NA	L	L–H	M	H	H
Urgency assessment	0.5	Y	0.2–0.5	H	M–H	H	NA	H	NA	L	L	L	L	H	L	H
Futures thinking	05.–2	Y	0.2–0.5	H	M	H	M	H	H	M	M	M	NA	M	H	M
Risk modeling	0.1	Y	0.1	H	S	M	M	M	M	NA	L	NA	M	H	L	L–H
Sensitivity analysis	0.1–0.5	Y	0.1–0.5	H	M	M	M	M	NA	M	M	M	M	M–H	H	H
Monte Carlo simulations	0.2–0.4	N	0.2–0.5	E	M	M	NA	H	NA	M	M	L	L	L	H	L
Risk factors	0.1–0.4	Y	0.1–0.5	H	S	M	M	M	M	NA	L	L	M	L–M	M	H
Risk response matrix	0.1–0.2	Y	0.1	H	S–M	H	M	M	NA	NA	M–H	M–H	L	H	H	H
Performance tracking	1.5	Y	1.5	M	M	M	M	H	M	H	H	M	M	M	M	H
Risk reviews and audits	0.1	Y	0.1	H	S	H	L	H	L	NA	M	L	H	H	M–H	H

N = no (not normally available)
Y = yes (normally available)
E = easy
H = heavy
M = Moderate
S = Slight

H = high
M = medium
L = low
NA = not applicable

H = high
M = medium
L = low

*Note that the thresholds of cost and implementation time are 0.1 and 3 resource months: how much effort it will take to implement the technique. Any activity that spans that range may be seen as something that expands (or shrinks) based on project size.

Table II.2   Technique Applications

TECHNIQUE	RISK MANAGEMENT PLANNING	RISK IDENTIFICATION	RISK QUALIFICATION	RISK QUALIFICATION	RISK RESPONSE PLANNING	RISK MONITORING AND CONTROL
	PREDOMINANT/SECONDARY USE					
Expert interviews	○	●				
Planning meetings	●	○	○		○	
Risk practice methodology	●		○	○		
Documentation reviews	○	●				○
Analogy comparisons		●	○	○	○	
Plan evaluation		●				○
Delphi technique	○	●	○	○	○	
Brainstorming		●			○	
Crawford slip method (CSM)		●			○	
SWOT analysis	○	●			○	
Checklists	○					○
Risk breakdown structure	○	●	○			○
Root cause identification and analysis	○	●	○		○	
Risk registers/tables	○	○	○		○	●
Project templates	●		○			○
Assumptions analysis		●	○	○		
Decision analysis—expected monetary value				●		
Estimating relationships	○			●		
Network analysis program		○		●	○	
Evaluation and review technique		○		●		
Other diagramming techniques				●		
Rating schemes	○		●	○		
Urgency assessment			●		○	●
Futures thinking	●	●	○		●	○
Risk modeling sensitivity analysis	●		○			
Monte Carlo simulations		●	○		○	
Risk factors				●		
Risk response matrix	○		●			
Performance tracking	○				●	
Risk reviews and audits	○					●

Legend: ● = Predominant use, ○ = Secondary use.

- Resource requirements
- Reliability
- Selection criteria

The chapters in Part II discuss and rate each risk technique in the context of these criteria. This analysis will not make selecting a technique an automatic decision, but it will provide project managers with an informed perspective to evaluate and choose approaches suited to the objectives of the risk management effort within a project's ever-present resource constraints.

The selection criteria for each technique receive extensive attention. Within the selection criteria, the three primary areas of analysis are resource requirements, applications, and outputs. The resource requirements include five subset areas of information for analysis:

- *Cost* refers to the cost of implementation in terms of resource months.
- *Proper facilities and equipment* is an equally crucial issue to technique implementation, raising the question as to whether most organizations have easy access to the facilities and equipment necessary to carry out the implementation. In most cases, the answer will be an attribute: either a project has these facilities (Y) or it does not (N).
- *Implementation time* is, in part, a function of the information developed under the cost criterion. If fewer resources are available, then the project may take longer than anticipated. If, however, more resources are available, then the time required may be trimmed.
- *Ease of use* refers to the level of training and education required before the technique can be implemented. It may also refer to the level of effort that may be involved in simply implementing the technique. Ease of use is designated as easy (E), heavy (H), moderate (M), or slight (S).
- *Time commitment* relates to the amount of oversight and involvement required of the project manager. If a project manager must make a long-term commitment, then this level may be considered heavy (H). If, on the other hand, the project does not require an extensive commitment, the project manager's involvement may be slight (S) or moderate (M).

In the requirements for applications, each area is evaluated on the level of support the technique can provide: high (H), medium (M), or low (L). There are seven subsets of information:

- *Project status reporting* refers to monitoring plans, costs, and schedules to ensure that standards are met and problems are identified for timely corrective action.
- *Major planning decisions* are those decisions in which a project manager may be willing to invest significant resources and personal attention.
- *Contract strategy selection* typically occurs several times through the life of a project. Different techniques can bring extensive influence to bear on the types of contracts selected for any given project.
- *Milestone preparation* is the development of significant and appropriate milestones within any project. Some techniques can facilitate this process, whereas others cannot.
- *Design guidance* refers to the level of insight that the technique under consideration can potentially provide for any given project.
- *Source selection* is the effort to determine which sources may be potential vendors for the project. The level of guidance a technique can provide in this area may range from nonexistent to significant.
- *Budget submittal* is the final area of concern under application. Many tools have the ability to generate copious financial data; other techniques are not financially oriented. A technique's ability to contribute to an accurate assessment of the project budget is evaluated here.

Outputs, in terms of information, are the last area reviewed in each technique's selection. As with the application issues, ratings of outputs are high (H), medium (M), or low (L). Three primary issues require consideration:

- *Accuracy* deals with the basic theoretical soundness of a technique and the presence of weakening assumptions that may dilute the value of information obtained in the analysis. Most

Table II.3   Project Phase Technique Application

TECHNIQUE	PROJECT PHASE				INFORMATION YIELD				
	CONCEPT	DEVELOPMENT	IMPLEMENTATION	CLOSEOUT	TECHNICAL	PROGRAMMATIC	SUPPORTABILITY	COST	SCHEDULE
Expert interviews	+	+	+	+	+	o	+	o	o
Planning meetings	−	o	+	+	+	o	+	−	−
Risk practice methodology	+	+	+	+	o	+	+	o	o
Documentation reviews	+	+	+	+	o	+	+	o	o
Analogy comparisons	o	+	+	+	+	o	o	+	o
Plane valuation	−	o	+	+	+	o	+	−	−
Delphi technique	+	+	o	−	+	o	o	o	o
Brain storming	+	+	o	o	o	o	o	o	o
Crawford slip method	+	+	o	o	o	o	o	o	o
SWOT analysis	+	o	o	o	o	+	+	o	o
Checklists	o	+	+	+	+	o	+	−	−
Risk breakdown structure	o	+	o	o	o	+	o	o	o
Root cause identification and analysis	+	o	o	o	+	o	o	o	o
Risk registers/tables	−	o	+	+	o	+	o	o	o
Project templates	o	+	+	+	+	o	+	−	−
Assumptions analysis	+	+	o	o	+	+	+	o	o
Decision analysis—expected monetary value	−	+	o	−	+	o	o	+	o
Estimating relationships	−	−	−	+	−	−	−	+	−
Network analysis	−	+	+	o	+	o	+	+	+
Program evaluation and review technique	−	+	+	o	+	o	+	+	+
Other diagramming techniques	o	+	+	o	+	o	+	+	+
Rating schemes	+	+	+	+	+	o	+	−	−
Urgency assessment	o	o	+	o	o	+	o	o	+
Futures thinking	+	+	o	o	+	+	o	o	o
Risk modeling	+	+	+	+	+	o	+	−	−
Sensitivity analysis	o	o	o	o	+	o	+	+	+
Monte Carlo simulations	−	+	+	−	−	o	o	+	+
Risk factors	−	o	+	+	−	−	−	+	−
Risk response matrix	−	+	+	o	o	o	o	o	o
Performance tracking	−	+	+	+	+	o	+	+	+
Risk reviews and audits	−	−	+	+	+	+	+	+	+

Legend: −=Relatively weak; o=Average; +=Relatively strong.

techniques present an obvious trade-off between ease-of-use or time commitment and the accuracy of analysis results.

- *Level of detail* concerns the extent to which outputs provide insight into cost, schedule, and technical risks. Techniques and how they are applied vary in the breadth, depth, and understanding that the outputs yield.

- *Utility* is a subjective factor that rates outputs in a general context of the usefulness to the project manager. Both the effort involved and the value of the information are considered.

It is important to note that some techniques have more applicability to specific project phases than others. Likewise, all the techniques do not yield the same information. Each technique's applicability for each project phase and the type of information likely to result are indicated in Table II.3. Since this table is a general summary, specific applications in some instances will continue to be exceptions to the guidance the table provides. Both project phase and the type of information desired must be considered in technique selection. For example, although networks do not help analyze risks for repetitive processes, they do have great value in planning and control to establish such processes.

Each chapter of Part II opens with a thorough discussion of a specific technique. The remainder of the chapter evaluated the technique by summarizing key characteristics to consider when deciding whether that technique is appropriate for your organization when dealing with the risk process involved.

4

EXPERT INTERVIEWS

Obtaining accurate judgments from technical experts is one of the most critical elements in both risk identification and risk qualification because

The information identifies areas that are perceived as risky

The interviews provide the basis for taking qualitative information and transforming it into quantitative risk estimates

Reliance on technical expertise here is mandatory. Since every project is unique, all information necessary for an accurate risk assessment cannot usually be derived from the previous project data. However, obtaining the information from experts can be frustrating and can often lead to less-than-optimal results.

Nearly all risk analysis techniques require some expert judgment. However, it can sometimes be difficult to distinguish between good and bad judgment, and therefore this aspect makes the approach and documentation even more important than usual. The project manager or risk analyst performing the task is likely to receive divergent opinions from many "experts," and as a result, the project manager must be able to defend the ultimate position taken.

Technique Description

The expert interview technique is relatively simple. Basically, it consists of identifying appropriate experts and then methodically questioning them about risks in their areas of expertise as related to the project. (Some methods for extrapolating this information are outlined in Appendix D.) The technique can be used with individuals or groups of experts. The process normally obtains information on risk associated with all three facets of the classic triple constraint:

schedule, cost, and performance. In addition, the process may identify risks associated with other environmental and organizational considerations.

When Applicable

This technique is recommended for all projects. Expert interviews focus on extracting information about what risks exist and how severe they may be. Interviews are most useful in risk identification but may apply in other processes as well. When questioning experts about risks on a project, it is logical to pursue potential risk responses and alternatives, as well as information pertaining to probability and potential impact. Expert interviews may also support the development of risk categories for the risk breakdown structure (see Chapter 15).

Inputs and Outputs

Expert interviewing has two prerequisites. First, the interviewer must prepare by researching the topic and thinking through the interview agenda. Second, the interviewee must be willing to spend the time necessary to disclose the information to the analyst or manager. Results of such interviews can be qualitative, quantitative, or both. Expert interviews nearly always result in inputs that can be used to develop a risk watch list. They may also result in gathering the base data to formulate a range of uncertainty or a probability density function (PDF) for use in any of several risk analysis tools. The range or function can be expressed in terms of cost, schedule, or performance.

Major Steps in Applying the Technique

Since expert interviews result in a collection of subjective judgments, the only real error would be in the methodology used for gathering the data. If the techniques used are inadequate, then the entire risk identification and quantification process will be less reliable. Unfortunately, no technique exists for ensuring that the best possible data are collected. However, several methodologies are available, but many must be eliminated because of time constraints. One combination of methodologies that seems to work well consists of the following five steps:

Identify suitable individual(s). Identifying the correct subject matter expert is crucial. It is relatively easy to make a mistake and choose an expert who knows only a portion of the subject matter. If any doubt exists about an expert's level of expertise, it is worthwhile to find one or two other candidates. The time used to identify individuals to interview will be well spent. A preliminary telephone screening usually lasting only a few minutes can give the analyst a sense of the interviewee's level of expertise and can help provide focus as questions are developed for the interview. When establishing the "right" individual(s), do *not* overlook the customer and its staff as potential interviewees. Frequently, customers will have the best available risk perspectives on a project because of their high levels of organizational awareness.

Prepare for the interview. Participants save time if all of them prepare adequately. Both the interviewer and interviewee must consider what areas to cover during the interview. The interviewer must know and practice the methodology that will be used to quantify the expert judgment and should develop an agenda or topics list to ensure that the discussion has clear direction. In addition, the interviewer should understand how the expert functions in the organization and how long he or she has been in the field. The interviewer must also keep the ultimate goals of risk identification, qualification, and quantification in mind during preparation.

Target the interest area. The first portion of the actual interview should focus on verifying previously identified risk information. This time should be kept brief unless there appears to be disagreement that would require additional information. Next, the interview should concentrate on the individual's area of expertise, which will confirm that the correct individual is being interviewed. More interview time can then be spent gathering information. If the interviewer discovers that the "wrong" expert is being interviewed, then the interview can be changed or ended, saving valuable time.

Solicit judgments and general information. It is important to allow time for the expert to discuss other areas of the project after completing the target interest areas. If for nothing else, the information gained can be used when interviewing other experts to stimulate thoughts and generate alternative opinions. Someone familiar with one area may identify risks in other areas because of the interrelationships of risks. In some instances, an expert from the "wrong" area may identify risks that would be overlooked by those who spend their work lives contending with certain common risks, making them oblivious to those risks. This information generally becomes more refined as more subject matter experts are interviewed. Experience shows that if the expert is cooperative, then the information given is generally accurate. Although additional clarification may be required or the expert may be unwilling to attempt quantification, identification of the risk remains valid nevertheless.

Qualify and quantify the information. This may be the most sensitive aspect of any risk analysis. After risk areas have been identified, an estimate of their potential impact on the project cost, schedule, and performance must be made. This requires that the expert considers the probability of a given risk event's occurrence and its potential impact. If the expert cannot provide a numeric value for the information, then suggest ranges of probability as well as ranges of impact consistent with the organization's values for qualification. For many risks, precise application of a numeric value may be impossible. In such instances, however, it may be reasonable to establish qualitative ranges (Chapter 25).

Use of Results

The uses of expert interview results are as varied as the experts who provide the information. Some expert interviews will be used to establish the basic framework of the risk plan, including probability and impact ranges and internal terms and terminology. Other expert interviews may serve the basic project risk identification or construction of the risk breakdown structure. And still others will lead to qualitative and quantitative assessments of the risks under evaluation. However, only rarely will *any* discussion on risk be conducted without some recommendations being offered on how the risks themselves might be managed and which response strategies might be appropriate.

Resource Requirements

Conducting an expert interview is a relatively easy task. Virtually, anyone can ask a series of questions and note responses. To generate *high-quality* data, however, each participant in the interview must possess some fundamental qualities. The interviewer must have the ability to assimilate information without bias and to report that information accurately and effectively in the context of the greater risk analysis. In addition, the interviewer should have the ability to follow up on insights that may expand or limit the range of issues to be discussed. The interviewee, in turn, must have the subject matter expertise directly related to the areas under consideration. If either party lacks these fundamental skills, then the expert interview cannot be wholly effective.

Reliability

When conducted properly, expert interviews provide very reliable qualitative information. Transforming qualitative information into quantitative distributions or other measures depends on the skill of the interviewer. Moreover, the technique is not without problems. These problems include

The wrong expert identified
Poor-quality information obtained
The expert's unwillingness to share information
Changing opinions
Conflicting judgments

Selection Criteria

As with each chapter on techniques, the expert interview technique is assessed using selection criteria relating to resource requirements, applications, and outputs for the technique. To compare expert interviews with other techniques, review Table II.1.

Resource Requirements

Interviewing experts requires three specific resources. The first is time. Although interviewing is one of the most common techniques for risk identification, qualification, and quantification, it is frequently misapplied because of time limitations. Planned interviews are sometimes shortened or skipped altogether. Methodically examining an entire project requires the time of several experts from both the project organization and the customer organization.

The second key resource requirement is the interviewer. Frequently, experts provide information that is not readily usable for a risk register or quantitative analysis. To encourage the expert to divulge information in the correct format and at the right level of depth, some modest interviewing skill is required. Even if an interviewer lacks this skill, the techniques can still yield some valuable information if enough time is taken.

The third key resource is the interviewee or expert. It is vital to remember that the expertise required of this individual is project specific. He or she need not have a keen awareness of the risk management practice or of the interviewing strategy and techniques. The only requisite traits that this individual should possess are a willingness to share information and the ability to translate his or her technical expertise into a language that other parties in the organization can interpret and understand. While some experts will have information specific to an extremely limited subject matter area, others will have the ability to provide information that spans the breadth of the project. Both have value, depending on the information needs of the organization and the project.

> *Cost* for expert interviews may range from minimal (1–2 days) to extended (2–3 months), depending on the needs of the project. The more skilled the interviewer is, then the less time required to accomplish the same level of depth in expert interviewing. Thus, it often behooves the project manager to pay a little more for a qualified interviewer for a shorter period of time.
>
> *Proper facilities and equipment* for expert interviews are generally minimal unless the interviews must be formally maintained. For a normal expert interview, the equipment will require not more than a few chairs, a notepad, pencil or pen, and a

recorder. While some interviewers may prefer to use a laptop, it actually can serve as a barrier to communication, as the interviewer can become distracted by the screen rather than focusing on the information shared by the interviewee (and the accompanying body language). In extreme cases, expert interviews may feature a bank of television cameras and a recording studio. If a panel of experts is brought together for the interviews, then a stenographer or court recorder may be used to generate a verbatim transcript of the information shared. But for the most part, expert interviews tend to be relatively easy to manage in terms of equipment and facilities.

The *implementation time* for an expert interview is a crucial consideration. However, if resources and facilities are available, the time should not be extensive. In this case, because there are normally only one or two expert interviewers, the time to implement is reflected in the time required under "Cost."

Ease of use is one of the most attractive features of expert interviews because virtually anyone with minimal training can conduct a passable interview. While it is easy, the best interviewers are those truly skilled enough to draw out deeper and more meaningful responses from the interviewees. The most effective interviewers are those who can put together a relatively open-ended question and get back a clear and specific response. One way to achieve this is by listening carefully to the interviewee's answers and providing feedback to clarify any outstanding issues.

The project manager's *time commitment* is sometimes based on the skill levels of the project manager as an expert interviewer. The time required of the project manager (assessed on a gradient of slight to moderate to heavy) is slight as long as he or she is not personally required to conduct the interviews or train the interviewers.

Applications

As stated earlier, the expert interview has the advantage of being applicable in a wide variety of situations. The applicability of the interviews is assessed on a scale of high, medium, and low.

Project status reporting refers to monitoring plans, costs, and schedules. Although the monitoring process is not a primary application of the expert interview, gathering the information essential to status reports is often a function of the interviews. From that perspective, project status reports would be difficult (if not impossible) to develop without some interviewing skills.

Major planning decisions often hinge on the opinions of a few key individuals associated with the project. As such, the expert interview may expedite the process and ensure full participation with the individuals involved.

Contract strategy selection does not rely as heavily on expert interviews as it does on other techniques, but the interviews can play a valuable role in building the support data to feed those other techniques.

Applying expert interviews in *milestone preparation* is direct and important. Since the objectives are to ensure that planning has been comprehensive and the system is ready to move forward into its next phase, in-depth consultation with both internal and external customers is vital.

Design guidance is frequently a function of expert interviewing. The interviews are useful for making decisions ranging from considering technology alternatives for major systems to choosing components. To understand how uncertainties relate to one another and how the alternatives compare, expert interviews are often used in the data-gathering stage.

Source selection is a prime application for expert interviews. In many cases, interviews determine which candidates to eliminate for a subcontract or consulting position. In addition, if the expert interview is conducted properly during source selection, then it can open new avenues for later negotiation with the source.

Budget submittal is a crucial step in project management, but it is not well supported by expert interviews because budgets work almost exclusively from purely quantifiable data.

Expert interviews also serve other applications. They can be used to establish the organization's risk tolerances and thresholds, as well as the general culture for risk. The interviews can be used to explore specific risk events or general risk strategies. As a tool, interviews have perhaps the greatest breadth of any of the basic risk management tools.

Outputs

Outputs of the expert interview are most often a collection of notes or an individual's evaluation and documentation of these notes, which have been organized in a comprehensible manner. Outputs can include both qualitative data and individual perspectives on quantitative data.

Accuracy deals with the basic theoretical soundness of expert interviewing. Since many consider expert interviewing to be extremely easy with a limited time commitment, its accuracy is often called into question. The bottom line remains that its accuracy is only as good as the blend of the interviewer *and* interviewee. If both of them are well versed in their respective skill areas, then the interview can have high accuracy. If, on the other hand, they have limited skill levels, then the interview may have low accuracy. In general, the expert interview must be considered less than purely quantitative because of the inevitable existence of individual bias.

Level of detail is not the greatest strength of the expert interview, but interviews may provide incredible depth that is not achievable through other techniques. Interviews may also be so superfluous that the information is useless. Again, the talents of the human resources drive the ultimate level of detail.

Utility is a subjective factor that takes into account both the effort involved and the value of the information. For most expert interviews, the documentation developed after completing the interviews becomes a crucial element in the project's records.

Summary

In determining the effectiveness of expert interviews, it is vital to evaluate the skills of both the interviewer and the interviewee. That information provides the best sense of how well (and how accurately) the insights required will be developed. Although team members with limited skill sets can reasonably handle expert interviews, those who understand the critical nature of the expert interview and the numerous applications for the technique will achieve the best results in the end.

5

PLANNING MEETINGS
The Risk Management Plan

Technique Description

Planning meetings are conducted to ensure the organization has a consistent vision in terms of the project's risk methodology, roles and responsibilities, timing, thresholds, reporting formats, and approaches to tracking. Planning meetings focus on bringing together key stakeholders on risk to determine the risk practices to be pursued and the approach to be used in pursuing them.

When Applicable

This technique is recommended for all projects. Planning meetings ensure a general team acceptance of risk management as a practice. The technique is most effective in the initial risk-planning stages but will apply in other processes as well. When conducting risk reviews and evaluations, the basic risk management plan may be reconsidered.

Inputs and Outputs

Planning meetings have a number of inputs. Foremost among them, the existing risk and project data should be researched and made available during planning meetings. In some organizations, such data will be scant; in others, they will be voluminous. Participants should come to the meeting with clear expectations that they will share their own perspectives on risk thresholds and organizational policy. Any risk templates or policies that exist organizationally must also be brought to the table for this process. When complete, the session(s) should close with a clear risk methodology for the project in question, as well as the roles and responsibilities, timing, thresholds, reporting formats, and approaches to tracking. The information should be well documented and available to all key project stakeholders.

Major Steps in Applying the Technique

Since planning meetings result in a project-specific version of what should be organizational practice, key concerns rest with the interpretation of the existing information. If, however, the existing information is misinterpreted, then the possibility exists that the risk management plan will not accurately reflect the organization's risk tolerances and thresholds. It is also possible for the project team to err excessively on the side of caution *or* instability. Some basic practices to ensure consistency are embedded in the following processes:

Review the project charter. The project team needs to ensure that there is unanimity of vision on the project objectives, as well as on the overall approach. In addition, the team must ensure that there is clarity on the duration and scope of the project manager's authority. The level of authority in part defines the capacity of the project team to manage risk effectively, whereas the project manager's ability to manage resources dictates the number and quality of the personnel responsible for risk management.

Assess the existing organizational risk-handling policies. Participants will save time if they take advantage of information that already exists on managing risk. Tools, techniques, and templates all work together to streamline the process. Predefined application of those tools expedites the decision-making process if team members are in a quandary as to how to ensure thorough identification, qualification, quantification, and response development. Limits on reserves, insurance, warranties, and other fundamental strategy issues may also be identified here. The project manager should make certain that all germane policy issues are clearly documented and noted in preparation for and during the meeting.

Identify resource support. In most organizations, some risk responsibilities have owners before the project ever gets under way. For example, legal departments take responsibility for all contractual issues. Human resource departments assume responsibility for health, welfare, and compensation risks. Senior management assumes risks that fall into the area of management reserves, the unknown unknowns of the project universe. In different organizations, different players have predetermined roles and responsibilities for risk. These players should be noted for future reference so that their expertise may be tapped and they can be aware of their role in working with the specific risks relative to the project in question.

Establish risk tolerances. Perhaps, the single most daunting task of the planning meeting is that participants from a variety of organizations who support the project should clearly identify what their risk tolerances are in terms of cost, schedule, performance, and other mission-critical areas. In many cases, individuals will find it difficult to deal with this abstraction as they wrestle with the notion of "how much is too much." To overcome this difficulty, the project manager may wish to identify a sample set of scenarios to test individual and organizational tolerance on various risk issues. A manager who cannot simply say "I won't accept a cost overrun of greater than 20 percent" may be able to share the same information when it is posed as a scenario (such as, "If a team member came to you and reported a 10 percent overrun, would you shut down the project? A 20 percent overrun? A 30 percent overrun?"). Such scenarios are not limited to cost or schedule alone. It is important to know what thresholds are for performance issues and for other issues of importance (politics, customer satisfaction, and employee attrition, for example). Risk tolerances should be identified for all key stakeholders as wide variations in perceptions of risk that can potentially skew data analysis later in the risk qualification process.

Establish risk thresholds and their triggers. On the basis of the risk tolerances (the points beyond which we cannot go), the team can now identify thresholds at which organization behavior should change. As practicable, thresholds should be established at such a point that a tolerance is being approached, but can still be avoided. If there are visible identifiers that clearly warn that a threshold has been breached, these triggers should be documented and communicated out to the broader set of project stakeholders to ensure the highest levels of visibility.

Review the WBS. As with most project management processes, the work breakdown structure is a key input to risk management. The WBS also clarifies the needs of the project at both the summary and detailed levels. The WBS generates insight on where and how the process will flow effectively and where temptation may exist to circumvent the best practice. Since any work associated with the project risk management plan will ultimately be incorporated into the WBS, a clear understanding of its content to date is appropriate here.

Apply organizational risk templates. Not every organization has risk management templates. Some risk templates provide general guidance, whereas others explain each step of the process in excruciating detail. The general rule for risk templates is that if they exist, then use them because they normally reflect the best practice in the organization as well as lessons learned.

Outputs from these meetings should include a clear approach as to how risk management will be conducted. At both micro- and macro-levels, stakeholders should have a clear understanding of how the remaining steps in the process will be carried out and by whom. According to the *PMBOK® Guide* (2013), the following elements become components of the risk management plan:

The *methodology* for project risk management will include a basic outline of both the process and tools for the remainder of the risk management effort. This may be a rudimentary explanation that risk management will consist of a risk identification meeting, some quick qualification, and a response development discussion. It may also be a complex series of steps including plans for prequalification of risk data, reviews using Monte Carlo analysis, and integrated analyses of risk strategies. In any case, the methodology should clarify the timing of when various steps in the process are going to be applied and the individuals who will have *responsibility*.

The risk management plan should incorporate detail on *roles and responsibilities* for risk practices throughout the project life cycle. The plan's roles and responsibilities section will include escalation practices (such as when it is time to notify the management that a particular risk event is imminent).

The risk management plan should have indicators as to how the risk *budget* will be established for both contingency reserve (reserves for overruns within the project) and management reserve (reserves for issues outside the project purview). Although the final monetary figure may not yet be assigned, the approach to risk budgeting should be documented.

The plan will include the *timing for risk practices*, including the frequency of risk identification, qualification, and response development and any organizationally specific triggers that may prompt an early recurrence of the cycle.

The planning meeting should clarify what risk documentation approaches will be applied, including documentation *formats*. Any risk *tracking* requirements should also be clarified during the session.

Although organizational risk *thresholds* are critical inputs to planning meetings, one of the outputs of the meetings should clearly be risk tolerances and thresholds at the project level. Project-specific risk thresholds give team members an indication of when differing levels of intervention are required.

Either in line with the thresholds or as a separate issue, the planning meeting(s) may generate specific metrics for *scoring and interpretation*. Common values for concepts such as "high probability" or "moderate impact" ensure that risk qualification will run more smoothly. Similarly, the application of risk models, discussed in Chapter 28, may be described here. Definitions of probability and impact, displayed in a probability–impact matrix, are often among the outputs.

Initial risk *categories* may also be generated during these planning meetings. These categories may be broken down into project areas, project-specific risk areas, or organizationally specific risk areas. These data can be displayed in a risk breakdown structure (see Chapter 15) to facilitate understanding of the relationships among the categories.

Use of Results

After planning meetings have concluded, the information should be distilled and documented for easy retrieval by anyone responsible for project planning. Some information will be used immediately (as with the application of risk model assessments), whereas other information will be used throughout the risk management process (such as risk thresholds).

Resource Requirements

Planning meetings require a panel of participants, which alone makes it a challenge. In many organizations, merely bringing together the key stakeholders early in a project can be the single greatest impediment to a well-run planning session. In addition, the planning session will require a facilitator with the capability to educe information on individual and organizational risk thresholds. That often requires the exploration of issues, scenario development, and analysis and interpretation of information. The facilitator should have the ability to build on the information and insights that the participants provide. In a perfect situation, the planning meeting will have a secretary or recorder responsible for capturing the risk plan information as it evolves. The recorder should be able to thoroughly document all planning meeting discussions.

Reliability

The reliability of the process largely hinges on the ability of the facilitator to elicit information from a group of participants. Drawing out scoring metrics and interpretation, for example, requires patience and a clear understanding of the information and insight being extracted. The reliability of the information and the risk plan that the planning meeting generates also depend on the depth of information and infrastructure already in place in the organization.

Selection Criteria

As with each chapter on techniques, planning meetings are assessed using selection criteria relating to resource requirements, applications, and outputs for the technique. To compare planning meetings with other techniques, review Table II.1.

Resource Requirements

Although the risk-planning meeting generally requires less than a half-day session, the assembled time is a critical resource, particularly given the number of participants involved. The time spent together is important for clarifying and resolving issues, as is *full* participation. Often, the challenge is ensuring that all participants are available and will be present at the same time.

The other key resource for a well-run session will be the facilitator. Although the project manager may assume this role at times, it is not uncommon to bring in an external facilitator familiar with the process and the organization. His or her chief skill is to ensure involvement by all participants and to facilitate group understanding of the process.

Cost for the risk-planning meeting will consist of the hourly wages for the participants and any fees associated with the facilitator.

Proper facilities and equipment for a planning meeting will ideally include an off-site meeting area (to minimize disruption) and the tools for recording the minutes of the meeting. Flip charts (or erasable boards) and a high-resolution digital camera will allow for inexpensive information capture from any group discussions.

The *time needed to implement* a planning meeting normally consists of a half-day of coordination to ensure all participants are aware of (and available for) the session and a half-day for implementation and postmeeting documentation capture.

Ease of use is high, as there are very few individuals who have not participated in meetings, which generate a relatively low-threat environment. As the goal of the planning meeting is not to critique but rather to gather and structure data, a skilled facilitator's presence makes the meetings relatively easy to run.

The project manager's *time commitment* is based in part on his or her role. If the project manager also serves as the facilitator and recorder, then the level of commitment is more significant. If a consultant or internal facilitator is running the session, then the project manager's time commitment is slight, saving for postmeeting documentation capture.

Applications

The planning meeting, as a component of building a sound project risk infrastructure, is primarily launched early in the project, ideally during the concept or ideation process.

Project status reporting refers to monitoring plans, costs, and schedules. This meeting will largely determine the structure of such status reports, particularly as they relate to risk. Levels of reporting and reporting requirements should be established during the planning meeting. The applicability here is high.

Major planning decisions are frequently based on the relative levels of risk involved in the project. They may also be rooted in the risk reviews, which are scheduled and structured during this process. The impact of planning meetings on planning decisions should be high.

Contract strategy selection does not heavily rely on planning meetings because procurement discussions in such meetings are normally extremely limited.

The planning meeting may establish review schedules for milestones, but otherwise, planning meetings do not have a significant role in *milestone preparation*.

Design guidance is an issue that can be and frequently is addressed in planning meetings because it often represents opportunities to bring together key players in an environment where they may freely exchange ideas.

Source selection is not a prime application for planning meetings as procurement representatives are rarely in attendance at such sessions. Although meetings are appropriate for source selection, planning meetings are not normally focused on the procurement process and thus have limited utility for source selection.

Planning meetings partially support *budget submittal*, but they are by no means the exclusive venue for preparing for such submittals. Planning meetings clarify the infrastructure essential to the project (and thus the base investment for the project as well). But planning meetings can rarely accomplish the in-depth research necessary to generate the quantifiable data associated with budgets. They may, however, generate information on risk budgets, such as the contingency reserve, which will become a component of the budget.

Planning meetings also serve other applications. They can be used to establish the organization's risk tolerances and thresholds, as well as the general culture for risk responses. The meetings can be used to explore specific risk events or general risk strategies. They present a wonderful opportunity to build the team and make team members risk aware.

Outputs

Outputs of the planning meeting are most often a set of minutes (or, in the extreme, a transcript of the meeting), as well as a draft of the risk management plan. Outputs can include qualitative data as well as group and individual perspectives on quantitative data.

> *Accuracy* addresses the viability and soundness of planning meeting data. Accuracy in the planning meeting environment is generally a function of the levels of information and insight available to the team members in attendance. Although meetings are easy to hold, there are limits to their accuracy if the wrong attendees have been enlisted to participate. Accuracy can best be ensured with a diverse participant set, with all equally committed to a thorough analysis of project risk. Divergent viewpoints limit the planning meeting propensity for groupthink and encourage full discussion on issues such as risk probability and impact. The skill of the facilitator will directly influence accuracy inasmuch as he or she will largely be responsible for directing discussions toward issues that are germane to the risk analysis. Even though planning meetings are a common and appropriate technique, outputs are not purely quantifiable.

Level of detail is a strength of the planning meeting if adequate time is allowed to explore the project risk culture, language, and environment. As multiple perspectives are brought to bear, there are greater opportunities to investigate in depth the risks and their potential impacts. As with accuracy, the skill of the facilitator will be a determining factor as to whether a desirable level of detail is achieved. More than the planning meeting duration, facilitator skill determines the degree to which this technique will extract and distill the appropriate information.

Utility takes into account both the effort involved and the value of the information. Planning meetings have high utility because the team members who participated in the process will likely be the same individuals responsible for using the information. Since they generate the information, they are both more aware of it and more likely to be able to apply the outputs.

Summary

The facilitator is one key to an effective planning meeting. However, a good facilitator will work specifically to identify risk issues in the organization and the potential impact of these issues with the team. A skilled facilitator will studiously avoid the desire of some team members to wallow in organizational issues, turning a healthy risk analysis into a "whine-fest." Instead, a skilled facilitator will directly focus on the issues, symptoms, and triggers that the team members identify and will explore in depth all facets of the project's risks. Those individuals without a visible stake will also achieve the best outcome.

6

RISK PRACTICE
METHODOLOGY

Organizational risk practices are frequently perceived as ad hoc phenomena, created on a project-by-project or on a project manager-by-project manager basis. Nothing could be further from the truth. Organizational risk practices are those that are consistent and work to ensure that

Risk management is applied
Risk management is applied to consistent levels of depth
Risk management is applied by taking advantage of organizational best practices

Although each project's risks are different (due to the unique nature of projects), a risk management methodology ensures a measure of consistency. Application depends on the project itself, but a sound methodology will encourage some deployment consistency. That consistency should also promote long-term knowledge transfer across projects.

Methodologies are practices that are rendered consistent within and across an organization in an effort to allow for greater continuity from project manager to project manager, project to project, and team to team. Misapplication of methodologies can sometimes lead to organizational infighting and blame, where the processes the methodology prescribes are viewed as responsible for failure to identify or mitigate particular risks.

The organization, the project office, or a pioneering few project managers with a passion for analyzing risk often establish methodologies. They can be developed from an organization's grass roots, or they can evolve from directives from the senior management. In either case, they hinge on buy-in at some level of the organization, and they must build on that buy-in to integrate other divisions, factions, and suborganizations within the organization. These organizational process assets are essential to building risk management plans and supporting risk management practice.

Technique Description

A risk methodology is made up of a series of pro forma steps that are to be followed based on the needs and the structures of the project(s) in question. Methodologies are as distinctive as the organizations that support them, but they have some basic components in common. Most methodologies will outline clear process steps, forms, and practices. Most of them will dictate (on a scaled basis) the frequency with which these components are applied. They may be stored and shared either in hard copy or electronically, but they do afford the organization a common repository both for the forms and for their completed counterparts.

As a skeletal example, such a methodology may include guidance and direction similar to the framework in Table 6.1. This methodology is not designed as a template but rather as a representative of what a sound risk methodology might include.

Although Table 6.1 does not show the level of detail that would be found in a risk methodology for a real project, it does provide a sense of what types of information may be incorporated. Some of the subelements of the methodology may evolve differently in different projects. In any case, all these elements should be incorporated in the risk management plan.

When Applicable

This technique is recommended for all projects (but, of course, only in organizations where methodologies are either in development or in place). Since the methodology represents the accumulated practices of the entire project organization, it is generally circumvented only in the most extreme circumstances. It is applicable on an as-described basis (such as whenever the methodology itself says it is appropriate, it is appropriate).

Table 6.1 Sample Risk Methodology

STEP	PROCESS GUIDANCE	TIMING	SPECIAL CONSIDERATIONS
Risk review	This step involves a thorough search of the *sample* database for past project experience with the same customer, product, or service. Outputs should be documented in the Risk-Review-Outputs directory of the PM office support folders.	Prior to risk modeling and at any phase-gate reviews	Note that not all customers within a given business entity are the same. A different project sponsor may radically change the level of project risk and opportunity.
Risk modeling	The *sample* risk model should be scored by at least two project team members who should represent potentially competing interests within the organization. Scoring guidance is provided with the tool.	Prior to project acceptance and prior to risk contingency funding approval	The risk model is designed to provide relative scores on potential project risks. It is not intended to provide guidance on a risk-by-risk basis but instead to afford the organization a perspective on the general level of risk.
Risk identification	*Sample* prefers application of the Crawford Slip and brainstorming techniques, while other approaches, such as nominal group and the Delphi technique, may be appropriate. Identification should involve at least four team members, preferably including at least one from the customer organization.	Early in the concept phase, at phase-gate reviews, and any time the project undergoes significant change	Changes in personnel and requirements are frequently just as harmful to the project and generate as much risk as changes in external influences, such as technology or physical conditions. When in doubt as to the appropriateness of risk identification, it should be conducted.
Risk qualification	All identified risks should be evaluated according to the *sample* scales for impact and probability. These scores should be documented and logged in the project risk subdirectory in the project office repository. The scoring metrics reflect the organization's risk thresholds.	After risk identification and at regular intervals (at least once each quarter of the way through the project)	If the *sample* scale discounts risks that are obviously high probability or high impact, contact the project office to identify the shortcomings in the practice and any recommendations for metrics to overcome those shortcomings.

continued

Table 6.1 *(continued)* Sample Risk Methodology

STEP	PROCESS GUIDANCE	TIMING	SPECIAL CONSIDERATIONS
Risk quantification	All H-H risks (as identified in risk qualification) shall be quantified to establish the expected value *(probability x impact)* of the risks and any contingency funding appropriate to their application.	After risk qualification	Sources for impact and probability data should be thoroughly documented. If such data are the result of expert interviews or other nonquantitative techniques, validate the data to the degree possible by getting second (and third) opinions.
Risk response development	At a minimum, strategies should be developed for the top 20 risks in the project. Strategies should be mapped against a strategy response matrix to ensure consistency and effectiveness of coverage.	After risk qualification and quantification	Those individuals or groups responsible for implementation should ideally develop strategies.
Lessons learned documentation	While most of this information will have been captured during the other stages in the risk process, it is important to close out the project with a comprehensive review of lessons learned. This should incorporate specific, actionable steps that can be pursued by other project managers on future efforts.	Regularly, as a component of the other steps, and at project termination	Lessons learned should capture a contact name, e-mail, and telephone number to ensure effective tracking.

Inputs and Outputs

Application of a risk management methodology has one key prerequisite: having a guide, a handbook, or an instruction on how the methodology will be applied. Without such guidance, any organizational development efforts for a risk methodology are rendered moot. The guidance may point to any number of other tools and techniques, such as expert interviewing, brainstorming, simulation analyses, or others discussed in this book. The key rationale for having a methodology is to ensure a measure of consistency in its application. Outputs from the process will include documentation for each step of the processes that the methodology identifies. Outputs will be methodology specific.

Major Steps in Applying the Technique

Since each methodology is different, the steps used will vary as well. However, some modest commonalities can be applied:

Review all steps before applying any of them. Inasmuch as many steps are contingent on other steps, it is important to have a comprehensive overview before attempting application of any single step. Since outputs of a single process may serve as inputs for many others, a holistic perspective is essential to proper use.

Check any information repositories. As both inputs and outputs will have common homes, it is important to make sure that information stores identified in the methodology are current and that they contain the variety and types of information the methodology describes.

Affirm forms and formats. Since function frequently follows form, it is important to know what forms and formats are appropriate for the project and whether these forms and sample applications in the formats are available. It is often reasonable to review application practice with those who have used it in the past to ensure the practices are still applicable and valid.

Identify archival responsibility. Someone in the organization must ultimately take responsibility to complete the forms, archive the information, and track risk information required under the methodology. The archivist can be either the greatest strength of such a methodology or its greatest weakness. In many organizations that have worked to implement methodologies, the initial implementation has gone smoothly, only to have poor follow-through and weak archiving damages the long-term application. In addition, the archivist frequently becomes responsible for identifying informational gaps, and in many ways, takes on the role of a caretaker for the methodology.

Establish a regular review. Although an effective archivist can be the strength of a good methodology, regular reviews ensure that no single imprint is impressed too heavily on the data generated through the methodology. Different perspectives on the information developed and retained ensure that the organization takes advantage of the breadth of its organizational memory rather than the depth of a single individual.

Use of Results

Methodologies are based on history. The only advantages from risk methodologies for new projects stem from information generated on *past* projects. As methodologies are put into practice, the history that they create becomes valuable only as it is applied. The old axiom, "Those who do not learn from history are condemned to repeat it," applies in both the business world and the project world just as readily as it applies to governments and civilizations.

Information from methodologies provides the background and history that allows a new team member to integrate into the project more quickly. It also permits a replacement project manager to better understand the breadth of what has transpired. The information should clarify the strengths of the relationships, as well as the weaknesses, and should afford the project team visibility on what is going on with other divisions, functions, and partners serving the same project. The methodology facilitates communication and does so in a manner that ensures that everyone in the organization knows where certain data types are stored and how they can be accessed.

Resource Requirements

Although resource requirements for following methodologies are methodology specific, two critical roles are the manager responsible for implementation and the project archivist. The project manager should ideally be someone who clearly understands both the informational requirements of the methodology and the rationale for collecting that information. Without a clear understanding of why the information is being collected, the project manager will have difficulty defending what is frequently a time-intensive process. The archivist's role, as cited earlier, is in many ways the cornerstone of a successful methodology. Capturing information thoroughly and in a timely manner leads to a much higher probability of success. Archivists who write in bullets and cite oblique references may satisfy the technical requirements of the methodology but will fall short in terms of serving most methodologies' intents. Complete sentences and exhaustive references to external sources build organizational memory, which is a key goal of a comprehensive risk methodology.

Reliability

Methodologies are as reliable as their historians. If an organization rewards their practice and uses information from the methodologies, then the methodologies are highly reliable. If, instead, the information is perceived as data for data's sake, then reliability will drop significantly as fewer and fewer team members actively pursue the information.

Methodologies are frequently the fruit of a self-fulfilling prophecy. When maintained and used well, they tend to attract better information and more thorough inputs. If, however, they are not maintained well, then fewer people will see their value and will actively make contributions. Weak inputs can drive a downward spiral from which a methodology cannot recover. If there is evidence that team members are actively investing time and energy in data entry, then the reliability of the methodology, on the whole, is probably high.

Selection Criteria

As with each chapter on techniques, the risk methodology technique is assessed using selection criteria relating to resource requirements, applications, and outputs for the technique. To compare risk practice methodology with other techniques, review Table 6.1.

Resource Requirements

Some resource requirements for methodology applications are actually somewhat more abstract than for some other tools and techniques discussed in this book. Specifically, the methodology infrastructure should be in place, a management champion should exist for that infrastructure, and time and personnel must be allotted to meet the methodology's requirements.

The infrastructure requirements are both physical and documentation based. The physical infrastructure requirements include a common data storage facility for risk information (and ideally, a data administrator to maintain the facility). The documentation infrastructure includes any program forms and formats that become the conduits for data entry.

The second key resource requirement is a management champion. Without executive support, long-term implications of a risk methodology can easily be lost in the short-term demands of a project. An effective management champion will know the reasons behind the methodology and the implications of subverting it. He or she will defend the application of the methodology in the face of adversity and will encourage peers to do likewise.

The other key resources are time and personnel. The archivist and project manager responsible for data gathering and data entry have weighty responsibilities to support the methodology, and without clear support and time, they will be unable to carry out these responsibilities.

> *Cost* for methodology implementation largely depends on the project. In a large-scale, multiyear effort, the costs of implementation are negligible. In a short, multiweek intervention, the costs of implementation may be perceived as significant. The more consistent the organization is in implementing the methodology and the more effective the organization is in facilitating quick, clear data entry, then the less time is required to generate the same level of benefit.

Proper facilities and equipment for a methodology generally include a network server or cloud-based interface that allows for consistent data collection and storage. Any forms or formats that have been developed will also be required, but they will ultimately become part of the interface itself. The system and organizational demands on facilities are initially moderate, becoming easier over time.

The *time needed to implement* a risk methodology is methodology dependent but, in the ideal, should be in proportion to the magnitude of the project. If the infrastructure is already in place, then the time needed to implement should be limited.

Ease of use on a methodology is moderate. Since the steps should be clearly spelled out, the actual application and documentation requirements take time and energy. The documentation requirements also require a deft touch for ensuring that all critical information has been captured. Again, the longer a methodology has been in place and the more consistent its application, then the easier it becomes to use.

The project manager's *time commitment* is largely based on the skills and abilities of the individual identified as a project archivist. A skilled archivist will guide the project manager to fill any informational gaps and will reduce the time and energy involved in research and analysis. A less-skilled archivist may need extensive support from the project manager and may significantly increase the amount of time the project manager will need to invest in data gathering and recording.

Applications

The methodology can be applied most effectively when it brings consistency from project to project and from project manager to project manager. The applicability of the methodologies is assessed on a scale of high, medium, and low.

Project status reporting refers to monitoring plans, costs, and schedules. The monitoring process is frequently a key function of the methodology and is a basic rationale as to why such methodologies are put in place. Project status reports heavily rely on methodologies, particularly for comparative analyses.

Major planning decisions should be rooted in history. The history is gathered in the repositories that the methodology supports. Thus, the methodology and major planning decisions should be inextricably linked.

Contract strategy selection does not rely heavily on methodologies, although any documentation or history on the application of the various types of strategies may prove advantageous to those responsible for contract strategy selection. Still, the relationship between the methodology and contract strategy selection is extremely limited.

Again, methodologies play a tangential role in *milestone preparation*. There is only limited information about milestones captured in most methodologies, and unless that is a focus of the methodology in question, there will be very limited applicability.

Methodologies do not directly support *design guidance*, although the insights from past data collection efforts may prove fruitful.

Methodologies do not support *source selection* unless there are specific elements built into the methodology to address procurement or contracting processes.

The methodology may support *budget submittal* if there are specific risk perspectives reflected in the methodology that focus on building contingency reserves or establishing budgetary practices.

Methodologies also serve other applications. Perhaps most importantly, they focus on the organization's lessons learned. They ensure consistent data collection and a clear means to report risk activity and to catalog specific project risk behaviors. As a tool, methodologies allow organizations to capture information that would otherwise be lost.

Outputs

Outputs of the methodology take on the forms prescribed within the methodology itself. Many organizations generate such information in electronic copy, storing it on the organization's server or cloud data storage site. The outputs can include both qualitative data and individual perspectives on quantitative data.

Accuracy of information from the methodologies is generally perceived as high, even though it is frequently borne out of a variety of qualitative techniques. The reason for this perception of high accuracy is that the information is generated in a consistent manner and is stored in a common repository. That works to create a sense of order (that might not exist if a single project manager simply generated the information for a single project).

Level of detail is a strength of methodologies because the descriptions of the steps within the methodology work to drive information to the level of detail appropriate for the information concerned.

Utility is a subjective factor that takes into account both the effort involved and the value of the information. Since organizations have seen fit to collect whatever information is gathered under the methodology, the utility of the data must be assumed to be high.

Summary

Methodologies are not the result of the work of an individual project manager. While the inputs reflect a single-project experience, the structure is a direct reflection of the informational needs and the vision of the supporting organization. And although an organization may have no long-term goals for the information, even a short-term rationale (such as multiproject resource management or risk contingency reserve determination) can make development of the methodology a sound, reasonable business practice.

7
DOCUMENTATION REVIEWS

In some projects, a documentation review is seen as an opportunity to infer information that otherwise does not exist about a project. In other projects, however, it is a sincere effort to ensure that the natural risks inherent in any given activity are identified, no matter where they are embedded within the project. Documentation reviews allow for thorough and consistent analysis of the breadth of support documentation in the project, ranging from the statement of work to the work breakdown structure to the project charter. Essentially, *any* project documentation may reflect an element of risk and should be reviewed as a simple best-practice evaluation of the project in its entirety.

Project documentation may vary from project to project, but any significant documentation either on the client side or from the project organization's data pool may harbor risk information that would be missed without a thorough review.

A project documentation review is more than a simple reading of the project's documents, but it is not a dissection or parsing of every word ever generated about the project. Rather, it is a balanced analysis of project documentation to identify any assumptions made, generalities stated, or concerns expressed that are not otherwise flagged in the requirements or the statement of work.

Although documentation reviews can include any number of different documents in the project, certain documents should be reviewed at a minimum: the WBS (if developed), the statement of work (or memorandum of understanding), the project charter, and any cost/schedule documents. Even though documents may be in various stages of development, they should be reviewed if they dictate project outcome or reflect project intent.

Technique Description

A project documentation review is a thorough reading of the pertinent documentation with one critical issue always in play: Does the information in this document identify potential risks that we may face on this project? This review can take place in a group setting or by having individuals analyze the documentation with which they have the greatest familiarity.

In a WBS, for example, a documentation review would involve a read through of all activities (at all levels) and for each one, and then asking the concurrent question: What are the risks?

The technique requires no special skills, only familiarity with the processes described by the documentation under review and a sense of what potential risks exist therein.

When Applicable

This technique is recommended for all projects when their initiating documents are complete. It is not essential that the WBS be fully developed, but it is helpful to continue the reviews as the project documentation evolves. Any risks ascribed to discoveries from a piece of documentation (or components thereof) should be cataloged and matched up with that piece of documentation.

Inputs and Outputs

Inputs for documentation reviews are rather obvious: project documentation. As stated earlier, any documentation designed to lend clarity to the project, its processes, or its objectives should be included in such a review.

Outputs will be identified risks, risk sources, and triggers captured during the analysis. They should be documented, cataloged, and readily available to anyone conducting further reviews of the same documentation at a later date.

Major Steps in Applying the Technique

Since documentation reviews are rather generally applied, the steps may vary somewhat based on the type of documentation undergoing review. However, there is some consistency that spans most of these reviews:

Identify the available pool of project documentation. This does not include every engineer's note and Post-it® written about the project. However, it should incorporate only information that directly contributes to the understanding of the project, its requirements, and the relationships between and among internal and external entities.

Identify appropriate parties to review the documentation. Some documentation will be so highly technical that only one or two staffers would have any idea whether any elements represent risk. The key is to match the individuals responsible for the document *to* the document.

Read the documentation with an eye to risk and document. As the document reviewer analyzes the documentation, it is important to keep the perspective on what risk(s) information contained in the document will generate. If that context can be kept in mind, then there are wonderful opportunities to plumb new depths to find risks from planning, contracting, and internal support perspectives.

Catalog any risk issues. As new risks, triggers, or symptoms are identified, the information should be captured and linked to the original documentation. In that way, anyone reviewing the documentation will be able to spot the concerns that have already been highlighted.

Communicate any new risks. Finally, the identified risks should be shared through any communication channels established in the project communications plan or in the project risk methodology. If the risks are not communicated to the other parties on the project, then the chances that the information will be used effectively are slight.

Use of Results

Information gathered during documentation review may represent the bulk of common risk knowledge on the project. If the common risks that are identified are the same risks that historically have caused the project organization the highest levels of concern, then this may be the risk technique with the lowest level of technical support required and the highest yield.

The information this technique provides should include virtually all obvious project risks. It should also generate a second set of risk information that is more project specific and more directly related to the documented understanding of various project parties. In best-practice organizations, outputs from documentation reviews will be directly linked to the original documentation used in the analysis.

Resource Requirements

Resource requirements for documentation reviews are specific to the documentation but are basically those individuals who have a level of understanding and familiarity with the documentation sufficient to identify anomalies and common concerns. Although the project manager will share responsibility for ensuring that the information is properly focused, the reviewer has the primary role in the review. The best reviewers will be those who can both identify risk issues and communicate them in ways that are significant and meaningful to the project team as a whole.

Reliability

Documentation reviews are as reliable as the information used to develop them. If the project has a rich documentation pool and those who understand the scope and nature of the work can tap that pool, then the review's reliability will be extremely high. If, however, the data pool is shallow or the reviewers are highly inexperienced, then outputs from the documentation review are less likely to be reliable.

Selection Criteria

As with each chapter on techniques, the documentation review technique is assessed using selection criteria relating to resource requirements, applications, and outputs for the technique. To compare documentation reviews with other techniques, review Table II.1.

Resource Requirements

The basic resource requirements for documentation reviews include the documentation and the personnel. The documentation needs to be centrally archived, available to the reviewers, and clearly related to the project, its approaches, and its personnel.

Documentation for such an effort may include, but is not limited to the

Work breakdown structure
Project charter
Contract
Memorandum of understanding
Statement of work
Requirements documentation
Network diagrams

Personnel assigned to review each of the documentation elements should be those individuals with a clear understanding of and experience with the documentation. They should be individuals who have the ability to communicate what aspects within the documentation they identified as risks and their reasons for doing so.

Cost for documentation reviews, particularly when weighed against the yield, is relatively small.

Proper facilities and equipment for documentation reviews normally consist of a common data repository, such as a network server or cloud storage that allows for consistent data collection and storage.

The *time needed to implement* documentation reviews tends to be one of the most attractive aspects of the technique. It is normally seen as a short-term effort that can be completed as team members have the time available to perform the work.

Ease of use is high for documentation reviews because they generally involve a simple read-and-review cycle. The most challenging and time-consuming aspect of the process is the documentation required to capture the reviewers' insights.

The project manager's *time commitment* depends on the degree to which the project manager performs the task independently.

The more team members are given responsibility for tasks associated with a documentation review, then the less time is required on the part of the project manager.

Applications

Documentation reviews are most effective when the data pool is deep and readily accessible. They allow for interpretation of project assumptions, and to a degree, validation of some information that is generated during the project life cycle.

Documentation reviews strongly support *project status reporting* because the reviews will normally identify any shortcomings in the existing base of project status information (as well as any unusual reporting requirements).

Major planning decisions, because they are based on project history, rely heavily on project documentation reviews. The reviews afford the organization an opportunity to clarify the foundation for such decisions and ensure that there is a clear interpretation of the documentation being evaluated.

Contract strategy selection may rely somewhat on documentation reviews, although the two are not inextricably linked. Since documentation reviews generally include the contract, some overlap here is almost inevitable. However, the degree of support is moderate at best.

Milestone preparation will get only nominal support from documentation reviews although the reviews may provide some insight as to the level of effort that is necessary for preparing for major project deliverables and events.

Design guidance should rely heavily on documentation reviews because the reviews should point to customer expectations, the overall project objectives, and the detailed implementation approach.

For similar reasons, documentation reviews can support *source selection* because the nature of the project work and the history of performance in achieving similar goals may go a long way toward establishing the best available sources for project performance.

Again, for many of the same reasons, documentation reviews support *budget submittal.* The documentation will include information on past performance, issues, and concerns, and as such, may provide strong support for budget submittals.

Documentation reviews constitute a key component of best-practice project management. Best-practice managers rely on history to determine future courses of action. They understand the value of the information that exists in a project and do not presume to do things the same way each time they tackle a new endeavor. To discern between situations where the same old approach is appropriate and a new action is called for, they must know and understand the parameters of the situation. Documentation reviews afford such a level of understanding.

Outputs

The outputs of the documentation review are more of documentation. They comprise supporting documentation that clarifies, interprets, and identifies risk, and establishes a common understanding of the existing documentation.

Accuracy of documentation reviews is largely reviewer dependent. A cursory review with no context to interpret the information may leave the organization with less valuable (and less accurate) information. On the other hand, a more exhaustive parsing of the documentation may generate far more accurate insight.

Level of detail is highly reviewer dependent. Some reviewers know how to examine project information for risk insights that will add to the understanding of the project. Others will keep the detail too high level to be of any significant value.

Utility is high for documentation reviews because newly discovered information is maintained and stored with the original documentation. It expands the organization's understanding of risk values and keeps risk visible in tandem with information where risk is sometimes seen as a secondary issue (as with the project charter).

Summary

To some degree, documentation reviews seem like the tedium of an ordinary project where ordinary practices include reviewing the paperwork. In some ways, that may be an apt description. But documentation reviews go beyond those limiting walls. Documentation reviews provide levels of depth and clarity that we might otherwise never capture. They provide a clearer vision as to what the project is intended to accomplish and how it will do so.

8

ANALOGY COMPARISONS

The analogy comparison and lessons-learned techniques for risk identification, qualification, and quantification are based on the supposition that no project—no matter how advanced or unique—represents a totally new system. Most projects originated or evolved from existing projects or simply represent a new combination of existing components or subsystems. A logical extension of this premise is that the project manager can gain valuable insights concerning various aspects of a current project's risk by examining the successes, failures, problems, and solutions of similar existing or past projects. The experience and knowledge gained or lessons learned can be applied to the task of identifying potential risk in a project and developing a strategy to handle that risk.

Technique Description

The analogy comparison and lessons-learned techniques involve identifying past or existing programs similar to the current project effort and reviewing and using data from these projects in the risk process. The term "similar" refers to the commonality of various characteristics that define a project. The analogy may be similar in technology, function, contract strategy, manufacturing process, or other area. The key is to understand the relationships among the project characteristics and the particular aspects of the project being examined. For example, in many system developments, historical cost data show a strong positive relationship with technical complexity. Thus, when searching for a project in which to analyze cost risk for comparison, it makes sense to examine data from projects with similar function, technology, and technical complexity. The use of data or lessons learned from past programs may be applicable at the system, subsystem, or component level. For instance, although an existing system's function and quantity produced differ, some key element may be similar in performance characteristics to that of a current project, thereby making the element a valid basis for analogy comparison. All in all, several different projects may be used for comparison to the current project at various levels of the end item.

When Applicable

Project managers can apply lessons learned or compare existing projects to new projects in all phases and aspects of a project any time historical data are useful. These techniques are especially valuable when a system is primarily a new combination of existing subsystems, equipment, or components. The value increases significantly when recent and complete historical project data are available. When properly done and documented, analogy comparison provides a good understanding of how project characteristics affect identified risks and serves as necessary inputs to other risk techniques.

Inputs and Outputs

Three types of data are required to use this technique:

   Description and project characteristics of the new system and its
      components (or approach)
   Description and project characteristics of existing or past projects and their components (or approach)
   Detailed data (cost, schedule, and performance) for the previous
      system being reviewed

The description and project characteristics are needed to draw valid analogies between the current and past projects. Detailed data are required to evaluate and understand project risks and their potential effect on the current project.

Often, the project manager needs technical specialists to make appropriate comparisons and to help extrapolate or adjust data from old projects to make inferences about new projects. Technical or project judgments may be needed to adjust findings and data for differences in complexity, performance, physical characteristics, or contracting approach.

The outputs from examining analogous projects and lessons learned typically become the inputs to other risk assessment and analysis techniques. The review of project lessons-learned reports can identify a number of problems to be integrated into a project's watch list or risk register. The length and volatility of past development projects provide information that helps build realistic durations in a network analysis of a new project's development schedule. Data from the lessons-learned review become the source of information for risk identification, qualification, quantification, and response techniques.

Major Steps in Applying the Technique

The major steps in using analogous system data and lessons learned include identifying analogous programs, collecting data, and analyzing the data gathered. Figure 8.1 shows a further breakdown of this process.

The first step is to determine the information needs in this phase of risk management. Information needs can range from preliminary risk assessment on a key approach to a project-wide analysis of major risks associated with the effort. The second step is to define the basic characteristics of the new system. With the new system generally defined, the analyst can begin to identify past projects with similar attributes for comparison and analysis.

Since they are interdependent, the next steps in this process are generally done in parallel. The key to useful analogy comparisons is the availability of data on past projects. The new system is broken down into logical components for comparison while assessing the availability of historical data. The same level of detailed information is necessary to make comparisons. On the basis of the availability of data, the information needs of the process, and the logical structure of the project, analogous systems are selected and data are gathered.

Data gathered for comparison include the detailed information being analyzed, as well as the general characteristics and descriptions of past projects. General project description data are essential to ensure that proper analogies are being drawn and that the relationship between these characteristics and the detailed data being gathered is clear. For the analogy to be valid, some relationship must exist

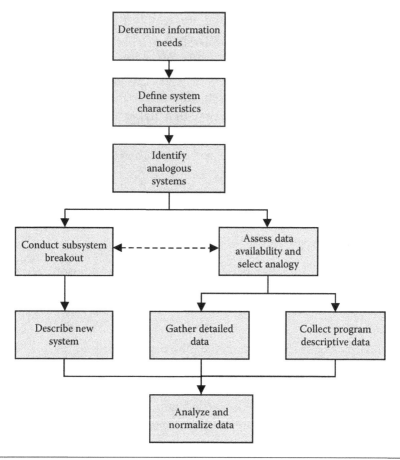

Figure 8.1 Analogy comparison.

between the characteristic being used to make comparisons and the specific aspect of the project being examined.

Often, the data collection process and initial assessment lead to further defining the system for the purpose of comparison. After this has been accomplished, the last step in the process is analyzing and normalizing the historical data. But comparisons to older systems may not be exact. The data may need to be adjusted to serve as a basis for estimating the current project. For example, in analogy-based cost estimating, cost data must be adjusted for inflation, overhead rates, general and administrative (G&A) rates, and so on, for accurate comparison. As a result, project managers frequently require technical assistance to adjust data for differences between past and current projects. The desired outputs provide some insight into the cost, schedule, and technical risks of a project based on observations of similar past projects.

Use of Results

As stated earlier, outputs from analogies and lessons learned typically augment other risk techniques. The results may provide a checklist of factors to monitor for the development of problems or a range of cost factors to use in estimating. Analogies and lessons learned generate risk information. Regardless of whether the information is used in a detailed estimate, in a technology trade-off study, or at a system level for a quick test of reasonableness, the results are intended to provide the analyst with insights for analysis and decision making.

Resource Requirements

Using analogous data and lessons-learned studies to gather risk data is a relatively easy task. Selecting proper comparisons and analyzing the data gathered may require some technical assistance and judgment, but the task is probably not beyond the capabilities of the project manager. However, the time and effort needed for an analogy comparison can vary widely. The resources required depend on the depth of data gathering, the number of different projects, and the availability of historical data. Consequently, a project team can expend much effort for a limited amount of information. That is why an initial assessment of data availability is important in selecting analogous programs to compare.

Reliability

Using analogy comparisons and lessons learned has two limitations. The first, availability of data, has already been discussed. If common project characteristics cannot be found or if detailed data are missing from either the old or new systems, then the data collected will have limited utility. The second limitation deals with the accuracy of the analogy drawn. An older system may be somewhat similar, but rapid changes in technology, manufacturing, methodology, and so on, may make comparisons inappropriate.

Selection Criteria

As with each chapter on techniques, analogy comparison is assessed using selection criteria relating to resource requirements, applications, and outputs for this technique. To compare analogies with other techniques, review Table II.1.

Resource Requirements

The *cost* associated with analogy comparison techniques is relatively low if the organization has been fastidious about retaining information from past projects. If there is a broad database from which to draw information, then the analogy techniques can be easily applied, assuming that the new project is even in part analogous to an older project. Unfortunately, most new projects are not wholly analogous and must be evaluated against piecemeal information. If the data are available, then the resource time consumed may be as little as a week or less. However, if the data are sketchy, then it can take multiple resource months to gather the data from the various departments or projects within the organization.

Proper facilities and equipment are rudimentary, consisting of little more than a server hosting historical project data and client computers with the appropriate database access tools, word processors, and project management applications.

The *time needed to implement* this approach is a direct function of the number of sources from which data are available and the number of team resources assigned to the activity. With a team of three or four data gatherers, even the most complex set of information may be compiled and reviewed in as little as a week or two. With a single individual assigned to the task, the resource hours assigned in the "Cost" category apply.

Ease of use appears to be a major advantage of the analogy approach, but that ease can be deceptive. Some project managers will be tempted to make across-the-board, one-for-one analogies for the entire project. But that is applicable only in the rarest of cases. The technique is appropriate, however, only if it is applied in the context of the new project under consideration. This may be evaluated in terms of the scale of the projects being compared, the time frames in which they are developed, or the resources applied against both. Thus, this technique often appears easier than it is.

The project manager's *time commitment* in this technique is a factor of how heavily involved the project manager wishes to become in analyzing the data. If the project manager wants to spend as little time as possible approving the work of the team, then the level of effort is nominal. It is recommended that the project manager invests at least several hours analyzing the analogous projects driving the conclusions.

Applications

For *project status reporting*, the analogy comparison technique can serve only as a defense of certain numbers that may have been used to establish the baseline for the project. Otherwise, analogy comparisons have little value when assessing the new project's current status.

Major planning decisions should rely very heavily on an organization's lessons learned. History is an excellent teacher, and using the organization's historical experience with similar projects can prove invaluable. If certain approaches have been attempted, then it is vital to find out whether they succeeded or failed.

As with planning decisions, the issue of *contract strategy selection* can be developed using analogy comparison techniques. If work with a similar client, similar project, or similar resources has failed in part due to using one contract strategy, then it is worthwhile to consider alternate strategies.

Milestone preparation is not an area in which analogy comparisons have much value unless a project was noted as exceptional in part because of its outstanding use of milestones. Generally, milestones are seldom major influences in a project's success or failure. In the rare case in which milestones have played a key role, then the analogy technique may apply.

Although *design guidance* does not rely exclusively on analogy comparisons, analogies should be an essential component of

any design decision. Too often, organizations fail to scruti-
nize the failings of past designs, only to learn later that the
project at hand is failing for the same reasons as a project just
a year or two before. Analogy comparisons will not provide
the complete picture on design guidance, but they will provide a sense of corporate history and experience.

Many organizations (like the U.S. government) make analogy
comparisons a key component of *source selection*. Terms such
as "past performance," "performance history," and "preferred
vendor" all reflect some analysis of analogous projects. These
are valuable analyses because organizations should not repeat
the mistake of dealing with a less-than-acceptable vendor.

For *budget submittal*, the analogy comparisons technique has
limited application except as a background for some of the
numbers that may have been incorporated into the budget.
Although analogies may be found, some independent extrap-
olation or evaluation of the data must also be conducted.

Outputs

The *accuracy* of the analogy comparison technique is less than
ideal. This technique relies not only on the accuracy of past
data but also on the accuracy of the interpretation of those
data, which incorporates two variables into the overall assessment of the data for the new project. Thus, the level of accuracy comes into question.

The *level of detail* that the technique generates is practically a
direct function of the volume of data the organization stores.
If an organization is meticulous in its project record keeping,
then the level of detail can be tremendous. If, however, the
organization has a limited, purely anecdotal history, then the
level of detail becomes low at best.

The *utility* of the outputs is based on both the quality of the analogous documentation and the relevance of the analogy. If both
are high quality, then the information obtained has the potential to be extremely useful. If, however, the relevance or quality
is in dispute, then the usefulness diminishes significantly.

Summary

In evaluating the potential use of analogy comparisons for an organization, the first step should always be an assessment of the volume and quality of the documentation to be used for analogies, including how recent it is. If the organization does not effectively maintain this information, then the analogy comparison technique may prove useless for virtually any application.

9

PLAN EVALUATION

This technique highlights and isolates risk disparities in planning. It evaluates project plans for contradictions and voids. Traditional, formal plans used to guide a project include, but are not limited to, the following:

Project
Cost management
Schedule management
Quality management
Communication management
Human resource management
Contract management
Stakeholder management
Test management
Training

Other documents are also essential to the success of the project and to such evaluations:

Work breakdown structure (WBS)
Project specifications
Statement of work (SOW)
Contracts
Other baseline documents

Although plans outline project implementation approaches, other documents represent critical communication with stakeholders about what is to be done. Flaws, inconsistencies, contradictions, and voids in these documents inevitably lead to project problems and introduce significant risk. Figure 9.1 illustrates the linkage between three key documents.

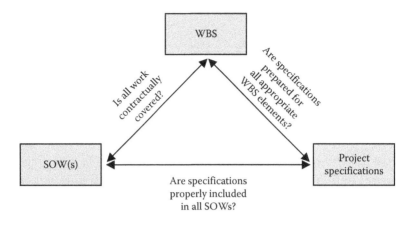

Figure 9.1   Plan evaluation technique.

Technique Description

The plan evaluation technique simply suggests a thorough, recurring internal review of all plans for correctness, completeness, and currency, together with a cross-check for consistency.

Using the WBS for Risk Identification

Proper development of a WBS represents a major step in risk control because it constitutes much of the project definition. Its quality—indeed its very existence—provides the planning framework that sets the standard for the future of the project. As a WBS is completed, a careful examination is appropriate, asking the following questions:

Are all elements of the WBS necessary and sufficient?
Is there a WBS dictionary, and does it adequately explain the content of each element?
Does the WBS represent what is to be done rather than who is to do it?
Are all elements of the WBS present?
Is the contracting strategy reflected in the project WBS?
Is any work to be done that is not reflected in the WBS?

The WBS offers a framework for organizing and displaying risk factors. The technique of downward allocation and upward summarization through the WBS can be used to highlight discrepancies in most of the project's performance parameters, such as efficiency, reliability, cost, and capability.

The WBS provides a sensible structure for treating technical risk. A systematic review for risk identification and preliminary rating of each WBS element will yield much information for the risk analyst.

The relationship between the WBS and the specifications is so important that mapping the relationships is a valuable exercise for the risk analyst. Mapping will highlight inconsistencies between the work to be done and the performance to be achieved. The levels of performance to be attained may also be reflected in the quality plan, if one exists, because careful examination of the quality plan may also have merit as a component of WBS analysis.

The project WBS eventually becomes the aggregate of all contract information, including subcontractors' plans. The risk analyst should review the WBS with the question "Who is doing what?" as a test of reasonableness of the contracting strategy. Finally, the WBS represents the framework for cost and schedule performance (although it is *not* a representation of the schedule itself). A survey of both cost and schedule reporting in the context of the WBS identifies possible blind spots in cost and schedule information. As part of this survey, the analyst can gain valuable insights by comparing the numbering schemes for the WBS, scheduling system, and cost-reporting system. Ease of translation among and ease of summarization within each of these numbering systems can indicate how well traceability among the WBS, schedules, and cost data can be maintained. Incompatibility introduces management risk into the project.

To extract additional risk from the WBS, any variety of techniques may be used, with each one posing the question, "What are the risks for this WBS element?" Expert interviews, brainstorms, and the Crawford slip method can all generate that information.

Using Specifications for Risk Identification

Some of the previous discussion deals with the important relationship between the WBS and the specifications and the need for compatibility. When that compatibility exists, the performance to be achieved can be related to the work to be done. Since the specifications represent the source of all technical performance requirements, they are the single most important source of information for the risk analyst attempting to identify, organize, and display items of technical risk. Each performance parameter of a given WBS element represents a possible focus for an expert interview on technical risk.

As with the WBS, a survey of the specifications is appropriate for risk identification, asking the following questions:

Do the specifications overlay the WBS so that performance requirements are specified for WBS elements?

Are all performance parameters identified even though they may not be specified (that is, given a discrete value)?

Can the risk of achieving the specified value for the performance parameter be sensibly discussed?

Is there a technical performance measurement scheme for each performance parameter?

Using Statements of Work (SOWs) for Risk Identification

The SOW is the one of the most important communication between the project organization and the customer. If the WBS and the specifications are complete and well developed, then SOWs are fairly straightforward. The risk analyst is primarily searching for gaps in coverage and should consider the following questions:

Does the SOW cover whole parts of the WBS that can clearly be evaluated against the specifications?

Does the SOW represent work that matches the project organization's assets and environment in terms of politics, contractual capabilities, and legal capabilities?

Is all work contractually covered?

Are the SOW requirements properly related to the specification?

Developing a Technical Risk Dictionary or Risk Register

A dictionary in project management can expand understanding and provide documentation and background on a specific project area. So far, this chapter has addressed the need to gather all project information with common descriptions into a common database. A technical risk dictionary, as conceptualized in Figure 9.2, offers the risk analyst

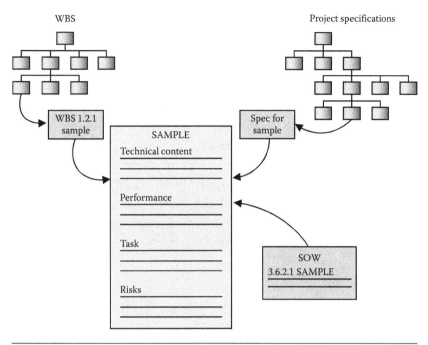

Figure 9.2   Technical risk dictionary.

a single place to gather this information for facilitating the risk identification and definition processes.

Until recently, creating a technical risk dictionary or risk register
has been a formidable editorial task. Advances in project management software, coupled with advances in documentation management, allow for integrated data within a single database, and in some
cases, a single file. In most popular project management software
packages, there are sufficient available text and numbers fields so that
the bulk or whole of the risk dictionary can be maintained in the same
file as the project plan itself. If the text and numbers fields are to be
used this way, then the same text field used for one element in one
project (for example, Text13 = Performance Risk) should be used for
the same purposes in all projects within the organization to facilitate
knowledge transfer. The responsibility for designating the application of such fields often falls to the project support office (PSO) or
project management office (PMO) to ensure consistency across the
organization.

Such information maintenance practices afford project managers a
"home" where their risk information can readily be shared with the

team and where risk identification and management can be integrated into day-to-day operations.

Using Other Plans for Risk Identification

"Risk Identification" in Chapter 3 discusses the use of a top-level risk matrix to highlight and isolate risks. The matrix relies heavily on goal definition and strategy development. The presumption is that the strategies expressed in the project plans are directed at meeting the project goals. Comparing the two can identify risks. The same thinking can be applied to lower-level risk matrices associated with any other management plans (communication, human resource, quality, testing, and so on) that are developed.

When Applicable

The plan evaluation technique is directed specifically at risk identification and is best used for technical risk. Its utility for cost and schedule risk is considerably lower. However, this technique could highlight missing information concerning deliverables that would affect cost and schedule risks. It is most applicable to the implementation phase of a project. As a risk identification technique, it requires the existence of the plans to be evaluated. As a strategy tool (to identify what risks can be avoided), it can be used during the project-planning process.

Inputs and Outputs

Plan evaluation operates on the collective body of documentation broadly referred to as project plans and includes primarily those documents listed earlier. Outputs typically include

Top-level risk matrix
Lower-level risk matrices
Technical risk dictionary
Updated versions of project plans

Major Steps in Applying the Technique

The major steps in plan evaluation are as follows:

Evaluate the WBS for completeness and correctness

Evaluate specifications for completeness, correctness, and compatibility with the WBS

Evaluate SOWs for completeness, correctness, and compatibility with the WBS and for inclusion of specification references

Evaluate other plans and develop a lower-level risk matrix for each

Use of Results

Plan evaluation is designed to improve the quality of and reduce the risks associated with the project plan. The technique also produces descriptive documentation on the technical performance, programmatic risks, and supportability risks associated with the project. The technical risk dictionary or risk register describes technical risks in a centralized location that is cross-referenced with the WBS. This technique can produce a single "official" list of project risks that will receive active management attention.

Resource Requirements

This technique requires a great deal of thought as well as experienced, knowledgeable personnel who are thoroughly familiar with the content of the total project. The project manager (or deputy project manager) leading a team of senior staff members would constitute the ideal team for this technique.

Reliability

The completeness and the farsightedness of the project plans drive the reliability of plan evaluation. If the numerous support plans are all well defined for a low-risk project, then only a handful of project risks will be uncovered. If, however, the support plans are well defined for a higher-risk project, then there is a likelihood that significantly more risks will become evident.

The major caution for using this technique is to avoid forcing the detailed project definition too early. Some inconsistencies exist due to poor planning, but others exist because of a legitimate lack of information.

Selection Criteria

As with each chapter on techniques, plan evaluation is assessed using selection criteria relating to resource requirements, applications, and outputs for the technique. To compare plan evaluation with other techniques, review Table II.1.

Resource Requirements

> With plan evaluations, *cost* constraints are extremely flexible. If the project manager determines that a comprehensive review of every piece of project-planning documentation is appropriate, then numerous resources will be required for an extended period of time. If, by contrast, the project manager determines that a high-level summary review is appropriate, then the resources required will drop significantly.
>
> Heretofore, the discussion in this chapter has focused on in-depth analyses; so, the assumption is that the analysis will be comprehensive. However, comprehensive evaluations may prove to be prohibitively costly because key resources will be required to justify their existing plans and reevaluate the plans' efficacy. To do a comprehensive evaluation, each team member responsible for a component plan will need to spend several days to a week analyzing his or her documentation and documenting those analyses. Consequently, using the full complement of plans described at the beginning of the chapter, an effort for a 1-year period may require 4–6 resource weeks.
>
> *Proper facilities and equipment* are limited to a sufficient number of personal computers to support all team members involved in the review. Team members will need access to the material-planning documentation, including the supporting documents (which would require word-processing applications), and the project management software program and files. This technique is not equipment intensive.

The *time needed to implement* this approach is highly dependent on the number of resources applied. To be effective, one resource should be designated for each major piece of documentation to be evaluated. However, most organizations are not willing to commit that level of staff to a single- evaluation effort. Thus, the work will be spread across a more limited base. In the ideal, this effort should be accomplished in 2 or 3 days using a skilled, broad-based team. Yet, with fewer resources, the effort may take as long as 4–6 resource weeks.

Ease of use is an issue with this technique because the project manager will clearly understand the level of effort required to analyze outputs; but, the management and team members may not appreciate the in-depth analysis essential for a clear understanding of the information. For some team members and stakeholders, the entire package may present information that does not meet their specific needs. For others, the material may be presented in a way they cannot understand. Thus, the proper sorting and filtering of the information is vital to the ease of use for this technique for all its recipients.

The project manager's *time commitment* is significant. Since the project manager normally understands the details of the plans, he or she becomes the focal point for all questions and clarifications that team members require. The project manager's ready availability facilitates the efforts of the technical personnel responsible for their respective support plans or project plan components.

Applications

Plan evaluations are essential to *project status reporting* because, without a thorough review of the project plans and their variances to date, it is impossible to evaluate project status in an accurate, historic context. In many ways, plan evaluations almost force the project team into developing status reports because that is the best application for the technique.

Major planning decisions should depend on a sense of project history and may be subject to the evaluations of specific project plans. The difference in the application with major planning decisions is that major planning decisions may focus on one particular aspect of the project (such as schedule, cost, or performance) and thus may not require the level of depth described in this chapter. The planning decision may also hinge on a single type of support plan or a single component of the project plan. Either way, plan evaluation ultimately provides the ideal support in major planning decisions, whether from a component of the plan or from the comprehensive plan evaluation.

Although *contract strategy selection* relies on the evaluation of the initial project plan, it is not normally considered a key application for plan evaluation. Plan evaluations are usually conducted after the project has been implemented to assess the effectiveness of the plan versus reality.

As with contract strategy selection, *milestone preparation* is most often a step conducted at the beginning of the project. However, there is a slightly closer link between milestone preparation and plan evaluation than what occurs with the contract strategy selection. Specifically, many plan evaluations will lead to corrective action, which often includes adding supplemental milestones to ensure that the corrective action is effective. As such, there is a modest correlation between this application and the technique.

Plan evaluations can support *design guidance* only during the early phases of the project, and even then, only to a limited degree. To provide guidance, the plans must show some direct link between the original design selected and the project plan or its supporting plans. If no such link exists, then the plan evaluation technique does not apply.

In *source selection*, there is little applicability for plan evaluation unless the selection occurs at midproject or in the context of multiple projects. The plan evaluation technique can afford insights into the needs of the project and the shortcomings of the existing vendor base. But for initial source or vendor selection, there is little applicability.

The plan evaluation technique does not affect *budget submittal* unless (as with source selection) the budget is an interim budget being submitted at midproject. In any other scenario, the plan evaluation technique has extremely limited applicability.

Outputs

Accuracy is a cornerstone of the plan evaluation technique. It is wholly designed to discover inaccuracies and to address them. Although much of the evaluation is subjective, the results tend to make the plans reflect the project better as it evolves.

The *level of detail* in the plan evaluation technique is exhaustive. The information drawn from the various plans and the assessment of these plans are most effectively realized when all the plans are assessed for their effectiveness to date. Although a simple WBS review might require moderate scrutiny, the level of effort and the depth of information developed in a comprehensive plan evaluation are extensive.

For areas in which the plan evaluation technique is logically applied, its *utility* is extremely high. Unfortunately, project managers may be tempted to use plan evaluation as a panacea for analyzing all project risks. Although plan evaluation applies well in some areas, it is inappropriate in others. The evaluation data are so in depth and diverse that they have the potential to be misinterpreted or misused.

Summary

In an ideal world where seasoned professionals of long tenure support a project manager, plan evaluations would produce few results for a significant level of effort. All planning documents would be created in proper sequence, each with reference to all that preceded it. Eminently logical contracts would be matched with masterful work statements and perfect specifications. In reality, however, as team members shift in and out of projects and as schedules and objectives change, plans often represent the only key to organizational memory. Since planning is conducted early in a project, any link to organizational memory later in the effort becomes significant.

The plan evaluation technique is extremely useful due to its clear strengths in so many applications and its relative value in terms of resource consumption and outputs. As long as the tool is used appropriately by the project manager, it is one of the most powerful techniques available.

10

DELPHI TECHNIQUE

Although people with experience in a particular subject matter are a key resource for expert interviews, they are not always readily available for such interviews; and, in many instances, they prefer *not* to make the time to participate in the data-gathering process. The Delphi technique works to address that situation by affording an alternate means of educing information from experts in a manner that neither pressures them nor forces them to leave the comfort of their own environs.

The Delphi technique has the advantage of drawing information directly from experts without impinging on their busy schedules. It also allows for directed follow-up from experts after their peers have been consulted. In the process, it also eliminates much of the potential for expert bias driven by the participation of multiple experts.

Technique Description

The Delphi technique derives its name from the oracle at Delphi. In Greek mythology, the oracle (of the god Apollo) foretold the future through a priestess who, after being posed a question, channeled all knowledge from the gods, which an interpreter then cataloged and translated. In the modern world, the project manager or facilitator takes on the role of the interpreter, translating the insights of experts into common terms and allowing for his or her review and reassessment. The cycle of question, response, and reiteration is repeated several times to ensure that the highest quality of information possible is extracted from the experts.

When Applicable

This technique is recommended when the project's experts cannot coordinate their schedules or when geographic distance separates them. The Delphi technique is also appropriate when bringing experts together to a common venue may generate excess friction.

Inputs and Outputs

The inputs for the Delphi technique are questions or questionnaires. The questionnaire addresses the risk area(s) of concern, allowing for progressive refinement of the answers provided until general consensus is achieved. The questionnaire should allow for sufficient focus on areas of concern without directing the experts to specific responses.

Outputs from the process are progressively detailed because all iterations should draw the experts involved closer to consensus. The initial responses to the questionnaire will generally reflect the most intense biases of the experts. Through the iterations, the facilitator will attempt to define a common ground within their responses, refining the responses until consensus is achieved.

Major Steps in Applying the Technique

The technique heavily relies on the facilitator's ability both to generate the original questions to submit to the experts and to distill the information from the experts as it is received. The process is simple but is potentially time consuming.

> *Identify experts and ensure their participation.* The experts need not be individuals who have already done the work or dealt with the risks under consideration; but, they should be individuals who are attuned to the organization, the customer, and their mutual concerns. Experts can be defined as anyone who has an informed stake in the project and its processes. Commitments for participation should come from the experts, their direct superiors, or both.
>
> *Create the Delphi instrument.* Questions asked under the Delphi technique must not only be sufficiently specific to elicit information of value but also sufficiently general to allow for creative interpretation. Since risk management is inherently an inexact science, attempts to generate excessive precision may lead to false assumptions. The Delphi questions should avoid cultural and organizational bias and should not be directive

(unless there is a need to identify and/or evaluate risk in a niche rather than across the entire project spectrum). If the answers are best provided in a specific format, that format should be a component of the guidance on how to complete the instrument.

Have the experts respond to the instrument. Conventionally, this is done remotely, allowing the experts sufficient time to ruminate over their responses. However, some organizations have supported encouraging questionnaire completion en masse during meetings to expedite the process. Regardless of the approach, the idea is to pursue all the key insights of the experts. The approach (e-mail, postal mail, or meetings) for gathering the experts' observations will largely determine the timing for the process as a whole.

Review and restate the responses. The facilitator will carefully review the responses, attempting to identify common areas, issues, and concerns. These will be documented and returned to the experts for their assessment and review. Again, this may happen by mail or in a meeting, although the standard approach is to conduct the Delphi method remotely.

Gather the experts' opinions and repeat. The process is repeated as many times as the facilitator deems appropriate so as to draw out the responses necessary to move forward. Three process cycles are considered the minimum to allow for thoughtful review and reassessment.

Distribute and apply the data. After sufficient cycles have been completed, the facilitator should issue the final version of the documentation and explain how, when, and where it will be applied. This step is important so that the experts can observe how their contributions will serve the project's needs and where their issues fit into the grander scheme of risks up for discussion.

Use of Results

The Delphi technique is frequently used when there are only a handful of experts who have an understanding of the project. It is also used when certain experts have insights about a particular aspect of the project that cannot be ignored. Although some other risk identification, assessment, and response development tools have broad application, the Delphi technique is a more exacting tool, drawing out only the responses or types of responses desired. The information acquired from the Delphi technique can be used to support risk identification, qualification, quantification, or response development.

Resource Requirements

The Delphi technique requires that a project has both a skilled Delphi facilitator and experts to support the process. The facilitator must have the ability to present the premise clearly in the Delphi questionnaire and then must have the capacity to refine and distill the inputs from the participants. The participants, in turn, must have an awareness of the area on which they are being consulted.

Reliability

The technique generates relatively reliable data (for a qualitative analysis) because multiple experts subject the information to at least three iterations of reviews. The iterative nature of the process and the requisite reviews tend to enhance accuracy, though the use of inappropriate experts or the development of poorly couched questions may produce less-than-optimal results. Still, because there are multiple reviewers, some built-in safeguards ensure a measure of reliability.

Selection Criteria

As with each chapter on techniques, the Delphi technique is assessed using selection criteria relating to resource requirements, applications, and outputs for the technique. To compare the Delphi technique with other techniques, review Table II.1.

Resource Requirements

The Delphi technique requires little more than basic office supplies. The infrastructure for the technique is minimal, as it is little more than a specially processed expert interview.

From a personnel perspective, the facilitator's greatest talent must be in distilling the information from one iteration of the approach to the next, achieving a balance of the information presented, and at the same time, not alienating the experts involved.

Participants in a Delphi technique analysis can derive comfort in the fact that their contributions, for the most part, will be anonymous because their inputs will never be directly presented to the other experts. The facilitator will filter and distill it first. Nonetheless, the participants should be reasonably skilled at documenting their contributions, as that is where the Delphi technique generates its value.

> *Cost* for the Delphi technique is minimal. Since most participants can complete the questionnaire at their leisure, there is little time pressure on the participant's side. The facilitator is also generally not time constrained in this practice and thus has some latitude to complete this effort when there is time to work on it. Even though the cost is minimal, the time to complete a Delphi technique process can be extensive, as it can continue for weeks if unmanaged.
>
> *Proper facilities and equipment* for the Delphi technique consist of little more than office supplies or e-mail for participants to record and return their responses to the facilitator. Most organizations already have such capabilities in-house.
>
> The *time needed to implement* the Delphi technique is the single most significant drawback of the approach. Despite that e-mail has created a faster way to accomplish the work, the technique still may take several days to complete. For some organizations, however, the quality of the data generated makes this trade-off worthwhile.
>
> Although the *ease of use* for the participants is high, the facilitator must be skilled in distilling and paraphrasing information. The facilitator must also ensure that the process stays on track. It is very easy to allow the Delphi technique to falter due to the time frames and distance involved.
>
> The project manager's *time commitment* is slight, with intense, short bursts of activity each time a cycle of responses is received.

Applications

The Delphi technique has broad utility because of its use of the experts' skills and insights. The applicability of the technique is assessed on a scale of high, medium, and low.

> *Project status reporting* is an area where the Delphi technique can provide more balanced insight than other tools can. Some projects falter because there is not a common understanding of the work accomplished, but the Delphi technique by its nature can reorient a team. Since the tool draws out consensus among the experts, it can facilitate in-depth analyses of project status. The tool's value here is medium.

> Since the experts in an organization tend to make *major planning decisions*, the Delphi technique can be seen as viable here. Particularly in situations where there is significant conflict over planning decisions, the Delphi technique has high applicability due to its capacity to elicit a common vision from a group of experts.

> *Contract strategy selection* is an area where experts are frequently tapped to make decisions, and likewise, conflict can be significant. As with planning decisions, the Delphi technique can serve extremely well in these situations, giving it a high value.

> Applying the Delphi technique in *milestone preparation* would probably have limited use and low value. While milestone preparation is a function of needs analysis, multiple experts are normally not required to ascertain the best times for milestones.

> *Design guidance* is a prime application for the Delphi technique. It is a creative endeavor requiring multiple perspectives. As such, the Delphi technique has high value as a classic tool for bringing different approaches to the fore and selecting the best possible approach.

> *Source selection* may be an application of the Delphi technique. If the experts in the technique are familiar with the needs of the procurement and if they are attuned to the organization's limitations, then the Delphi technique may be appropriate. However, the tool's utility here is medium at best.

> *Budget submittal* is a quantitative process and thus cannot take full advantage of the Delphi technique.

The Delphi technique is peerless in allowing for thoughtful review of the subject matter experts' insights. As such, organizations may be able to use this technique to establish risk responses, to identify risks, or to assess risk performance to date. However, the drawbacks associated with the timing of the process tend to limit its utility. When time is not of the essence, however, the Delphi technique can create some of the most thorough qualitative analyses available to the project manager.

Outputs

The outputs of the Delphi technique are sets of modified responses to the questionnaire. Although participants generate these responses, the facilitator has the ultimate responsibility to produce final outputs based on an amalgam of responses from subject matter experts to each question or issue.

> The *accuracy* of the Delphi technique is qualitatively rooted and is perhaps the single most accurate qualitative tool because it draws on multiple experts to establish its conclusions.
>
> *Level of detail* is a strength of the Delphi technique because there are rarely limits on the insights that the experts can share. As the process goes through multiple iterations, the level of detail can increase if the questions are expanded or the follow-up is particularly detailed or provocative.
>
> *Utility* is a subjective factor that takes into account both the effort involved and the value of the information. The Delphi technique tends to generate highly utilitarian information as it is revised several times before the outputs are finalized.

Summary

The Delphi technique is time consuming; but, it is a sound, structured practice for drawing out insights from professionals who might otherwise not contribute to the project's body of knowledge. It affords the facilitator the opportunity to review multiple perspectives before coming to grips with the middle-of-the-road perspective that Delphi tends to generate. The technique can be applied in a variety of situations, but for each, the time constraint must be given serious consideration.

11

BRAINSTORMING

Brainstorming is a classic technique for extracting information. Although it may not be the most efficient tool or the most thorough technique, its familiarity and broad acceptance make it the tool of choice for many risk analysts. And while it may be viewed as a generic tool, the fact that most participants are aware of the process and the tool's nuances make it desirable in a variety of risk management settings. Since risk is a future phenomenon and everyone has the ability to intuit some aspect of the future, brainstorming as an ideation tool is a logical application.

Brainstorming can be used in a variety of risk management practices, including efforts to identify risks, establish qualification schemes, clarify quantification assumptions, and generate potential risk responses. It can draw on project team members, management, customers, and vendors. Virtually any stakeholder can contribute.

A brainstorm is more than a basic core dump of information. It is rather the expression of ideas that then feeds other ideas and concepts in a cascade of data. It encourages team members to build on one another's concepts and perceptions. It circumvents conventions by encouraging the free flow of information.

Technique Description

Brainstorming is a facilitated sharing of information—without criticism—on a topic of the facilitator's choosing. It educes information from participants without evaluation, drawing out as many answers as possible and documenting them. There are no limits to the information flow or direction. Brainstorming is designed to encourage thinking outside of conventional boundaries so as to generate new insights and possibilities.

For risk identification, the facilitator might ask as an example, "For the *y* component, what are the risks? What bad things could happen?" Participants can then fuel their imagination with ideas as the facilitator documents or catalogs each new suggestion.

The technique requires limited facilitation skills and familiarity with any premise being presented to the group (for clarification purposes).

When Applicable

This technique is applicable in virtually every step in the risk management process. Its broad utility makes it appealing in a variety of settings and sustains the following process steps:

Risk identification, to establish a base pool of risks or to create the risk categories (associated with the risk breakdown structure (RBS))

Qualification, to work toward terms and terminology as to what constitutes high, medium, and low in the various categories of risk

Qualification, to capture environmental assumptions and potential data sources

Response development, to generate risk strategies and to examine the implications thereof

Inputs and Outputs

Inputs are the basic premise of a brainstorm itself: a single, comprehensive idea to be presented to the group of participants.

Outputs will depend on the premise presented but may also include identified risks, risk sources, categories, triggers, qualification approaches, assumptions, risk responses, or other data captured during the analysis. The outputs should be documented and cataloged for future application.

Major Steps in Applying the Technique

Since brainstorms are well understood in most environments, this analysis will focus on their application in a risk setting.

Establish the basic premise of the risk brainstorm and prepare the setting. This involves making certain that a means exists to capture and catalog the information as it is presented. Few facilitators are sufficiently skilled to both record information and elicit responses from a group at the same time. Questions posed to the group should not be biased in any direction.

Identify appropriate participants. This is sometimes a function of group dynamics rather than project insight. Some individuals function well in a group setting and contribute readily, whereas others do not. Identify individuals who are likely to contribute and add value to the ideas being presented. A negative attitude or an overzealous contributor can spoil an otherwise-effective brainstorming session.

Explain the rules of brainstorming to the group. Emphasize that *all* ideas will be recorded because all ideas have some measure of value. Reinforce that everyone should have the opportunity to participate and that no pressure should be brought to bear that would stifle anyone. Any critiques of information or insight should be postponed until after the brainstorm.

Solicit information from the group. Share the premise(s) of the brainstorm and draw out information from the participants. Also, if there is a specific form or format required for responses from the group, that format should be identified at the outset (e.g., *Risk should be stated as cause and effect or "if-then" statements*). As an idea is shared, it should be repeated (to ensure accuracy) and documented (preferably in view of the large group as a whole). Participation should be allowed to flow freely within the group, but the facilitator needs to ensure that all participants have equal opportunity to provide their contributions.

Review the information presented. As the group runs out of insights or as the session nears a close, the premise should be re-presented after a thorough review of all the ideas shared so far. Any new insights should be captured at this time. In some organizations, this will be used as the one and only opportunity to critique the ideas presented earlier in the brainstorm.

Communicate the information. After the session is complete, the information distilled from the brainstorm should be circulated to all participants for their records. This affirms that the information was actually captured and provides a sense of how the information will ultimately be used. If data from the brainstorm are to be captured within the project plans or the risk plans, then the data should be sorted and filed with the project documentation.

Use of Results

Information gathered during the brainstorm will vary in levels of quality. For example, some risks identified may be on the fringe ("Locusts could attack, devouring all the project documentation"); and others may be overly obvious ("If the vendor delivers late, then we could run into schedule delays"). The information will be used best when it is assessed for validity and then documented and applied within the project plan.

Brainstorming frequently captures the most obvious risks or the most self-explanatory qualification approaches. On the other hand, this technique will also generate information that might otherwise be missed entirely. Thus, a key role for the facilitator is to ensure that the information is captured well and applied appropriately.

Resource Requirements

Resource requirements for brainstorms include a facilitator, a group of participants, and the physical facilities to assemble them and document their outputs. The best participants will be those who are willing to set aside any biases they may have toward a particular perspective and who are willing to contribute freely on the premise presented.

Reliability

Brainstorms generally have low reliability. Although some of the insights generated will be extraordinarily valuable, it is a matter of "separating the wheat from the chaff." To arrive at a handful of key nuggets of information, the facilitator of the brainstorm may also catalog dozens of lesser ideas.

Selection Criteria

As with each chapter on techniques, brainstorming is assessed using selection criteria relating to resource requirements, applications, and outputs for the technique. To compare brainstorming with other techniques, review Table II.1.

Resource Requirements

The basic resource requirements for brainstorming include the participants, the facilitators, and the materials with which their insights will be captured. The tools for data capture are normally nothing more than flip charts, an erasable board, or a laptop computer.

The personnel participating in the brainstorming session should have a basic understanding of the premise(s) that the brainstorm addresses and a willingness to share their insights. They should also be individuals who have the ability to communicate in a manner that allows others to understand what they are sharing but without sounding critical of others' inputs.

Cost for brainstorming is relatively small. The sessions are generally conducted in conjunction with other project activities.

There is normally no capital investment required in terms of *proper facilities and equipment* for brainstorming. Most facilities have documentation equipment and a meeting room adequate to the task.

The *time needed to implement* brainstorming is not as abbreviated as some may think. This technique is not inherently a quick endeavor but depends on the participants and their willingness (or eagerness) to share information. Exhausting the pool of ideas of some groups may be a relatively short effort; yet, for others, exhausting their creative energies can take several hours.

Ease of use is high as most business professionals have, at one time or another, participated in one or two brainstorming sessions. Familiarity encourages use, and as such, brainstorms are widely applied. The key challenge for most facilitators will be to control the group's urge to critique input as it is provided.

The project manager's *time commitment* largely depends on whether the project manager is the facilitator of the session, which happens in many cases. The project manager then becomes responsible for developing the premises for discussion and for postsession information distillation. As such, there is a modest commitment on the part of the project manager when a brainstorm is conducted.

Applications

Brainstorms are effective when they are directed at a clear, easily discernible goal, which is crucial. Without an objective for the outputs, risk brainstorms can easily deteriorate into complaint sessions.

Project status reporting receives limited support from this technique because quantifiable data are normally preferable for status reports. While some types of qualified data may be appropriate in this area, outputs from brainstorms are not among these types.

Major planning decisions are not closely tied to brainstorms, though some implications of such decisions could be reviewed in a brainstorming environment. Again, the qualitative nature of the technique limits its utility here.

Contract strategy selection, such as major planning decisions, may benefit from a brainstorm in terms of a review of implications. However, brainstorms are not a key tool to be applied here.

Milestone preparation receives only nominal support from this technique as the general nature of a brainstorm's outputs does not lend itself to the specificity associated with milestone preparation.

Design guidance may draw strongly on brainstorms because there is frequently a need to examine the breadth of options at an organization's disposal. Since the design is a creative endeavor, the creative energies of brainstorming may work to the organization's advantage here.

Brainstorming generally does not support *source selection* except for open discussions of the implications of selecting certain sources.

Budget submittal is not normally seen as a brainstorming situation because both inputs and outputs in the budget process are highly quantitative.

Although brainstorms have limited utility for many of these areas, they are virtually without equal in environments where quick analysis is needed and individuals with a willingness to participate are available. For risk identification, qualification scheme discussions, and risk response development, brainstorming can produce volumes of valuable information from which the best available responses can be derived. Brainstorms afford new perspectives, which are essential to the success of any risk management effort because risk management is a foray into the unknown.

Outputs

The outputs of brainstorming are generally a list of insights on the premise presented.

Accuracy of brainstorms is generally seen as low. Since many weak ideas are generated with the good, some view brainstorming as highly inaccurate. If, after the brainstorm, the facilitator can cull through and select the truly valuable data, then the accuracy of the process can increase significantly. On the whole, however, the process generates imprecise and potentially ambiguous data.

Level of detail is normally premise dependent. If the premise of the question put forth in a brainstorm is nebulous, then the level of detail will be weak. If, however, the premise is focused, then the level of detail for outputs will be more focused as well.

Utility is high for brainstorming despite its other shortcomings. Since the tool and the application are familiar in a variety of different areas, project managers frequently lean toward brainstorms as the tool of choice.

Summary

Brainstorms often open the door to a free and candid discussion of risk and risk issues. For that feature alone, they increase value. However, they also add to the body of knowledge about a given project or risk area. They encourage new perspectives and a new understanding of risk. They can also lead to new approaches in risk qualification, quantification, and response development. In all those regards, the brainstorm technique serves as a foundation tool for risk management.

12

CRAWFORD SLIP METHOD (CSM)

Gathering data is one of the greatest challenges in risk management as there is a propensity for risk identification and risk information gathering to become a negative influence on team members and their attitudes about the project. The Crawford Slip Method (CSM) is a classic tool for collecting information without the negativism inherent in many risk discussions.

CSM has a variety of advantages over other information-gathering techniques. These include its ability to aggregate large volumes of information in a very short time and its complete avoidance of group-think, where team members become embroiled in a particular tangent and cannot extract themselves.

Technique Description

With proper facilitation, CSM is an easy technique to apply. The basic approach involves establishing a clear premise or question and then having all participants in the process document on a slip of paper their response to that premise. Using the same premise, the process is repeated 10 times (per Crawford) to extract all the information available. Although there may be a great deal of similarity among the initial slips, those generated later tend to identify issues and risks that otherwise would never have surfaced. Applications for risk management often cut the number of cycles to 5 because team members frequently lack the fortitude to formulate 10 responses to each premise.

When Applicable

This technique is recommended when team members are available to provide inputs, as there are limits to their desire to share information in a group setting. CSM is also appropriate when there is a need to generate a large volume of information in a short span of time.

Inputs and Outputs

The key input for CSM is a clear premise. If the premise or question posed to the group is not detailed, clear, and well crafted, then the method will generate either poor or the wrong outputs. The premise should clearly state the information sought and the environment or assumptions surrounding the information. This context should be documented for the facilitator so that he or she can refer to it while working through the iterations of the process. The premise should also incorporate the format in which the responses should be generated to ensure all the required information is gathered.

Outputs from the process will be a significant number of slips of paper from the participants, preferably arranged according to the premises presented. The participants may arrange or organize the slips during the working session, or the facilitator may arrange them at some later time. The quality of outputs will correlate directly to the precision with which the premise was stated and the direction provided to the participants. Poor explanations on how to write risk statements or how to identify the information in question will invariably lead to inferior outputs.

Major Steps in Applying the Technique

The technique relies heavily on facilitator skill and the ability of the facilitator to follow the process. That process requires the facilitator to direct a nonspecific or nonthreatening question to the group and allows for individual responses, one at a time, on paper from each participant. This process ensures consistent levels of inputs from each participant and also builds the largest volume of information possible. The process, in its simplest form, consists of six steps:

> *Bring together those participants with an awareness of the issue at hand.* Even though complete subject matter expertise is not essential, awareness is. Those participating in any type of risk information-gathering effort should have at least a superficial cognizance of the concerns in the project.

Identify the primary rationale for the process. Regardless of whether CSM is being applied to identify risks and risk triggers, recognize risk sources, or develop risk responses, participants need to be aware of the reason for their involvement. Since the process is designed to elicit their perceptions, they clearly need to know what insights they will be expected to share.

Issue slips of paper. Although literature on CSM specifies the exact size of the paper to be used and the number of slips appropriate to the method (Siegel and Clayton 1996), for project risk analysis, these decisions rest largely in the hands of the project manager. In many instances, ordinary "sticky notes" will be sufficient and effective to serve the purpose. The number of slips will determine the volume of the outcome.

Explain the process. The facilitator will direct participants that they will be expected to contribute one idea per slip of paper and that the facilitator will specify what information is to go on the slip and when. In intervals of roughly one minute each, the facilitator will state a question or premise (such as, "What risks do we face on the Nancy Project?"). The participants will write down a single thought, set that slip aside, and prepare to write another idea on the next slip. If necessary, the facilitator will explain how the statements should be written and what constitutes an appropriate response. Explaining that a risk statement consists of the event that will happen and its consequence can be important for ensuring that the statements are couched appropriately (rather than as one- or two-word responses to the premise).

Begin the process and cycle through it iteratively. The facilitator will then walk participants through the process. Each participant should have one response per slip, and no slips should be lost. The number of cycles will determine how much information is generated.

Gather and/or sort the data. After sufficient cycles have been completed, the facilitator may simply gather the data and terminate the session; or he or she may instruct participants to sort their slips either into preordained categories or into groups that seem to have natural affinities. The information gathered now represents a current body of insight from individuals familiar with the project.

Use of Results

The uses of CSM results are generally applied in establishing an initial pool of risk events associated with the project or the options available to respond to risks on the project. The body of information will sometimes be sufficient to develop preliminary risk reports (general overviews of the body of risks on a project), or it may require distillation prior to such use. When being used to develop risk responses, CSM may serve to generate a volume of options that may be reviewed later using tools such as the risk response matrix (Chapter 32).

Resource Requirements

Once understood, CSM is perhaps the simplest of the high-volume, information-gathering techniques. If the facilitator knows the premise of the session and has the ability to communicate precisely the types of outputs participants are to produce, then the sessions tend to be extraordinarily productive. Often, the key rests not in the CSM facilitator but rather in the participants selected to participate in the process. Their level of awareness will determine the quality of information produced. If they have project awareness plus a basic understanding of the risks that the project may face (or how to resolve them), then they may be able to make significant contributions through CSM.

Reliability

The technique tends to produce highly variable data, largely because of the volume of information produced. Although that may be perceived as a weakness of this approach, in this situation it is actually a strength. Risks are frequently discounted as being "too remote" or "too far-fetched" until they actually occur. Since the process generates such a large volume of risk data, it tends to capture ideas from the sublime to the ridiculous; and because the process is anonymous, it frequently collects information from those who would not readily participate in a more public venue, like a brainstorm.

Selection Criteria

As with each chapter on techniques, CSM is assessed using selection criteria relating to resource requirements, applications, and outputs for the technique. To compare CSM with other techniques, review Table II.1.

Resource Requirements

The resources essential to CSM are extremely limited. The technique requires paper slips, pens or pencils, a facilitator, and participants. It may also employ a predetermined set of risk or risk response categories for sorting information, but that is optional.

The basic tools of CSM are office supplies. Although books on what is sometimes referred to as the "mass interviewing technique" suggest specific sizes for the paper, such decisions largely rest in the hands of the facilitator. The paper should be sufficient in size to capture the information requested and manageable for any later sorting required. Different colors of paper may be used to identify specific questions or respondents, if desired.

As mentioned earlier, facilitation skills required for CSM are minimal. If the basic premise questions are clearly established and the participants are told precisely what format their final responses should take, then facilitation becomes extremely easy. The only management required of the facilitator is directing participants who either fail to complete their slips or who jump ahead in the documentation process.

CSM participants should be aware that they will be expected to contribute to the process. In many other, more public idea-generation techniques, such pressure is not brought to bear as more reticent participants can waive participation. In CSM, however, all participants are expected to contribute equally.

Finally, some CSM sessions will incorporate predetermined sorting criteria for cataloging the data after the session. If such sorting is required, then the definitions for the categories should be clearly stated before sorting begins. Beyond the CSM-specific requirements, the demands for the technique are slight.

- *Cost* for CSM is extremely minimal. CSM sessions are frequently measured in minutes rather than hours. Although multiple participants are essential to CSM success, their time commitment for the process is limited based on the number of iterations.
- *Proper facilities and equipment* for CSM consist of a room large enough to accommodate all the participants invited to the session. There should be sufficient pencils or pens and slips of paper to ensure that all participants can respond to all iterations for the question(s) posed.
- The *time needed to implement* a CSM is perhaps its most attractive quality. Compared to any other technique discussed in this book, CSM requires less time to generate more information.
- *Ease of use* is another attractive trait because CSM can be incorporated into other meetings where the appropriate personnel are brought together to work on the project. The key is in establishing the clear premise for the session and the outputs desired from the participants. If that information is clearly expressed at the beginning of the session, then the process will be relatively easy to deploy. The only challenge, however, may come from those individuals who are not anxious to take part. The facilitator may have to reinforce the rationale for the session and the value of each participant's inputs.

The project manager's *time commitment* is extremely slight.

Applications

CSM can be used in a number of different situations, but it does not have the broadband utility of more general techniques such as expert interviews. CSM's applicability is assessed on a scale of high, medium, and low.

Project status reporting is not a strength of CSM. Since CSM generally focuses on educing insights about approaches or concerns, it does not attain the level of specificity required for project status reporting. Its value here would be extremely low.

Major planning decisions tend to rely on quantitative data rather than volumes of qualitative information. For this process, the value of CSM is low.

Contract strategy selection tends to rely heavily on quantitative information. CSM has extremely limited value in this regard.

Applying CSM in *milestone preparation* would be largely a misapplication of the tool. While milestone preparation is normally born out of a careful needs analysis, CSM is more of an ideation tool rather than an analysis tool.

Design guidance may take advantage of CSM because design development is frequently a function of reviewing options and assessing possibilities. Since design guidance is more of a creative endeavor that requires inputs from diverse sources, CSM can have medium utility here.

Source selection is not an application of CSM. Source selection should be conducted against a predetermined set of criteria and should not rely primarily on fresh ideas to determine the best available source.

Budget submittal is a quantitative process and thus cannot take advantage of CSM.

However, CSM does serve two primary applications. It is used for risk identification, both alone and in conjunction with other project management tools (such as the work breakdown structure). In that environment, it is virtually peerless in its ability to generate large volumes of risk statements in a nonthreatening and positive way. In addition, it is impressive in its ability to capture a variety of risk management strategies and responses. CSM's ability to draw out insight without alienating the participants is striking.

Outputs

CSM's outputs are stacks of paper slips, each slip with a single idea or piece of information, which may or may not be sorted into preordained categories. Generally, the information gathered tends to be qualitative and represents individual perspectives. Ultimately, the data generated should be incorporated into the risk lists or risk register.

The *accuracy* of CSM is largely dependent on the insight of the process participants. It generates qualitative information that, although valuable, may not be considered highly accurate.

Level of detail is a true strength of CSM, particularly in regard to the amount of time invested. Unlike other tools that are limited by the group's ability to catalog information serially, CSM allows for an expedient collection of significant volumes of data, often yielding details that would otherwise be missed.

Utility is a subjective factor that takes into account both the effort involved and the value of the resulting information. The utility of CSM data is rooted in part in the background of the participants and their knowledge of the project and its risks. How CSM data are distilled, sorted, and interpreted may also drive its utility. Given the volume of information involved, effective interpretation of the data is critical to the outputs' utility.

Summary

The keys to the success of the Crawford slip method are the clarity of the premises presented, the backgrounds of the participants, and the distillation of the outputs. However, because of the efficiency of the process, occasionally, there is a temptation to draw it out for a longer period of time than is necessary. Nevertheless, the method's strength is its efficiency. With properly staged questions or premises, CSM builds a substantial volume of valuable data in a very short time.

13
SWOT Analysis

Strengths, weaknesses, opportunities, and threats—SWOT analysis—is essentially a directed risk analysis designed to identify risks and opportunities within the greater organizational context. The main difference between this and other analysis techniques is that SWOT reinforces the need to review risks and opportunities from the perspective of the organization as a whole rather than just from inside the project vacuum.

Technique Description

The technique consists of four brief idea-generation sessions held to populate the analysis documentation with answers to these questions:

What are our organization's strengths?
What are our organization's weaknesses?
What opportunities does this project present in that context?
What threats does this project present in that context?

Using the answers to these four questions, the project manager can discern any specific cultural, organizational, or environmental issues that may either enable or cripple the project in question.

When Applicable

This technique is recommended early in the project as an overview analysis or to establish the general risk (and opportunity) environment. Since an SWOT analysis is seen as a big-picture tool, it is not designed to draw out detailed project risks. Thus, its greatest utility is near the inception of the project.

STRENGTHS	WEAKNESSES
OPPORTUNITIES	THREATS

Figure 13.1   SWOT grid and format.

Inputs and Outputs

SWOT analysis has four key types of inputs. The inputs comprise the questions cited above. The SWOT facilitator poses these questions to either individuals or groups, eliciting as many concise, incisive responses as possible.

These responses are then presented in a four-square grid, designed to allow for analysis and cross-reference. The grid is laid out in the following format (Figure 13.1).

Major Steps in Applying the Technique

SWOT analysis is a subjective tool; so, practices on completing the grid may vary with the facilitator. Nonetheless, the steps for completing the tool are rather consistent:

Identify the SWOT analysis resource(s). Selecting the right subject matter experts to complete the SWOT analysis is important. This is not a good tool to use with someone who is unfamiliar with the organization or the environment. Therefore, it is important to work with individuals who understand the culture in which the project will function because they will have a better sense of the strengths and weaknesses portions of the analysis.

Ask about the organization's strengths. This should be within the project context, but it is still imperative for the facilitator to reinforce the fact that the question is not about the project but about the organization. What does the organization do well? Sometimes, there is a temptation to be modest about organizational capability; this is not that time. Strengths should be articulated from the perspectives of both those working within the organization and with their customers.

Ask about the organization's weaknesses. Although this is in the project context, it is essential to educe as much information as possible about where the organization fails to perform well. Honesty and candor are critical. This should not be used as an opportunity to complain about the organization but, instead, to identify weaknesses that make the organization less capable in the eyes of its employees, its customers, and the public.

Ask what opportunities the project presents. This should not be exclusively a monetary issue. The financial value of the project is important, but it is not the only reason for pursuing any piece of work. Are there promotional opportunities associated with the project? Are there opportunities to build the client base? Are there opportunities to win hearts and minds inside the organization? Be sure to examine the potentially positive influences both internally and externally.

Ask what threats could imperil the project. Invariably, there are scenarios where any project could fail. The key is to define these scenarios and to identify the specific threats that exist that could do harm to the project or, because the organization pursues the project, do harm to the organization.

Use of Results

SWOT analyses are normally used to present project information to the management. The idea behind an SWOT analysis is not to build a strong case either for or against the project (although that frequently occurs) but rather to present the pros and cons of a project openly. The SWOT analysis is sometimes used to encourage the management to alter some environmental factors from the strengths and weaknesses sections that will directly influence the project. In some instances, the project manager also perceives it as a self-protective measure to ensure that if those environmental influences do harm to the project, then the management was alerted to them early and proactively.

Resource Requirements

An SWOT analysis, as with most of the qualitative tools, requires individuals with only modest knowledge of the project and the organization in which it will be performed. Obviously, the greater the depth of organizational background, then the greater the depth of the analysis. The facilitator's principal skill is in asking the questions and thoroughly documenting the responses.

Reliability

SWOT analyses are highly subjective, and as such, they can be somewhat unreliable. However, because they are broadly used and generally accepted as business practice, they frequently assume an aura of acceptability that they may not merit. The more reliable and insightful the participants in the analysis are, then the more valuable and reliable the analysis becomes.

Selection Criteria

As with each chapter on techniques, the SWOT analysis technique is assessed using selection criteria relating to resource requirements, applications, and outputs for the technique. To compare SWOT analysis with other techniques, review Table II.1 in Part II.

Resource Requirements

The only resource requirements for SWOT analysis are the facilitator, the participants, and the grid. The key to success will be the quality of the participants.

The facilitator has two main roles: listening and documenting. Since the questions in an SWOT analysis are standardized, the facilitator's primary function is to capture the insights of the participants. A good archivist will have the ability to document information as it is being shared. As a safeguard, the facilitator should occasionally provide feedback as to what has been documented to ensure that it adequately reflects what the participants said.

The participants' primary function is to share their insights about the organization and the project. As such, the best resources will be those with familiarity in both areas.

The grid is a standard format for capturing basic project documentation. The four quadrants should ideally appear on the same page so

Table 13.1 SWOT Matrix

	OPPORTUNITY WE MAY FIND NEW STAFF	OPPORTUNITY WE MAY DISCOVER A NEW PROCESS	THREAT WE MAY LOSE PERSONNEL	THREAT WE MAY DAMAGE THE CLIENT'S FACILITY	THREAT THE CLIENT MAY IDENTIFY AN ALTERNATIVE VENDOR
STRENGTH: We have a superb marketing team					+
STRENGTH: We offer outstanding employee benefits	+		+		
WEAKNESS: Management tends to micromanage on-site personnel		−	−	+	
WEAKNESS: We use outdated processes		+	−	−	−

that the insights within the four quadrants can be cross-referenced and compared during any post-SWOT analysis. The grid is sometimes expanded into a matrix (see Table 13.1) to allow for extended cross-reference of strengths and weaknesses on one axis and opportunities and threats on the other axis. The intersecting boxes are then marked with plus signs (+) to indicate areas of specific potential improvement and minus signs (−) to indicate potential areas of harm.

Cost for an SWOT analysis is minimal because the document is designed to capture incisive, short statements from the experts. As no special facilitation skills are normally required, there is no expense for an outside facilitator.

Proper facilities and equipment for an SWOT analysis are minimal because the process requires only the space in which to conduct it.

The *time needed to implement* an SWOT analysis is an aspect in the technique's favor. SWOT analyses are normally events lasting less than an hour. Although they can take longer with more participants, lengthier discussions may not have any significant value because the SWOT analysis outputs are designed as a single grid populated with brief insights on the four areas.

Ease of use is an attractive feature of the SWOT analysis because it is quick, requires no special tools, and generates a familiar piece of project documentation (a grid). Since no special facilitation skills are required and the grid is self-explanatory, the SWOT analysis has an extremely high ease of use.

The project manager's *time commitment* is slight even if the project manager assumes the role of an SWOT analysis facilitator. Since the analysis is brief and the questions are preordained, the time commitment of those conducting the analysis is limited as well.

Applications

The key application of the SWOT analysis is early in the project to draw attention to the organizational or environmental influences on the project. In many ways, the SWOT analysis is as much a presentation tool as an analysis tool. Because of the ability of the SWOT analysis to draw attention to the organization's issues and concerns that will potentially affect the project, the tool is more valuable than an analysis of risk alone. Since the tool presents this information concurrently, it affords the project manager the opportunity to present risk in a greater context.

An SWOT analysis does not generally affect *project status reporting*. Unless the analysis is updated at the time of the status report, the two bear little or no correlation.

Major planning decisions may rely in some measure on an SWOT analysis because the tool is good for high-level presentations of information as well as high-level analysis.

The SWOT analysis would only affect *contract strategy selection* if specific contract types or specific types of contract work were identified as strengths or weaknesses within the analysis. Otherwise, the two are relatively unrelated.

Using an SWOT analysis in *milestone preparation* would be a misapplication of the tool.

Design guidance can take advantage of the SWOT analysis because the design may in some measure be a function of the organization's strengths and weaknesses and how they play into the opportunities and threats that the project presents. The SWOT analysis allows for high-level defense of design strategies or challenges to these strategies.

Source selection, like contract strategy selection, would be affected only if specific sources or types of sources were identified as strengths or weaknesses within the analysis.

It is not likely that an SWOT analysis will directly affect *budget submittal* as budgets are derived almost exclusively from purely quantifiable data.

SWOT analyses are powerful in presenting information in the aggregate. They juxtapose information that otherwise would not be examined in tandem. That is important because context frequently influences risks. As a tool, SWOT analyses have limited utility, but for presenting information as described herein, they are invaluable.

Outputs

The outputs of the SWOT analysis are normally posters or graphic displays that present the four-quadrant grid. The outputs are normally qualitative and reflect the biases or concerns of the facilitator and those who provided the inputs.

The level of *accuracy* for the SWOT analysis would be low because the tool is highly subjective and relies on the perceptions of those who generated it. While the analysis presents valuable insight, the accuracy of the insight hinges almost exclusively on the skills and expertise of those who provided the inputs. If they provide accurate information, then the outputs will be accurate. If, however, their information can be called into question, then the outputs may be called into question as well.

Level of detail for the SWOT analysis is low because the tool is designed primarily for high-level analysis. The SWOT analysis is designed to address sweeping organizational issues rather than details within the project.

The *utility* of the SWOT analysis can be high in organizations where presentations dictate future action. The SWOT analysis is an accepted presentation format for risk information, and as such, may make risk discussions more palatable than other approaches.

Summary

Owing to its high-level nature, SWOT analysis has limited utility. But because of its general acceptance in the business community, SWOT analysis can be effective in drawing the management and executives into risk discussions in which they otherwise would not be interested. If the management has a propensity for analyzing information at the macro level, then the SWOT analysis may be a tool of choice. Otherwise, the data evaluated in an SWOT analysis can frequently be extracted and presented using other tools.

14

CHECKLISTS

Technique Description

Checklists are classic tools of risk identification, drawing on the experience of other project managers and past projects to ensure a level of consistency in early risk analysis. They consist of simple lists of questions or statements based on lessons learned from earlier projects, which allow the project manager to build early risk lists that reflect risks faced on previous projects.

When Applicable

This technique is recommended for all projects in organizations where checklists have been developed. Some external organizations, such as the Software Engineering Institute (SEI), have developed generic risk identification checklists for all projects in a given field (such as SEI's taxonomy-based risk identification checklist). The technique is normally applied early in a project, though checklists can also be used at midterm and final project evaluations. PMI® recommends applying checklists each time a project-closing procedure is conducted and also emphasizes that the lowest level of the risk breakdown structure (see Chapter 15) may be applied as a risk checklist.

Inputs and Outputs

The inputs to build the checklists are the past experience of project teams and clear documentation of their experiences. After the checklists have been created, however, the inputs to applying checklists are nothing more than the checklists themselves. The project manager and the project team should take the checklist and openly, honestly discuss the concerns that the tool addresses.

Depending on the construction of the tool, the checklist may do little more than generate red flags to warn of categories of concern or specific risks. If the tool is software driven and more complex, then it may also provide a list of recommended basic actions to guide the project manager and the team toward best-practice experience in handling any of the risks or risk areas identified in the tool.

Major Steps in Applying the Technique

Operating under the assumption that a checklist has already been created, the process associated with checklists is among the simplest of all the risk tools:

Review the risk checklist. Ensure that the project team is working with a checklist that is appropriate to the environment, the culture, and the project in question. Since some risk checklists are designed to address issues within a given organization or within a given project type, it is important to work with a tool that is appropriate to the project at hand.

Answer the questions or check the appropriate boxes on the checklist. Checklists normally come with guidance to direct the user on the appropriate application. Such applications consist of simple question-and-answer sessions or rating schemes to assess the likelihood of encountering some common risks.

Review and communicate the guidance provided. Even though checklists normally include some direction about how to complete them, they also include guidance on how to apply the findings. In some cases, these findings may represent nothing more than a list of commonly identified risks (or risk areas) for the project. However, some of the more advanced checklists will also embed suggestions on the standard internal practice and procedure for resolving or managing the risks identified. Guidance of *any* nature should be communicated to the team.

Organizations looking to build their internal risk practice can frequently develop that practice by generating checklists. Checklists are often among the first steps that a project office takes to build a broader understanding of the depth of risks within the organization and the support that they can provide in ameliorating some of those risks.

Use of Results

Since checklists are first applied early in the project, outputs can be used to provide a general understanding of the nature of risks and the concerns in the project in a nonthreatening manner. Data from risk checklists tend to cause less anxiety because the questions asked (or statements made) are applied equitably to all projects and the outputs are normally familiar to the organization. Outputs at the end of the project should be used in any reevaluation of the checklists for additions or deletions. Checklist analysis should not be considered a panacea for risk identification. Efforts should be made to identify risks not directly called out in a checklist.

Resource Requirements

Checklist reviews normally require only two participants. At least two people should review a series of checklist responses to ensure that personal biases do not influence the outputs. The only other resources required are the checklist(s) and a tool for storing the outputs of the process.

Reliability

The reliability of the process pivots on the quality of the checklist. A sound checklist built to reflect the organization's culture, nature, and project history will build an excellent set of initial project risks. A checklist that a single individual crafts after a single project without considering the organizational culture will have limited reliability. The best checklists are those that capture experience from a variety of projects and project teams. Answered candidly, checklists of that caliber can generate extremely positive and reliable (although not inherently comprehensive) results.

Selection Criteria

As with each chapter on techniques, the checklist technique is assessed using selection criteria relating to resource requirements, applications, and outputs for the technique. To compare checklists with other techniques, review Table II.1.

Resource Requirements

The checklist has among the lowest resource requirements of any risk tool unless there are unusual resource demands peculiar to the individual list. Except when extensive research is required to answer the questions in the checklist, the time commitment is limited. And unless particular skills are required to answer the questions in the checklist, no special talents are required for the personnel working with the tool.

Cost for completing a checklist is extremely low because it expedites the process of preliminary risk analysis by suggesting a host of predetermined risks that are already appropriate to the organization and its projects. The initial costs of *developing* a checklist will be more substantial, however, and will require a much higher resource commitment.

Proper facilities and equipment for completing a checklist are nominal. The only real equipment required is a pencil or pen unless, of course, the checklist is online, in which case a computer is required.

The *time needed to implement* checklist completion largely depends on the research required to complete the checklist questionnaire. That, in turn, hinges on the number of questions the questionnaire asks. In any case, most questionnaires can be completed in a day at the extreme.

Ease of use is high as the tool is directive and the questions are specific. Even a novice project manager can normally apply a risk checklist with nominal direction.

The project manager's *time commitment* again depends on the research required to complete the checklist. If the checklist asks questions that do not require extensive analysis, then the time commitment is nominal. If, on the other hand, the questions or issues statements in the risk checklist require analysis, customer questions and answers, or a thorough grounding in a new technology, then the time commitment will clearly expand. Yet, in most instances, the time commitment is slight.

Applications

Depending on its design, the checklist can have a variety of applications. The key, however, is to use the checklist for the purposes for which it was built. Using the wrong checklist at the wrong time can lead to confusing and misleading outcomes.

  Risk checklists support *project status reporting* only when status is their primary intent. If the checklist is designed to investigate project data integrity or the overall risk levels, then it can have high applicability here.

  Major planning decisions are normally not based on checklists. Major planning decisions are generally tied to the specifics of a project, whereas checklists are more general in nature.

  Contract strategy selection may rely in some measure on checklists if the checklists are specifically designed to internally address contract types, together with the risks and issues regarding certain contracts, clauses, or approaches.

  Like contract strategy selection, checklists can support *milestone preparation* if the checklists are specifically designed to support that purpose. Generally, however, the connection here would be extremely weak.

  Checklists do not support *design guidance* unless they are specifically tailored to support design issues.

  Checklists may support *source selection* as they expose risk issues in a general sense, which may apply specifically to a source under consideration.

  A risk checklist does not support *budget submittal* unless it is used to establish project contingency reserves. Some checklists may be used in that manner if the contingency reserve is directly tied to the number or nature of questions that are checked affirmatively.

Risk checklists are normally used to establish whether certain concerns have been addressed. As with the specific project areas discussed above, it is possible to have checklists that are specific to a need. For most checklists to be effective, however, they need to be more general in application. They are used to identify risk considerations on the project as a whole and to facilitate gap analyses. In many instances, the project manager will use the questions or statements in a risk checklist as a defense for including a particular risk as a project consideration. The argument that "the checklist even asks whether it's going to be a problem" is one that is not uncommon in project risk discussions.

Outputs

Risk checklist outputs are generally derived according to the guidance provided with the particular checklist. In some cases (as with SEI's taxonomy-based risk questionnaire), the outputs will be strings of yes or no answers supported by explanations as to why a yes or no answer was reached and some follow-up as to what action will be taken. In some automated tools, the outputs may be combinations of graphic displays and lists of action items. And in still others, the checklist will merely indicate which actions have been taken and which have not.

   The *accuracy* of checklists is normally relatively high. Questions are couched in an unambiguous manner. Outputs are normally predetermined. Inputs are simple and readily answered from the base of project information. From project to project, there is consistency.

   Level of detail is wholly dependent on the depth of detail within the spreadsheet/checklist itself. Some checklists include hundreds of questions or statements, whereas others incorporate as few as 10. The level of detail is based on the type of tool applied. The greater the level of detail the checklist demands, then the greater the level of detail in the analysis.

   The *utility* of checklists is extremely high because they have been reviewed, validated, and applied on multiple projects. They normally address the breadth of an individual organization's risk and risk areas and draw on the expertise of the organization's veterans for establishing the "right" questions. They can be applied on different project types and allow for more of an "apples-to-apples" risk comparison without a significant investment of time or money for the analysis.

Summary

Checklists are powerful, easy-to-use tools for risk identification and analysis when organizations take the time to build them. The major investment in any good checklist is the initial development of the checklist and the occasional interim review of its application. Project offices or veteran project managers are frequently the arbiters of whether a checklist serves the organization's needs. Although it is impossible to build a checklist to identify every risk or to cover every category, it is possible to cover most risks endemic to an organization.

15
Risk Breakdown Structure

Some method of categorization or sorting is necessary and inevitable when identifying risk. Since risks naturally lend themselves to categorization and distillation, one tool—the RBS—has evolved in recent years to serve that end. Introduced (in its current form) by Dr. David Hillson in 2002 at the PMI® Annual Seminars and Symposium (and adopted in the *PMBOK® Guide*, third edition in 2004), the RBS is a hierarchical decomposition of the risks into logical, natural groupings associated with a project or an organization. (The Software Engineering Institute's *Taxonomy-Based Risk Identification* actually developed the earliest RBSs in 1994.) The goal of the tool is to enhance understanding and recognition of risks in a project within the context of a logical framework.

Technique Description

The use of the RBS actually comprises two stages, first in development and later in application. The first stage, development, involves creating the hierarchy itself, either based on past experience or on the relevant concerns of the organization. In organizations where the RBS has been employed for some time, this step may not be necessary, as a standardized hierarchy may already exist. However, for those projects where a new hierarchy must be developed and for those where the risks are sufficiently unique that past hierarchies do not apply, development of the RBS may be considered essential. In the second stage, application, the RBS serves as a resource for risk identification, analysis, and reporting.

When Applicable

RBS development is relevant when both sufficient risks and risk sources exist to warrant a thorough analysis of these risks from a variety of perspectives and when there is significant project change. RBS development is most appropriate when an RBS does not previously exist for the organization or when the organizational RBS is not germane to the project under consideration. RBS application is apropos when the structure is already in place and there is a need to conduct risk identification and in-depth analysis on risks by subject area, functional area, or, most suitably, risk areas and categories.

Inputs and Outputs

Inputs into risk breakdown structure *development* may include a list of risks or, more appropriately, a list of risk sources that are endemic to the project or the organization. Inputs into risk breakdown structure *application* include the list of project risks, the RBS itself, and an objective for the application. If there is no specific rationale as to why the RBS is being deployed, then its use may be potentially inappropriate.

Outputs from risk breakdown structure *development* include a hierarchy of risk sources either for a project or for an organization as a whole. The hierarchy may be displayed as an organizational array (like an organization chart in Figure 15.1) or as an outline with progressive decomposition. Outputs from risk breakdown structure *application* may include a more extensive list of risks and/or a list of risk categories that have the potential to exert the greatest influence on project outcomes.

Major Steps in Applying the Technique

Risk breakdown structure development is a powerful exercise for reviewing areas of concern and identifying potential relationships among these areas. The risk breakdown structure may be developed either from the top down or from the bottom up, much like the work breakdown structure. In a top-down development process, the key is

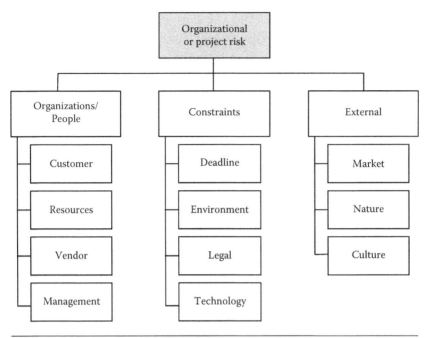

Figure 15.1 Sample risk breakdown structure.

to have an acute awareness of the primary categories of risk sources that exist within the organization:

Identify general categories of risk sources. These sources should represent the large-scale concerns that the organization faces on a regular basis for most, if not all, projects. These may stem from client relationships, the environment, management, the industry, the technologies, the projects, or a host of other considerations. They should, however, optimally represent only a handful (three to five) of categories that capture the essence of risk within the organization.

Within each category, identify subgroups. As with a WBS, the key here is to create discrete groups of risk sources. The risk sources represent comprehensive subsets of the higher category that capture all areas of potential concern within that category. The subgroups may then be further defined into progressively smaller sub-subgroups until a satisfactory level of decomposition has been achieved.

However, if developed from the bottom up, the RBS can be created by moving the lists of risks (identified using the Crawford Slip Method, brainstorm, or other idea-generation techniques) into progressively more general sets with each capturing the nature of the subset below it until a handful of large, logical categories has been derived.

Gather project risks identified. Use virtually any idea-generation technique to identify relevant risks.

Exhibit the risks. Using a process known as "affinity diagramming," have each team member individually post one risk on a wall, corkboard, or another surface. Then, have the next team member position one risk to where it fits into logical, natural groupings. (This is frequently done in silence to preclude extensive discussion and time-wasting arguments over risk placement.) Continue the cycle until all risks have been posted in natural groupings. Next, create titles for each group. (These titles represent the lowest level of the RBS.) For the titles, identify any logical "parent" groupings of risk sources. After the titles have been arranged into larger parent groups, label these parent groups. If sufficient diversity of parent groups still remains, then generate additional parent groups for these subparent groups.

Review the parent groups and subgroups with the participants. Ask whether the breadth of risk areas within the organization (or within the project) has been sufficiently identified.

The *application* of the RBS is sometimes the inverse of the development process. From the designated categories, the question "What types of____risks exist here?" is asked by inserting each category label in the blank. This creates more detail in terms of the risk areas that are common either to the organization or the project. Yet, beyond basic risk identification, the tool may also be applied in assessing the relative weight of particular risk areas. In applying the RBS, it is necessary to

Identify the risks. If qualification criteria have been established, establish the probability and impacts of the risk and assign their relative weights as described in Chapter 25.

Sort risks into the lowest level of the RBS.

Sum the total number of risks in each category/area at the lowest level. If the risks have been weighted in a qualification process, then sum their weights.

Characterize the value. The value will illustrate either the risk source with the greatest volume of risk or the greatest *weighted* volume of risk and may serve as an indicator of the risk source requiring the greatest attention.

Utilize the values. If the values are summed to the highest level of the RBS (that is, the project level), then the values (weighted or total) may be used to compare the relative level of project risk to the relative level of project risk on other projects.

Use of Results

The risk breakdown structure can serve as both a presentation tool (to highlight significant sources of risk) and as a tool to drive exploration into more risks or the nature of risk sources. As a presentation tool, the RBS provides a clearer understanding of what the various risk sources entail and can be used to explain how these sources impel risk in a variety of different areas. To explore more risks, the risk breakdown structure can be used as guidance for any information-gathering technique simply by asking the question "What specific risks can be identified associated with [the risk area from the RBS]?" Thus, a very expansive list of risks can be generated by repeating that question for each risk area within the structure. Furthermore, as a tool to explore the impact of risk sources, the RBS can be used as a means to evaluate which risk sources have the most inherent risks specific to the project. Those areas where more specific risks have been identified eventually serve to point out potentially greater sources of risk for a particular project.

Resource Requirements

The resources for the risk breakdown structure tool include the software required to generate a hierarchical diagram plus the individuals with the ability to discriminate among different risk sources and how risk events should be categorized within these sources.

Reliability

The risk breakdown structure is reliable because it primarily serves to reorient information rather than to create large volumes of new data. As such, it is as reliable as the inputs used to create it.

Selection Criteria

As with each chapter on techniques, the risk breakdown structure is assessed using selection criteria relating to resource requirements, applications, and outputs for the technique. To compare the risk breakdown structure with other techniques, review Table II.1.

Resource Requirements

- The *cost* of building an risk breakdown structure is partially driven by familiarity and past use. In organizations where RBSs have already been created, the experience and familiarity with the tool will expedite its use (and reduce costs). On the other hand, a first-time effort in building an RBS will be marginally more time consuming and expensive but will definitely not be prohibitive.
- There are no special equipment needs for this technique because it is primarily an administrative burden. The only requirement for *proper facilities and equipment* is having the software to capture the hierarchical diagram.
- The *time needed to implement* the risk breakdown structure is tied in part to the volume of risks identified on the project and the depth of information available. The greater the number of risk events that are identified, then the longer the sorting process into the RBS will take.
- The risk breakdown structure has moderate *ease of use*. Since the tool is unfamiliar to many professionals, training on its use and implementation may increase the amount of energy required to implement. In organizations where the tool is familiar, however, the ease of use is high.
- The project manager's *time commitment* to the risk breakdown structure again hinges on familiarity with the tool. As the tool

becomes more customary (and the process for sorting risk events into the RBS becomes more of a commonplace), the project manager's time commitment is accordingly reduced.

Applications

The risk breakdown structure contributes to most application categories in Table II.1.

For *project status reporting*, the RBS permits reporting on risk events by a source, thus allowing for a more organized reporting process. If, however, the risk sources are used as components of status reporting, then the RBS can prove invaluable.

Major planning decisions require an understanding of whether any new risk sources are being generated. The RBS identifies those risk sources that are already under consideration.

The RBS does not support contract strategy selection.

The RBS does not support *milestone preparation*.

The RBS can support *design guidance* by identifying specific areas of risk that may either influence or may be influenced by the design. When designers know the sources of risk identified in the RBS, they have the ability to recognize when their designs may generate a higher likelihood of risk events within those sources.

Since a large component of *source selection* is directly tied to risk transfer and/or avoidance, identifying contract sources that are also not significant risk sources is crucial. This makes the RBS highly applicable here.

Budget submittal has little or no relationship to the RBS.

Outputs

Outputs from the risk breakdown structure are both the hierarchical diagram and any information garnered through analysis of that diagram.

Accuracy of the risk breakdown structure increases as the volume of risk events captured by the diagram expands. As more risk events help to illuminate a greater breadth of risk sources, the accuracy of the diagram is enhanced when a greater number of risk events are identified and sorted into the tool.

The *level of detail* obtained through RBS analysis ties to the level desired. Since the RBS can be broken down into progressively more discrete sets and subsets of risk sources, the level of detail hinges on the level of depth applied with the tool.

The *utility* of the RBS is high because analyses can be conducted at a variety of levels at different points during the project life cycle. It serves to sort risk information, identify and reinforce sources of risk, and highlight areas of potential concern (and thus, areas of potential common mitigation).

Summary

Compared to other risk analysis applications, the risk breakdown structure is a relatively new tool. Nevertheless, it has proved its value over the years through the Software Engineering Institute's taxonomy of risk and through more recent work by Dr. David Hillson's refinement of the tool. The RBS is at its strongest when it is used to clarify and sort risk information into a common, distinct repository for risk information that validates what the organization should be examining, as well as those risk sources that may not exist in a given project. When applied in conjunction with effective risk identification and idea-generation techniques, the RBS can be a particularly powerful tool.

16

ROOT CAUSE IDENTIFICATION AND ANALYSIS

Identifying the root cause of any set of risks means that those causes, no matter how ingrained in an organization, can be recognized as separate and distinct causes of risk. They are the drivers and the contributory factors for making risk events come to pass. The key to *root* cause identification is to find those causes that are truly at the heart of driving risk. Root cause identification and analysis does not seek to discover what may occur or how it may occur. Instead, the emphasis is on *why* a given set of risks may occur (and as a result, it should be able to address that why in terms of ensuring that it is recognized and dealt with).

Technique Description

Similar to risk identification, root cause identification and analysis is an exercise in exploration. It is a shared quest for the causes behind risk. Rather than trying to understand the nature of a given risk event and/or its potential impact, root cause identification and analysis examines the nature of why risks are happening (or may happen) and what can be done to alter the environment to minimize or eliminate the cause.

When Applicable

Root cause identification and analysis is applied when direct action to resolve a risk seems inappropriate, unwieldy, or temporary. By way of example, shooing away a rabbit may temporarily eliminate the risk that a vegetable garden will be eaten, but it does not address the root cause. Root cause identification and analysis would instead address why rabbits are in the garden in the first place or why the food supply for rabbits is sufficiently deficient elsewhere that the garden seems an attractive option. Root cause identification and analysis examines causal factors to create a proactive shield around a particular subset of risks and can be appropriate when there are sufficient answers to the question of why risks may occur.

Inputs and Outputs

Inputs into root cause identification and analysis are data. Those data include more than just the risk events under consideration. They are also lists of answers to the "why" question. For the garden example, the questions would represent an effort to backtrack and try to determine some of the causes.

The data include not only a host of potential impacts from the risk events but also myriad factors that may be causing them.

Outputs from root cause identification and analysis will include specific causal factors that may be responsible for enabling or increasing the probability (or impact) of single or multiple risk events. Outputs often take the form of a causal factors chart. A causal factors chart starts with the potential problem on the top or right, breaking down the causes to the bottom or left until the root causes are identified (as illustrated in Figure 16.1).

Those root causes may be converted into a checklist format to determine whether they are present or prevalent within a given project. The

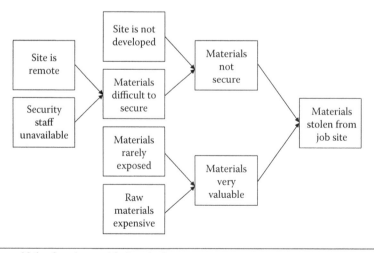

Figure 16.1   Sample causal factors chart.

checklist that is generated from these outputs is then used to identify whether the project is at greater risk for the ultimate risk or outcome and asks questions such as

Is the site remote?
Is security staff unavailable?
Are raw materials expensive?
Are these materials that are rarely exposed and available?
Is the site undeveloped and unpopulated?

A series of "yes" responses would be indicative of an environment where there is a much higher likelihood of having materials stolen from the job site than one in which a series of "no" responses could be achieved.

Major Steps in Applying the Technique

Root cause identification and analysis works through the "causes of causes of causes." It is an effort to progressively elaborate on the reasons why a particular risk or series of risks could or will occur.

Gather data. A broad range of data, including the risk events, the causal factors, and the root causes, must be collected. This is done by applying idea-generation techniques and by consistently re-asking the question why. By repeatedly inquiring why certain risks and causes may exist, the technique sifts out inappropriate responses, and it then becomes possible to work down to the root causes. Some proponents of root cause identification and analysis believe the "why" question must be asked at least five times to achieve certainty that the root cause has been discovered.

Chart the causes of the risk events. This process involves ensuring that each risk event's causes (and the causes of those causes) are provided in sufficient detail that analysts can determine the environment that makes the risk more likely or more threatening. This process may evolve over time as more information becomes available or as further investigation exposes further causes. What results is a sequential diagram reflecting the logic that dictates whether a risk event is highly likely to occur or likely to occur with a significant impact.

Map the causes. Continue mapping until there is sufficient detail to determine what the root causes (driving forces) are.

The list of root causes can later be used in a variety of fashions, including developing checklists, creating recommended actions, or establishing project policy to reduce the effects of the risk event. The information can also be utilized for presentations to identify key causal factors, paths through the root causes that drive those factors, and potential resolutions. Because the information is mapped through paths of how and why risk events may happen, the rationale for resolution(s) becomes more readily comprehensible.

Use of Results

Root cause identification and analysis can be used both as a justification for mitigation strategies and approaches and to clarify risk environments. Moreover, the process can support team members, who feel a need for greater exploration of risk events before declaring them as "likely" on a given project, as well as management in its defense of corporate strategy, which serves to preclude some causal factors from evolving.

If a checklist is developed as a result of root cause identification and analysis, then the checklist can become a more standardized tool to determine which common risk events are more likely than others to occur on any given project.

Resource Requirements

The resources for root cause identification and analysis include the software required to generate any graphics, plus the individuals with the ability to investigate risks.

Reliability

Root cause identification and analysis is only as reliable as the efficacy of the investigators in their ability to discern the true causal factors for risks and other causes. If they know the risk environment and can do an effective analysis thereof *and* have the ability to interpret the causes of risk accurately, then the reliability of root cause identification and analysis is high. Although single risk events may have multiple root causes, the reliability is high in terms of identifying at least some of the root causes.

Selection Criteria

As with each chapter on techniques, the root cause identification and analysis technique is assessed using selection criteria relating to resource requirements, applications, and outputs for the technique. To compare root cause identification and analysis with other techniques, review Table II.1 in Part II.

Resource Requirements

The *cost* of conducting root cause identification and analysis is low. Because it is primarily a function of personnel time to develop the analysis and because there are a limited number of individuals required to participate in the process, costs here are limited as well.

There are no special equipment needs for this technique because it is primarily an administrative burden. For *proper facilities and equipment*, the only requirement is to have the software to capture the data and the diagram.

The *time needed to implement* root cause identification and analysis is tied in part to the volume of risks identified on the project and the depth of information available. The more risk events that are identified, then the longer the effort will take to explore their root causes.

Table 16.1   Sample Root Cause Identification and Analysis

QUESTION	OBSERVATION
Why are the vegetables in the garden half-eaten?	There is a rabbit hopping around the garden.
Why is there a rabbit in the garden?	There are a lot of rabbits, an ample food supply, and no deterrent.
Why are there a lot of rabbits?	They breed in the warren near the oak tree.
Why are there no deterrents?	Rabbit-proof fences are ineffective.

The root cause identification and analysis processes have high *ease of use*. Because the technique largely consists of asking the question why, it represents a rudimentary approach to analyzing the background of risks.

The project manager's *time commitment* to root cause identification and analysis hinges on his or her role in the process. If the project manager is solely responsible for conducting the analysis and identifying the causes, then the time commitment can be significant. If, however, the project manager is responsible *only* for shepherding the project team through the process, then the time commitment is low.

Applications

Root cause identification and analysis contributes to most application categories in Table II.1 in Part II.

For *project status reporting*, the root cause identification and analysis technique allows for reporting on the causes of project risks, thereby generating an in-depth status report with a stronger data set.

Major planning decisions require an understanding of whether new risk sources are being generated. The process identifies those risk sources that are already under consideration.

Root cause identification and analysis can tangentially support *contract strategy selection* if contracts have historically been a source of risk.

Root cause identification and analysis does not support *milestone preparation*.

Root cause identification and analysis can support *design guidance* by identifying design elements that may be sources of risk. By knowing the root causes of risk, designers have the ability to recognize when their designs may contribute to driving those causes.

As with contract strategies, root cause identification and analysis can support *source selection* if vendors have historically been a source of risk.

Root cause identification and analysis has limited utility in relation to *budget submittal*.

Outputs

Outputs from root cause identification and analysis are the diagrams generated and the list of root causes associated with the project's identified risk events. That list of root causes may also generate a checklist of specific activities or behaviors to consider when moving forward on the project.

The *accuracy* of root cause identification and analysis increases as more root causes are identified. Because no root cause identification and analysis is truly exhaustive, the accuracy of the process may always be the subject of some speculation. However, accuracy is enhanced as more root causes are identified because a greater likelihood exists that the most significant (or *right*) cause(s) will be identified.

The *level of detail* obtained through root cause identification and analysis is high because the technique demands further parsing of risk events and the rationale for their existence.

The *utility* of root cause identification and analysis is high because analyses can be conducted at a variety of levels at different times during the project life cycle. It serves to reinforce the origins of risks and improves the option set available for mitigation or analysis.

Summary

Root cause identification and analysis has a long history as quality tools. The technique is respected as a sound practice for divining why risks may happen on a given project and what environment will make those risks more likely to happen. Because the entire technique hinges on asking why risks occur, it is a practice that most teams can easily understand and accept. Moreover, it is also an approach that most managers can facilitate, inasmuch as the effort is largely one of repetition and rote analysis.

17

RISK REGISTERS/TABLES

Capturing and storing risk information in an accessible, understandable format is crucial to any project where risk management will be applied. Risk registers are tables where project risk information (including data on everything from the risk event to the ultimate outcomes) is housed. Risk registers may be real or virtual, but they are essential elements of a risk practice, in that they are the repositories for information garnered using virtually all other approaches and techniques.

Technique Description

Risk registers are constructed as either word processing or spreadsheet tables to accommodate risk information. The register may include the label for the risk event, its nature, probability, impact, mitigation strategy, owner, as well as a host of other information (Figure 17.1). Virtually all risk data are logged in these tables to ensure a consistent understanding of the breadth of risks on a given project and how they are being analyzed and handled.

When Applicable

Risk registers are almost always applicable. Although they do not generate new information, they instead contain information garnered during other steps in the risk management process. Risk registers become progressively more applicable as a project evolves and as the information sets they house become progressively richer. They are also helpful as historical documents from past projects because they provide a sense of an entire project's risk history from startup to closure.

Risk Event	Date		Root Cause(s)	Probability	Impact
	Identified	Reviewed	Resolved/Closed			

Risk Event	Identified	Reviewed	Resolved/Closed	Root Cause(s)	Probability	Impact
<<Bad thing>> may happen, causing <<impact>>	First date recognized	Scheduled date or time period for review	Date of final review or total resolution	Cause or causes identified in root cause analysis	Likelihood of occurrence (H/M/L)	Severity of impact in value or H/M/L

Strategy		Owner	Outcome
Considered	Applied		
Approaches given serious consideration for risk resolution	Approach applied	Individual with direct responsibility for risk event and outcome	Nature of final outcome either in terms of impact or strategy efficacy

Figure 17.1   Sample risk register (partially complete with data instructions).

Inputs and Outputs

Inputs into risk registers comprise all information collected during other processes and arranged in tabular format. Inputs vary from organization to organization but can include a wide array of data. Some information that may be captured in a risk register include

Risk event
Date identified
Root cause(s)
Probability
Impact
Overall risk level
Priority
Strategies considered
Strategy selected
Owner
Date for review
Date for resolution/date resolved
Outcome

The breadth of a risk register is largely dependent upon the organization it serves. However, every column included in a risk register represents another input that must be considered in terms of data collection, evaluation, and retention.

The output from the risk register is the register itself. Because of the capabilities of most spreadsheet and word processing programs, data may be filtered in a variety of fashions. The key is to ensure that a common understanding exists of how the data from the tables will be applied. The outputs, as indicated earlier, can be maintained either as hard copy or in software. Software may include word processing, spreadsheet, or project management programs. In project management software, information may be linked to the tables or embedded in text fields that are resident within the software itself. Particularly if the latter approach is applied, then long-term knowledge management practices (consistent protocols for retention, acknowledged application of fields, protocols for access, and so on) should be used.

Data in these fields provide risk history and a clear road map for dealing with the risks as identified (as well as the organization's informational expectations).

Major Steps in Applying the Technique

Risk registers evolve over time as more information becomes available. The key to creating an effective risk register is not to attempt to populate the entire table right away. Instead, information should be embedded into the tool as it becomes available. Major application steps include

Identify risks and incorporate them in the "Risk Event" field. As stated earlier, risk events should be identified using a consistent syntax to ensure that the risk event is clearly identifiable in terms of cause and impact.

Capture the initial date the risk was identified, and log in the "Date Identified" field.

Identify the date for the next review of the risk, and log in the "Date Reviewed" field.

Identify the date the risk was resolved or acknowledged as terminated, and log in the "Date Resolved/Closed" field.

Assess the root causes of the risk event (as described in the previous chapter), and log in the "Root Cause(s)" field.

Identify the probability, and incorporate the relative probability for the event in the "Probability" field. The probabilities, as discussed in Part I, should be created according to either their actual, statistical likelihood or according to a high/medium/low/remote scheme as discussed in Chapter 25, "Ratings Schemes."

Identify impact, and incorporate the impact for the event in the "Impact" field. The impacts, as discussed in Part I, should be created according to either their real impact value (in terms of cost and/or schedule) or according to a high/medium/low scheme as discussed in Chapter 25, "Ratings Schemes."

Identify the overall risk, and incorporate the relative score (normally determined through an evaluation of the combined probability and impact), and log in the "Overall Risk" field).

Identify the relative priority (relative to the other risks identified and their overall risk scores), and assign the priority in the "Priority" field.

Identify potentially effective strategies for the risk (as discussed in Part I), and log in the "Strategy Considered" field.

Identify strategies to apply to the risk, and log in the "Strategy Applied" field.

Identify a risk owner responsible for tracking and mitigation, and log in the "Owner" field.

Determine the outcome of the risk event, and log in the "Outcome" field.

Again, these steps do not occur all at once but instead will be applied over an extended period of time as the information sets become available. The key is to ensure that information is captured in a consistent fashion and that it is maintained in a repository where others in the organization may ultimately access it for organizational memory, knowledge management, and lessons learned.

Use of Results

Although the risk register has a wide variety of applications, it serves primarily as a library and information tool for the project plan. In many organizations, the risk register is considered the primary manifestation of the risk plan. As such, the register is used to communicate risks, strategies, ownership patterns, and other vital information about the organization's project risk approach. From an historical perspective, the results are also used as an archive of what risks were anticipated on a given project, how they were handled, and their ultimate outcomes. The risk register or an update thereof is considered a critical output of every stage of the risk management process after the risk management plan is established.

Resource Requirements

Resources for the risk register include software required to generate the tables (and to store information for the permanent archive) and the individuals having the ability to catalog and sort information from many other processes into the tables. For the most part, administrative competence is the only skill required.

Reliability

The risk register is highly reliable as a repository because it encourages consistent and effective information storage. Inasmuch as it draws on information garnered from other processes and analyses, its role as "data warehouse" renders it highly reliable. As long as there are periodic information backups and they are retained in a relatively secure environment, then the risk register is a highly reliable tool.

Selection Criteria

As with each chapter on techniques, the risk register is assessed using selection criteria relating to resource requirements, applications, and outputs for the technique. To compare the risk register with other techniques, review Table II.1.

Resource Requirements

  The *cost* of implementing the risk register is low. Because generating and storing information in the table is primarily an administrative function, administrative personnel can conduct the work. Their investment of time is the time to log the information. Likewise, because the process requires the participation of a limited number of individuals, costs here are limited as well.

  No special equipment needs exist for this technique because it is primarily an administrative burden. For *proper facilities and equipment*, the only requirement is to have software to capture the data and the table.

  The *time needed to implement* the risk register is significant, but it occurs in very small increments throughout the life of the project. Were all the work lumped into a single experience, then the time required would be high. However, the fact that data should be input into the register in small degrees on a regular basis renders the time needed during those steps as low.

The risk register has high *ease of use* because it is primarily a data entry function.

The project manager's *time commitment* to the risk register is significant when considered in the aggregate. However, on an incremental, per-use basis, the project manager's time commitment to the tool is very small.

Applications

The risk register supports most application categories in Table II.1.

For *project status reporting*, the risk register can be filtered to highlight either risks resolved or risks at a given level of threat (impact or probability or both).

Major planning decisions require an understanding of risk in an across-the-project context, a perspective that the risk register affords.

The risk register can support *contract strategy selection* if the "Risk Event" and/or "Risk Source" fields are filtered for the term "contract" to highlight only those risks related to contracts and contract types.

The risk register does not support *milestone preparation*.

The risk register can support *design guidance* if the "Risk Event" and/or "Strategy" fields are filtered for the term "design" to highlight any risk events or strategies that may have a direct relationship to the design process.

As with contract strategies, the risk register can support *source selection* if "vendor" becomes the filter term.

The risk register may support *budget submittal* if the "Risk Event" and "Strategy" columns are filtered for those that incorporate the terms "cost," "budget," and/or "allocation."

Outputs

The output from the risk register is a spreadsheet or table that serves as the master repository for all risk information. Depending upon how the spreadsheet or table is analyzed, the output may be complete or filtered for specific terms as discussed in the *Applications* section above.

> *Accuracy* of the risk register is high, as it reflects the aggregated information from many other processes. Operating under the assumption that outputs from those processes were accurate should be reflected in the risk register.
>
> The *level of detail* in the risk register is extremely high, as it embodies the full breadth of risk information in the project.
>
> The *utility* of the risk register is extremely high, as it can be applied with a few, some, or all other tools in this book. The risk register becomes the tabular home for other risk information collected through other processes.

Summary

The risk register is common to a host of different project management processes because it is a documentary tool that evolves over the life of the project. As the project progresses and the risk register becomes progressively more complete, it also serves to provide a history of the project (in terms of risk) and to reflect the risk strategies and owners that have been effective (as well as those that have not).

18
PROJECT TEMPLATES

This technique is based on the notion that many organizations use templates to facilitate planning and to minimize risk. Templates are essentially nothing more than fully developed plans, forms, or outlines that provide structure for an organization's project managers. These templates often manifest themselves as elements of a much larger project methodology (discussed in Chapter 6). By properly applying these templates (or merely recognizing their existence), it becomes possible to mitigate additional risk and apply best practices to existing risks.

Technique Description

The technique consists of examining a series of templates covering specific areas that may present technical risk to a project. Each template examines an area that frequently spawns risks and then describes methods (or provides examples) to avoid or control that risk. Many risk descriptions and solutions are rooted in lessons learned from other projects. Some examples of areas that such templates may cover are illustrated in Figure 18.1.

When Applicable

Project templates should be used for most projects, either independently or in conjunction with another technique. Templates are generally built in response to past incidents as a means to preclude a risk that has already befallen an organization. Organizational templates specifically contain *extremely* valuable information because they are based on actual experience. The information can be pertinent for any size project at any phase of development. Because the technique views project management as a complete process, the solutions presented

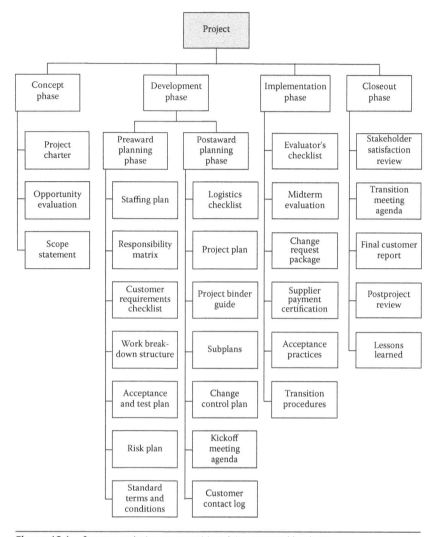

Figure 18.1   Common project management templates, arranged by phase.

reflect the interdependency of each part of the cycle. In other words, a conscious effort is made to present a solution that lowers the total risk for the entire project and not merely for short-term problems.

Inputs and Outputs

Each template will require inputs specific to that template. In a perfect world, all templates necessary to succeed would already exist in an organization, complete with guidance on how to apply them to every type of project. This effort is normally under the purview of senior project managers or a project office.

The application of templates requires discipline. Time must be committed to reading the templates, as well as the organizational methodologies driving them, and then to using that information to examine risk within a given project. Practical outputs of the technique are basic lists of risks built from past experience.

Major Steps in Applying the Technique

Because methodologies and templates cover areas common to nearly every project, each template should be reviewed for applicability. The project manager determines whether the template is appropriate to the project and its specific risks. After reviewing the template, the project manager or the team members responsible should evaluate the project in terms of solutions or risk mitigating actions that the template would prescribe. A periodic review of all templates is recommended with updates as the project progresses. In some cases, simply applying the template or reviewing its contents will be sufficient to identify (or in some cases, even mitigate) risks.

Use of Results

Results from templates can be used in a variety of ways:

In presentations to higher levels of authority
To influence the team members' current level of activity in an area
For continued monitoring of progress in each project area

In many instances, templates are used to modify team member behavior by reinforcing what data must be gathered or by encouraging certain documentation practices.

Resource Requirements

Because the inputs are template specific, most of the inputs are also specific to the individuals responsible for the given template. For example, if procurement templates (such as Supplier Payment

Certification) are applied, then some procurement staff support may be required. Although inputs may be required from a variety of functions, using templates should not necessitate substantial special skills or extra resources.

Reliability

Two cautions apply when using this technique:

> Project participants should not assume that templates contain all possible risks within a given area. Although common problems are frequently identified, this technique does not generate an exhaustive list of risks.
>
> Templates may not contain information regarding several programmatic risk areas that should also be examined.

Selection Criteria

As with each chapter on techniques, the project template technique is assessed using selection criteria relating to resource requirements, applications, and outputs for the technique. To compare project templates with other techniques, review Table II.1.

Resource Requirements

> The additional *cost* associated with project templates is small. This technique requires little additional resourcing beyond what is normally necessary to manage a project properly. The time consumed is nominal as long as the work is done continuously and incrementally.
>
> There are no special equipment needs for this technique because it is primarily a small administrative burden. For *proper facilities and equipment*, the only requirement is to locate the files, databases, or shelves housing the information.
>
> The *time needed to implement* project templates is actually a function of the project manager's level of discipline coupled with the nature of the templates themselves. Project templates must be reviewed (and comparative project progress must be analyzed) regularly against each of the template areas.

Project templates have extremely good *ease of use*. They do not require special skills beyond being able to comprehend the information requested for each particular template. In fact, they are designed to prevent organizations from regenerating established protocols each time a new project arises.

The project manager's *time commitment* to the templates is moderate because the project manager invariably will spend some time selecting the appropriate templates for the project and will also be responsible for reviewing the templates as they are completed. The time investment is well worth the return, however, because the project team develops information that virtually anyone in the organization's project support structure can understand.

Applications

Project templates can be used in most application categories in Table II.1. The technique is only indirectly useful in the budget category because it deals with preventive technical aspects rather than cost issues. It can, however, provide insight into the impetus behind both cost and subcontractor actions in situations involving vendors.

For *project status reporting*, project managers often find it helpful to build their status reports in formats that others have designed. This convention of building on past efforts within the organization becomes more time- and cost-effective as the organization develops. As a project template, project status reports will inherently highlight some issues that have arisen in the past.

Major planning decisions require a sense of organizational history, which project templates offer as well. If an organization has project templates in place either on an ad hoc basis or as part of a methodology, then the templates can expose issues that have driven major decisions in the past.

In most cases, *contract strategy* selection has some type of existing templates. Project templates encourage consistency in contract development and organization from project to project.

Milestone preparation often requires the use of project templates. Templates are often structured around milestones to specifically meet internal or external reporting needs. Templates for these events are commonplace and thus become critical tools for the project manager. By using templates (such as closeout checklists, annual budget review formats, or decision point analysis grids), the project manager can ensure that all reports, components, or completion criteria for a particular milestone are prepared in a timely fashion.

In terms of *design guidance*, project templates have clear utility. But there is a caveat: Project templates rely on history, and the latest developments in technology design often drive design. As such, the information that the template requires may not be congruous within current desired designs. In most cases, however, project templates are a good fit for design guidance because even as technology changes, many of the same questions or issues continue to apply.

Source selection requires rigorous procedures if vendors are to be assessed fairly and consistently. Project templates may include those procedures.

Budget submittal is not a clear use for project templates. Although the templates facilitate formatting, they do not generally include relevant historic cost data. That information can be obtained only through rigorous analysis.

Outputs

If the user properly documents results from a review of project templates, then the outputs will provide a set of traceable management data that can be used to make sound decisions on a variety of customer, personnel, and technical issues.

Accuracy of the project templates technique is a direct function of the project manager's adherence to the approach. There is often a temptation to skip templates that do not seem to address the project at hand; but if that is done, it may result in missing some key problem areas.

The *level of detail* obtained through project templates can potentially be exhaustive. If there is a complete methodology, then the project templates will provide the project manager with a sense of most risks encountered in the organization's past. If a single template is used or only one area is covered, then the level of detail can diminish significantly.

The *utility* of project templates is in their capacity to save the project manager from rediscovering organizational issues that may have a negative effect on the project. Because such templates are normally based on the experience of an organization's more talented project managers, they save the current project manager from constantly evaluating and reevaluating the project and the organization to ensure that every potential risk area has been addressed.

Summary

When using project templates, the key is the requisite discipline for going through the process in small, manageable steps. If a project manager or team attempts to complete all project templates at one time, then the task will invariably be overwhelming and enormously time-consuming. If, instead, the effort is conducted incrementally over time, then the administrative burden is reduced and the technique becomes far less onerous for long-term utility and application.

19
ASSUMPTIONS ANALYSIS

The critical element of assumptions analysis is assumptions identification. This technique entails conducting a thorough review of all project assumptions and validating or invalidating them. In either case, the information is published and shared across the team to communicate issues that should be considered in the project plan and in all customer and team member interactions.

Technique Description

Assumptions analysis consists of building project documentation that provides consistent interpretation of the project environment. Although the documentation may take a variety of forms, the key is to apply it consistently. If all projects within an organization use the same documentation structures to capture assumptions, then it is much easier to interpret the information consistently. The technique also involves analysis of the data captured within the documentation to establish each assumption's validity.

When Applicable

Assumptions analysis is applicable at the beginning of the project and any time there is a change in the project environment. It is also applicable when major decisions must be made, inasmuch as the assumptions under which the project operates often affect decision-making processes. Because decisions frequently influence assumptions sets, the earlier that assumptions can be identified and documented, the better. However, there is sometimes a tendency to shift assumptions based on project urgency. If assumptions have already been documented, then that tendency can be thwarted to some degree.

WBS	Task Name	Assumptions
1	**Media Campaign**	**The business need is for a June 1 Completion Date**
1.1	**Marketing Plan distributed**	**This milestone was achieved by the Marketing Dept.**
1.2	**Corporate Communications**	**Corporate Communications will be exclusively internal**
1.2.1	Corp Comm Kickoff	The kickoff will be internal personnel
1.2.2	Comm Plan	Plan delivery will be in soft copy format
1.2.3	Packaging	No custom packaging is required
1.2.4	Datasheets	Data for datasheets will be largely developed by Marketing
1.2.5	Reseller kits	Reseller kits will be the standard format, supplemented by custom content
1.2.6	Competitive comparison	Complettive analyses will be based on the standard Acme format
1.2.7	Demo script	Demo scripts will be approved on the first draft
1.2.8	Working Model	The "working model" will consist of a working model of the product to be promoted by the campaign
1.3	**Advertising**	**All internal advertising costs will be assumed as part of the contract and will not be billed separately**
1.3.1	Develop creative briefs	Customer will have only one review cycle to analyze creative briefs

Figure 19.1   Assumptions documentation.

Inputs and Outputs

Inputs into assumptions analysis consist of project assumptions. Those assumptions are not the exclusive province of the project manager, the project team, or the customer. Instead, they should be educed from as many different parties as can be identified. Other inputs into assumptions analysis include any background or supporting documentation that can prove or disprove assumption validity. Some of these inputs may derive from the lessons learned of other projects; other inputs are drawn from project-specific research.

Outputs from assumptions analysis will frequently be embedded in the risk register, the notes fields of project management software (as illustrated in the sample in Figure 19.1), or in the caveats and codicils within a memorandum of understanding. Ideally, they should be captured in a consistent document format.

Major Steps in Applying the Technique

Assumptions analysis is a general practice that leads to both broad and specific statements about the project environment that are then used in establishing the parameters for project plans. Even though approaches may vary, the processes remain similar from activity to activity.

Identify environmental conditions unique to the project. Although natural organizational conditions may drive some project assumptions, unique environmental conditions tend to drive less obvious assumptions. By identifying what makes the project unusual within the organizational environment, it then becomes possible to begin a discussion on what qualities or traits of that environment need to be clarified or rendered consistent for everyone involved in the project.

Determine what issues within that environment will be prone to misunderstanding or miscommunication. Assumptions are often established or recognized through conflicts of understanding between two individuals. Thus, assumptions are more readily captured when multiple parties participate in the assumptions documentation process. By reviewing project documentation and parsing unclear terms, the project team can ferret out some of the assumptions the project requires.

Catalog the assumptions. As shown in Figure 19.1, assumptions can be captured within the project plan by using project management software. They can also be documented in forms or lists, but the documentation should be retained with the project plan and should be readily accessible to anyone performing work on, receiving deliverables from, or making changes to the project.

As much as practical and possible, validate the assumptions. However, not all assumptions can be validated; some simply must be established in their own right. But for some other assumptions, it is possible to investigate and determine whether they are accurate or reliable. The degree to which this step of the process will be conducted depends largely on the amount of time and effort that will need to be expended to validate the information (and the potential value of it).

Use of Results

Assumptions from assumptions analysis should be retrieved whenever a need exists for better understanding the project, its plan, or its background. Typical situations where assumptions documentation might be used include

Project selection
Contract negotiations
Resource allocation meetings
Change or configuration control board meetings
Project evaluations
Customer reviews
Performance assessments
Project termination

The key is that assumptions documentation provides greater clarity for decision making and a mutual understanding of terms, practices, and characteristics.

Resource Requirements

The resources for the assumptions analysis technique are merely those individuals with the ability to generate an independent interpretation of project information. The solution, however, is to find those individuals whose interpretations will be widely understood and accepted by the broadest possible body of project stakeholders.

Reliability

The assumptions analysis process is reliable in that it generally increases the reliability of other activities and processes. Assumptions analysis focuses on increasing accuracy and ensuring consistent understanding of information, therefore rendering more of the project's overall information pool more reliable.

Selection Criteria

As with each chapter on techniques, the assumptions analysis technique is assessed using selection criteria relating to resource requirements, applications, and outputs for the technique. To compare assumptions analysis with other techniques, review Table II.1.

Resource Requirements

The *cost* of conducting assumptions analysis is closely related to the unfamiliarity of the project and its environment. Thus, the more original content that is associated with the project, then the more assumptions will need to be developed. The more assumptions are generated, then the more assumptions analysis must be conducted. Even so, reviewing project terms, practices, and processes should still be considered commonplace, and thus the additional cost is relatively limited.

There are no special equipment needs for this technique because it is primarily an administrative burden. For *proper facilities and equipment*, the only requirement is to establish a repository for documenting any assumptions.

The *time needed to implement* assumptions analysis is tied to the novelty of the project or the nature of the environment. The more original the project or the less understood the project environment, then the more time required for the analysis.

Project assumptions analysis has extremely high *ease of use*. Because assumptions are documented in a format that is readily accessible to the project team and because assumptions are directly related to areas of concern and confusion in the project, this clarification process adds value precisely where it is needed most.

The project manager's *time commitment* to assumptions analysis hinges on the novelty of the project and the uniqueness of the environment. The more singular the effort is, then the more time is required in the analysis.

Applications

Assumptions analysis contributes to most application categories in Table II.1.

For *project status reporting*, assumptions frequently determine how information will be expressed in the reports as well as the status itself. Although assumptions analysis does not generate status report information, it helps establish validity of the status reported.

Major planning decisions require a clear understanding of the project environment, which an unambiguous, shared grasp of the project's assumptions greatly facilitates.

Assumptions made about client behavior, project duration, and process approach may determine, in part, *contract strategy selection*. Because all those issues may be clarified somewhat during assumptions analysis, there is a strong application here.

Milestone preparation sometimes relies on a shared sense of what a given series of activities entails. Again, assumptions analysis can be extremely beneficial in this area.

Design guidance is a function of understanding client requirements, which is frequently rooted in assumptions. Thus, assumptions analysis is crucial here. In this instance, it is particularly important to ensure that the assumptions associated with both functional and technical requirements are dissected to address their potential impact on project design.

Because a large component of *source selection* is directly tied to assumptions on activities and performance, assumptions analysis heavily supports this area. For this application, however, it is especially prudent to assess the validity of assumptions based on the organization's knowledge of the sources under consideration and the volume of the information base available regarding those sources.

Budget submittal also relies heavily on assumptions analysis. The vital questions for many of these assumptions are "Where did the data originate?" and "How reliable are those sources?" This information should be documented along with the budget so that the validity of the assumptions applied can be analyzed for future reference.

Outputs

Outputs from assumptions analysis are frequently in the form of one- or two-line statements regarding anticipated performance, activity, behavior, or environmental conditions. These statements are (ideally) linked to the source documents under evaluation (for example, if the assumption is about a budget element, then it is documented with the budget).

Accuracy of assumptions analysis is tied to the volume and the accuracy of the supporting data available. The more valid the data that are available, then the more accurate the analysis will be. Accuracy also ties to the skill of the evaluators. Expert evaluators (or those with a history on the subject matter in question) will tend to generate more accurate assumptions assessments.

The *level of detail* obtained through assumptions analysis ties to the level desired. If assumptions analysis is conducted at the work package level of the work breakdown structure, then the level of detail will be exacting. If, however, the assumptions analysis is simply conducted on the project objective or the scope statement, then the level of detail will not be as thorough.

The *utility* of assumptions analysis is high because the analyses can be conducted at a variety of levels at different points during the project life cycle. It serves to refine requirements, cement understanding, and generate common interpretations of what may potentially be indistinct data.

Summary

Assumptions analyses take on a variety of forms within different projects and organizations. Although some assumptions analysis occurs almost unconsciously, the most effective assumptions analysis will be performed with multiple parties and with extensive documentation. That documentation will ultimately be stored where those who can put the information to use can readily retrieve it. If assumptions analyses are done simply for their own sake and the documentation is not generated or retrieved regularly, then the process has extremely limited utility.

20
DECISION ANALYSIS
Expected Monetary Value

Decision analysis can be used to determine strategies when a decision maker is faced with several decision alternatives and an uncertain or risk-filled pattern of future events. Before selecting a specific decision analysis technique, the kind of situation must be considered. Classifying decision-making situations is based on how much is known about those future events that are beyond the decision maker's control (known as states of nature). Thus, the two types of situations are as follows:

Decision making under certainty (when states of nature are known)

Decision making under uncertainty (when states of nature are unknown)

The decision analysis techniques appropriate for risk identification, quantification, and prioritization are those that consider decisions made under some degree of uncertainty.

In situations where good probability estimates can be developed for states of nature, the expected monetary value (EMV) method is a popular technique for making decisions. In some instances of decision making under uncertainty, the decision maker may not have the ability to assess probabilities of the various states of nature with confidence.

Technique Description

In general, three steps are involved in formulating a decision theory problem using the EMV method:

Define the problem.

Identify alternatives that the decision maker may consider (feasible alternatives may be denoted by d_i).

Identify those relevant future events that might occur and are beyond the decision maker's control (may be denoted by s_j).

In decision theory terminology, an outcome that results from a specific decision and the occurrence of a particular state of nature is referred to as the *payoff* (denoted by V). The formula $V(d_i, s_j)$ denotes the payoff associated with decision alternative d_i and state of nature s_j.

By way of example, a project manager must decide which method to use for a business trip. A car trip would take 4 hours, with a 5 percent probability of delays of 1 hour or longer. A plane trip would take 3.5 hours (including travel time to and from the airport), with a 30 percent probability of delays of 2 hours or longer. In this scenario, d_i is the project manager's decision to drive. Based on expected values, the plane trip would have taken 4 hours 6 minutes [3.5 hours + (120 minutes (0.30))]. According to expected value, the car trip should take 4 hours 3 minutes [4 hours + (60 minutes (0.05))]. The alternative selected (s_j) and how it turned out is the fact that the project manager had no delays and arrived in 4 hours. Note the characteristics. The decision alternative d_i could be determined at any point in time. The state of nature, s_j, remained unknown until the risk had come and gone. The payoff, $V(d_i, s_j)$, is the 4-hour trip, completed successfully.

When Applicable

The EMV method applies during any project phase, though it typically would be generated at the onset of the project to identify the probabilities and relative costs associated with particular courses of action. Because decision analysis models can be portrayed as decision trees, they can be applied to network analysis. Probability-based branching in a network is an example of using decision analysis in a network analysis framework.

Inputs and Outputs

Inputs to the EMV method consist of the decision alternatives to be considered (what options the project manager has), the states of nature associated with the decision alternatives (what can happen), and the probability of occurrence for each state of nature (what are the chances that a given scenario will happen). Outputs of the EMV method are the expected payoff values for each decision alternative under consideration.

Major Steps in Applying the Technique

The EMV criterion requires that the analyst compute the expected value for each alternative to select the choice that yields the best expected value. Because, ultimately, only one state of nature (or outcome) can occur (that is, only one given scenario can come to pass), the associated probabilities must satisfy the following condition:

$$P(s_j) \geq 0 \quad \text{for all states of nature}_j$$

$$\sum_{j=1}^{n} P(s_j) = P(s_1) + P(s_2) + P(s_3) + \ldots + P(s_n)$$

For this equation

$$P(s_j) = \text{probability of occurrence for the state of nature}(s_j)$$
$$n = \text{number of possible states of nature}$$

The expected monetary value of a decision alternative, d, is derived through the following equation:

$$\text{EMV}(d_i) = \sum_{j=1}^{n} P(s_j)V(d_i, s_1)$$

In other words, the EMV of a decision alternative is the product of the payoff and the probability that the payoff will occur. Put more simply, the EMV of a decision to buy a scratch-off lottery ticket is the sum of its probabilities and potential impact. Consider this example, where a single ticket has the following probabilities:

WINNINGS	PROBABILITY	EXPECTED VALUE
$1	0.25	$0.25
$10	0.01	$0.10
$1,000	0.0001	$0.10
$1,000,000	0.0000001	$0.10
0	0.7398999	$0

EMV = $0.25 + $0.10 + $0.10 + $0.10 + $0.00 = $0.55

The sum of all the probabilities equals 1.0; all the states of nature are accounted for; and all the expected values sum to $0.55. Although there will never be a single ticket with a $0.55 winner, if enough tickets are purchased over time, however, then their average value will ultimately be about $0.55.

The probability is expressed as the percentage for each potential state of nature (or outcome). The following is an example of a situation in which the EMV method can be used to make a decision.

Consider the decision of whether to purchase either Acme or Nadir water pumps for a fleet of 400 trucks based on the failure rates of the pumps, their relative maintenance cost in the first year of operation, and the purchase price. Historically, the trucking organization has saved time, energy, and risk by replacing all water pumps in the fleet at the same time.

Acme water pumps cost $500 each and have a failure rate of 5 percent in the first year of operation. Reinstalling a failed (and then rebuilt) Acme pump costs $150. Maintenance on pumps that do not fail is $100 per year. Acme reimburses all maintenance costs on failed pumps.

Nadir water pumps cost only $485 each but have a failure rate of 15 percent in the first year of operation. Reinstalling a failed (and then rebuilt) Nadir pump costs $200. Maintenance on pumps that do not fail is $100 per year. Nadir also reimburses all maintenance costs on failed pumps.

A decision table can be constructed that presents this problem with respect to two decision alternatives and the respective states of nature. Figure 20.1 depicts the decision table for this problem and the associated analysis.

The analyst has the option of building a table or a decision tree or of creating both based on personal preference. The decision tree graphically represents the decision under consideration (see Figure 20.2). Although the tree itself may never be drawn, all relevant events must be listed and analyzed to determine problems that can occur as the process reaches each decision point. Every outcome must be considered, and there must be a path through the tree to every possible outcome or payoff. Experts are consulted to identify each problem and possible outcome, as well as to assign probabilities to the various

Decision Alternatives   **States of Nature**

	Fail	Maintain
Buy Acme $d_1 = \$200,000$	$P(s_1) = 0.05$ 400 trucks (0.05 failure rate) ($150 per repair)	$P(s_2) = 0.95$ 400 trucks (0.95 maintenance rate) ($100 per maintenance event)
Buy Nadir $d_2 = \$194,000$	$P(s_1) = 0.15$ 400 trucks (0.15 failure rate) ($200 per repair)	$P(s_2) = 0.85$ 400 trucks (0.85 maintainance rate) ($100 per maintainance event)

Analysis

EMV (Buy Acme)

$200,000	400 pumps ($500 each)
3,000	400 trucks (0.05 failure rate) ($150 per repair)
38,000	400 trucks (0.95 maintenance rate) ($100 per truck)
$241,000	

EMV (Buy Nadir)

$194,000	400 trucks ($485 each)
12,000	400 trucks (0.15 failure rate) ($200 per repair)
34,000	400 trucks (0.85 maintenance rate) ($100 per truck)
$240,000	

If objective is based on a 1-year time frame and cost alone, buy Nadir.

Figure 20.1   Decision table.

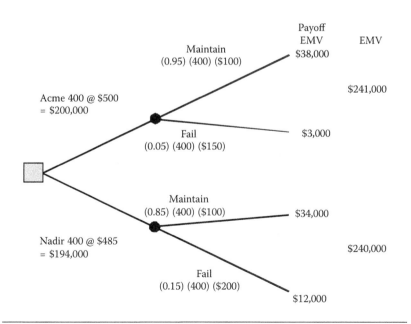

Figure 20.2   Decision tree.

problems and outcomes. Any realistic number of sequential outcomes can be evaluated.

Use of Results

Given the expected monetary values of the decision alternatives, the analyst's selection of the appropriate choice is predicated on whether the objective is to maximize profit or to minimize cost. In the sample problem, because the objective was to minimize cost, the analyst would select the alternative with the lowest EMV. When the difference between decision alternatives is slight, however, other programmatic factors may be considered when making the decision.

In the example provided, the apparent price gap between the two pumps has shrunk from $6,000 (the difference when only purchase price is considered) to $1,000 (the difference when expected monetary value—also called expected value—is factored in). It allows the decision maker to question whether the increased quality that an Acme pump affords is worth the additional expenditure of $1,000 to the organization.

Resource Requirements

With respect to resource requirements, the EMV technique is simplistic and can usually be calculated easily *after* obtaining the inputs to the model. Resource requirements for gathering those inputs may be more significant. As decision problems become more complex with an increasing number of decision alternatives and states of nature, the time required to create decision tables or decision trees will also increase.

Reliability

One of the most attractive features of the EMV method of decision analysis is that after obtaining respective inputs to the model, no ambiguity exists regarding the analysis. The reliability of the results is based on the validity of the inputs to the model. If analysts can realistically define all relevant decision alternatives, states of nature, and respective probabilities, then the model will reflect reality.

Reliability can improve from a probability perspective in a qualitative environment when consistent probability values are assigned to qualitative terms. For example, if "high probability" is always equated to 79%, then calculations can be done consistently across a project or across an organization. The key to improving EMV reliability in a qualitative venue is establishing a consistent numeric value for the qualitative terms.

Another significant benefit of the EMV method is that it can readily be portrayed in a diagram, facilitating a conceptual understanding of the problem, the alternatives, and the analysis.

Selection Criteria

As with each chapter on techniques, decision analysis is assessed using selection criteria relating to resource requirements, applications, and outputs for the technique. To compare decision analysis with other techniques, review Table II.1 in Part II.

Resource Requirements

   Decision analysis *cost* includes only the time to gather the data and to conduct the analysis. A skilled analyst merely requires a limited amount of time to assess the data available and to review its validity.

   The *proper facilities and equipment* requirement is limited to accessing enough computers to support analysts in developing the information.

   The *time needed to implement* this approach is highly dependent on the level of depth required and the quality of outputs the organization mandates.

   Ease of use in decision analysis is based on the skill level of the analyst. When reviewed against other techniques, this approach has a significantly shorter learning curve and thus does not require someone who is experienced in conducting decision analyses over an extended period of time. The technique can be taught effectively, and because the results are quantitative, they are easier to review for flawed analyses.

The project manager's *time commitment* to this particular technique is very limited. The project manager is normally responsible only for a final review of the outputs.

Applications

Decision analysis is frequently used as a tool to establish appropriate levels of contingency funding for projects. By applying EMV to the risks in the project and establishing the EMV for the project's major risks, it is possible to use decision analysis to ascertain the magnitude of an appropriate contingency budget. In the ideal, such a budget would incorporate from the EMV of any concurrent opportunities as well as risks to balance the project's potential windfalls against potential problems.

Decision analysis lends itself well to all the following applications:

For *project status reporting*, decision analysis allows the project manager to provide quantitative information on future events. Because few techniques provide that information, decision analysis provides valuable data essential to quality risk management.

Major planning decisions should hinge on the potential for success. Because decision analysis reviews the potential for success, it is invaluable. Inasmuch as contingency funds sometimes become a determining factor in major planning decisions, the role of EMV in that regard comes to the fore as well.

Contract strategy selection is keyed to the potential success of the buyer, vendor, contractor, or subcontractor(s) involved. Because monetary decisions often drive contracts, EMV and decision trees can help determine whether the contract strategy is appropriate to the value of the contract.

As with contract strategy selection, *milestone preparation* is most often a step conducted at the beginning of the project. Here, decision analysis has limited utility unless it is applied to schedules to determine the potential for success in terms of the schedule. However, if the milestones are budget driven, then decision analysis becomes even more appropriate.

Design guidance can stem directly from decision analysis because various designs will have different implications in terms of the potential for profits and the potential for technical success.

In *source selection*, decision analysis applies if a history or data record exists for the vendors under consideration. If that information is available, then decision analysis can be effectively applied. However, such evidence is often primarily anecdotal and, as such, does not work well with this technique.

Decision analysis may directly affect *budget submittal* because some organizations use decision analysis as part of the consideration for budget allocations.

Outputs

Outputs from decision analysis can be extraordinarily helpful or utterly useless. Nonetheless, its critical value in terms of outputs remains the quality of the inputs.

Accuracy is highly analyst and data dependent. If the project can be modeled accurately, then the outputs will be errorless; the inverse is also true. To generate effective, accurate information, the data must come from a valid, reliable source and must be analyzed by someone who clearly understands the implications of the technique.

The *level of detail* is based on what the project manager deems necessary. Decision analysis is fully scalable: It can be conducted on a broad scale or at a detailed level. As such, it offers an advantage over techniques that can be applied at only one end of the range.

The *utility* of decision analysis is not as high as with many other techniques because it does not provide the same diversity of outputs or address the myriad questions that other techniques do. Instead, it works best when it provides intense focus on a single issue.

Summary

Decision analysis affords project managers a multi-perspective analysis on a single issue. It does not answer broad, far-reaching project management questions. Instead, it draws on specifics to fill in the nuances of the larger picture. Decision analysis also gives the project manager some quantitative information to present in case of any significant conflict. If decision analysis is used to examine the appropriate questions using the proper inputs, then it can become a powerful tool for the project manager. The keys to making decision analysis effective are to use the tools properly and to ensure that the information being analyzed is current, valid, and accurate.

21

ESTIMATING RELATIONSHIPS

The estimating relationship method enables project personnel to evaluate a project, and based on that evaluation, to apply an equation to determine an appropriate contingency or risk funds budget. When using this method, the contingency fund represents the amount of funding (above that determined by cost analysis alone) required for work associated with unanticipated risks within the scale and scope of the project. The contingency fund requirement computed is usually expressed as a percentage of the baseline cost estimate. The technique is called an estimating relationship method because it uses some of the same techniques associated with cost estimating relationships (CERs) used in parametric cost estimating.

Technique Description

The CER method is based on the observation that costs of systems seem to correlate with design or performance variables. Independent variables, often called explanatory variables, are analyzed using regression analysis to describe the underlying mechanism relating such variables to cost. This approach to cost estimating is widely accepted and easy to apply, even for complex functions.

This ease of application makes it natural to apply the same techniques to estimate costs that result from risks. The approach attempts to discover which project characteristics can be refined into discrete variables, which can then be correlated with the historically demonstrated need for contingency or risk funds. Regression analysis using actual contingency fund figures from past projects (as expressed as a percentage of total costs) is performed to develop an equation with which to estimate contingency fund requirements for a new project not in a database.

The application of this technique is described below. In an example describing this application, project personnel evaluate four project and subcontractor characteristics known to affect the level of uncertainty. Each characteristic is assigned a value based on a scale provided for that characteristic. For this example, the four characteristics and their values are: engineering complexity (0 to 5); organizational proficiency and experience (0 to 3); degree of system definition (0 to 3); and multiple users (0 or 1). The sum of these numerics is entered as the value X in an estimating equation such as the following:[*]

$$y = (.0192 - 0.037X + 0.009X^2)\ 100$$

This formula determines the percentage contingency fund requirement, y. The model shown in this example is usable only for X values between 2 and 12 because lower values indicate essentially no need for contingency funds.

In some organizations, the formulae may not involve regression analysis and thus the calculations may be considerably simpler. The contingency percentage may simply be determined as X times .01. The key will be to ensure that the terms and terminology for the values that support the X variable are consistently defined as discussed in Chapter 25, "Rating Schemes."

When Applicable

This method of estimating the additional funding needed to cover anticipated risks has limited application. It can be used only if the research to establish a valid historical relationship between the key project characteristics or contract characteristics of similar projects and contingency fund requirements has already been done. The method is most applicable in circumstances in which good historical project description and contingency fund requirements are available for several similar projects. If the required risk funding estimating relationship is available, then this method has the advantage of being both quick and easy to apply.

---

[*] The figures in this equation were derived in the U.S. Department of Defense environment by the Defense Systems Management College. As such, they may or may not be appropriate within your organization. They are based on the collective experience of the organization and the implications of those characteristics within their project environments.

Inputs and Outputs

The inputs for an estimating relationship model, such as the equation under the heading "Technique Description," consist of judgment values characterizing the four project or contract factors described in the example.

Regarding outputs, the estimating relationship method provides a percentage that is applied to the estimated baseline cost to determine the amount of total or contract contingency funds required. This percentage value is computed using an equation similar to that used in the example, with the X value being the sum of the four factor values project personnel have determined.

Major Steps in Applying the Technique

When an appropriate contingency estimating equation is not available, the first step in using this method is by far the most challenging: to develop an equation relating project characteristics to contingency fund requirements. The most difficult part of this step is finding valid historical characteristics and contingency fund data for enough similar projects to carry out regression analysis. Data from a minimum of 10 past projects should be used to develop an estimating relationship equation.

The second part of this step is to determine the project or contract characteristics that drive contingency fund requirements and for which historical data have been collected. After collecting the historical data, using regression analysis to identify these characteristics is relatively simple. The summing of judgment values for each of the four project characteristics (as done in the previous example) is merely one way to develop one or more independent variables for an estimating relationship for contingency fund requirements. Geometric mean or weighted average techniques (like PERT) could also be used. Multiple regression analysis techniques frequently are used for parametric cost estimating.

The final step is to use the prediction equation derived through extensive analysis of past projects (coupled with the current project characteristic information) to compute a percentage for the contingency funds needed to cover anticipated additional costs associated with risk. It may be useful to vary the project description characteristic data somewhat and recompute the estimating equation to assess the impact of such changes on the computed contingency fund requirements. This sensitivity analysis is usually prudent because of the uncertainty associated with predicted project or contract characteristics.

Use of Results

To cover funds needed for risk, a percentage of the estimated contract or project cost is added to the basic cost estimate. For example, if the contract cost estimate is $100 million and the prediction equation provides a result of 20 percent, then $20 million would be added for risk, making the total estimated contract cost $120 million.

Resource Requirements

After a suitable contingency fund requirement prediction equation is available, only a few hours are required to apply this method. Most of the effort required involves interviewing project personnel to obtain their insights into the contract or project characteristic values to be used. If a prediction equation needs to be developed, then it would require 1 to 3 months of a skilled analyst's time, depending on the difficulty in acquiring the needed data. However, if the required data are not available, then it becomes impossible to produce a satisfactory prediction equation.

Reliability

This method provides results that significantly increase cost estimates* to allow for risk. Because the additional funds are based primarily on judgment values, they are subject to question. It would always be prudent for the project manager to have upper management review and approve the method (including the prediction equation to be used) before using it as the basis for a viable request for addition risk funding. The method can be used only where adequate historical data are available to develop a sound contingency fund requirement prediction

---

* This is based on extrapolating historical data that may include costs for risks that have already been experienced.

equation. The reliability of this approach increases with time and use. As more projects apply the equation, the technique becomes a more dependable tool to establish the appropriate level(s) of contingency funding.

Selection Criteria

As with each chapter on techniques, estimating relationships are assessed using selection criteria relating to resource requirements, applications, and outputs for the technique. To compare estimating relationships with other techniques, review Table II.1.

Resource Requirements

The *cost* of the estimating relationship technique depends largely on the availability of a parametric cost model specifically designed to estimate contingency reserve or risk funds as a function of one or more project parameters. If such a model is not available, then 1 to 3 resource-months may be required to develop it. If the required historical data are not available, then generating the required cost model may be impossible. On the other hand, if a satisfactory model is available, then it generally takes only a few days at most to apply it.

The *proper facilities and equipment* requirement relates primarily to databases with the appropriate information and the tools themselves. Otherwise, very little equipment is required. The model equations are usually so simple that a calculator is adequate to compute required contingency reserve fund requirements.

The *time needed to implement* the technique can range from a matter of days to as long as 3 months depending on the maturity of the organization in terms of the technique. If the technique has been developed and exercised regularly, then only a few days will be required. Otherwise, a 1- to 3-month window is required to develop the appropriate information.

Estimating relationships have high *ease of use* because after they are built, they require only the appropriate calculations to be developed. Ease of use after the models are constructed becomes a function of ease in data gathering.

The project manager's *time commitment* is extremely limited, but there are some responsibilities for the project manager. The project manager must support the technique's use so that key project personnel will provide the cost analyst with time judgments or information needed as inputs for the model.

Applications

This technique does not support *project status reporting* well. However, it may support midterm status if the criteria used to populate the cost model (the X value) are designed to decrease the contingency required as the project and its environment are more clearly understood.

The only *major planning decision* that the technique supports is determining the extent of contingency reserve or risk funds to be included in the initial budget request or baseline budget.

Contract strategy selection may hinge in small part on the level of risk funding required for the project. Otherwise, there is no relationship between the technique and this application.

This technique does not support *milestone preparation* and *design guidance*.

Source selection may be a critical input to the technique, but the estimating relationship outputs do not support it.

Budget submittal is the primary application for this technique. By computing the level of contingency reserve or risk funds required, the project manager can develop a budget that incorporates and reflects risk issues and allows for the vagaries of real-world project management.

Outputs

The *accuracy* of the technique is considered low, primarily because the historical databases on which such models are based are small. The accuracy also comes into question because accurately defining what funds were spent to address risk on past projects is often difficult.

This method provides a *level of detail* that is unacceptable to the detail-oriented analyst. It provides little or no information with respect to which parts of the project are at greater risk and, therefore, more likely to require additional funding.

Because so few models of this type are available and even their uses are subject to question, the overall *utility* of this method must be considered low. Nonetheless, the tool has utility in organizations willing to commit to the models over the long term. With greater use and application, CERs can become self-fulfilling prophecies in terms of setting reasonable levels of contingency and then applying it consistently.

Summary

Many project managers do not understand the estimating relationship method well. Some survey respondents indicated that they had used this technique when they had really used parametric cost estimating methods for some or all project cost estimates. Such analysis is more accurately described as all or part of a life-cycle cost analysis. The use of parametric estimating methods defines the estimating relationship method to estimate risk or contingency reserve fund requirements. Currently, few parametric cost models are available with which to do this.

22
NETWORK ANALYSIS (EXCLUDING PERT)

A quality schedule—fundamentally a time-scaled and integrated structure of project objectives—is critical for effective project planning, implementation, and control. It includes activities and events that must be accomplished to achieve the desired objectives. Many project managers are familiar with the concept of network-based scheduling in project management. Network-based schedules formalize the project's internal functions and processes and generate graphics that depict the project's activities and their relationships (predecessors, successors, and parallel tasks). Network diagrams are valuable because they

Alert functional managers and team members to their dependency on other functions and teams

Establish project completion dates based on performance rather than arbitrary deadlines

Illustrate the scope of the project

Provide a sense of resource requirements over time, particularly when multiple resources will be deployed on multiple tasks simultaneously

Facilitate risk review scenarios

Highlight activities that drive the end date of the project

The following actions are essential to successful network development:

Engage team members and their management (as appropriate) who will perform the work

Determine the appropriate level of detail (aggregate, intermediate, or work package)

Identify relevant activities

Define relationships among the activities
Forecast activity duration

In many cases, project managers assume responsibility for planning, scheduling, and controlling projects that consist of numerous separate jobs or tasks that a variety of departments, project offices, and individuals perform. Often these projects are so complex or large that the project manager cannot possibly remember all the information pertaining to the plan, schedule, and progress of the project. In these situations, the Program Evaluation and Review Technique or PERT (see Chapter 23), critical path method (CPM), and precedence diagramming techniques have proved to be extremely valuable in helping project managers carry out their management responsibilities. The value of the tools is in their ability to depict relationships among activities and to provide a clear understanding of how the project will evolve as an integrated whole. Figure 22.1 represents an activity-on-arrow (either PERT or CPM) network. Figure 22.2 represents the same network as a precedence diagram.

The significant output of a network analysis is a clearly identified critical path, which consists of those activities that must be finished on time or the project will be delayed. Activities in the critical path compose the longest single path through the network. Their total duration represents the project duration. Most project management software highlights critical path activities so that they can be recognized for their importance. Although these tools help identify some potentially higher-risk activities, they also distinguish those activities with free time or slack. Thus, activities not on the critical path can afford some modest schedule slippage without affecting the overall project schedule.

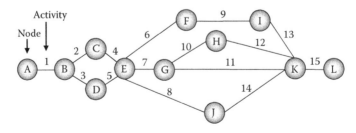

Figure 22.1   Project represented as an activity-on-arrow network.

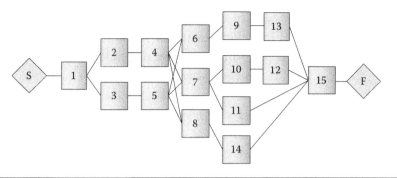

Figure 22.2   Project represented as a precedence diagram.

Technique Description

The original networking technique was based on the arrow diagramming method (ADM) or activity-on-arrow method of representing logical relationships between activities. ADM represents all predecessor and successor activities as finish-to-start relationships. Successor activities are not initiated until the predecessor is complete. However, because this form of relationship is not always true for predecessor-successor activities, other networking methodologies were developed to reflect more accurately the realities of those dependencies. Newer computer-based networking systems use the precedence diagramming method (PDM) or activity-on-node diagram to represent network logic. PDM allows greater flexibility than ADM in describing predecessor-successor relationships. With PDM, the following relationships can be described in addition to the finish-to-start relationship:

Finish-to-finish: Successor activity cannot finish until after the predecessor has been complete.

Start-to-start: Successor activity cannot start until after the predecessor has started.

Start-to-finish: Successor activity cannot be completed until the predecessor has started.

Most network-based risk models use PDM. The description that follows is based on PDM networks because they dominate as both scheduling and risk tools.

To reflect the realities of risk-related issues more accurately, network diagrams have been enhanced over the years. Logic has been added to increase the functionality of network analysis as a risk analysis tool. In probability-based networks, uncertainty manifests itself in two ways. First, there may be uncertainty related to cost, schedule, or technical performance. Generally, technical performance is considered a fixed parameter, whereas time and cost vary. Second, the start of some successors with a common predecessor may be based on the predecessor's success (that is, if the predecessor fails, then the successor may never begin). In some cases, the failure of a predecessor dictates an entirely different course of action. Some network models allow for iterative, probability-based cycles. It has become possible for the project manager to evaluate potential cost and time frames by ascribing percentage chances to the probability of achieving certain task outcomes. The project manager can then work through the model to determine the probability of achieving cost or schedule targets for the project as a whole.

A key issue in network development is selecting the appropriate level of detail. As with most project work, it is accepted practice to establish general process flows before working at the work package level. By their very nature, high-level networks embed significantly greater uncertainty. Detailed networks require a higher level of effort to generate but minimize the uncertainty associated with the relationships in the project. Realistically, as project requirements and information become more readily available, network models should evolve to greater levels of detail.

When Applicable

Networks are formulated based on project activities, interrelationships among activities, and constraints, such as time, money, human resources, technology, and so on. Because all projects have these characteristics, network analysis applies universally. Using the technique is easier if network-based project schedules already exist because analysts can then make logic modifications so that network data can be incorporated into risk analysis software programs as appropriate. If a network does not already exist, then one must be created to apply this technique. The time saved by transforming an existing network rather than creating one provides a strong argument for network-based project scheduling from the beginning of the project.

Inputs and Outputs

The inputs for the development of network models may be as simple as inputting activities, relationships, and duration. Some network models are far more complex, using inputs including probability density functions. (Appendix D discusses some techniques available for quantifying expert judgment.) Initially, inputs to the network model may be qualitative judgment that must be transformed into quantitative information. Thus, it is imperative that all individuals who fill a relevant project role provide inputs during the development process. Their contributions affect the credibility of the resulting network. Standard outputs from network models include task start and finish dates as well as overall project duration. Models that incorporate risk factors and risk data often count probability curves, bar charts, histograms, and cumulative density functions as components of their outputs. These are discussed in greater depth in Chapter 30, "Monte Carlo Simulations."

Even the most rudimentary of project scheduling tools provide valuable risk outputs. The clear definition of the early start and early finish of each activity, as well as its late start and late finish times, is frequently a risk indicator. Some activities that will have no free time (float) are low risk because the best and brightest individuals within the organization perform them. Other activities with nominal levels of float may pose far greater risks when less skilled personnel perform them. Networks highlight when an organization faces countless concurrent activities (and thus higher managerial risk). They clarify when a single activity has multiple successors (and thus higher dependency risks). They also elucidate when a single activity has multiple predecessors, thus creating a merge bias because of path convergence. (Merge bias is the concept that multiple paths merging together will create a higher likelihood of delays on the merge point if that merge point is studied using any simulation-based or probabilistic analysis.) In addition, networks highlight when multiple activities are being conducted serially, thereby generating greater risk on an entire string of work to be done. As a result, information derived from networks can be used to analyze and adjust labor, material, and time allocations.

Major Steps in Applying the Technique

The first step in this process is for the analyst to manually develop a rough-cut network. To develop a realistic model of the project, the analyst must identify all relevant parameters, such as activities, relationships, and probabilities associated with work or dependencies. As practicable, all relevant project personnel should participate in developing and validating the network.

Participants should work together to build network diagrams in an open setting by first identifying the work to be performed and then following up with an analysis of the relationships among the activities. This should be "penciled in" on an erasable board or flip chart before being committed to a computer tool.

After the rough-cut network has been developed, the analyst can enter the information into a computer for evaluation. Most project management software packages will conduct a rudimentary schedule analysis that provides the basic information needed for a high-level risk assessment. As more information becomes available, other computer modeling techniques, such as PERT and Monte Carlo simulations, can be applied.

Use of Results

The outputs of network analysis are extremely useful to the project manager. The study of networks for their inherent risk generally provides a far greater understanding of the sources and degree of risks. Results of the risk analysis process provide the information required to execute the risk response control phase of risk management effectively.

Resource Requirements

Because the project team builds most network analyses, costs should be estimated from a human resource perspective. A comprehensive network analysis for a major project may require definition of between 200 and 1,000 activities, plus weeks of preparation, information gathering, and expert interviews to establish risks inherent in individual activities and to construct the network. Obtaining the information to build the network generally entails more time and rechecking than initially might seem necessary. This is because the project plan usually undergoes continual revision and definition and the support team may not fully understand relationships among project activities.

Although the difficulty and time required for network definition can pose a problem, the effort of constructing a consistent and acceptable network model forces the responsible participants to plan effectively and to understand how their own segments of the project fit into the whole. Project managers have indicated that this benefit alone can justify all the effort in accomplishing a formal network risk assessment.

Reliability

The reliability of network risk analysis is a function of multiple factors. Developing a network that accurately reflects activities and relationships among activities is crucial to the resulting network analysis. Thus, it is imperative that all relevant project personnel provide inputs to developing and modifying the network. Defining relative levels of risk for the cost, schedule, and performance aspects of each task in the project can be done either here or later in a Monte Carlo analysis. The data are helpful here, even if they are not yet built into probability density functions (PDFs) because the more reliable the network is, then the more dependable the network analysis will be.

Selection Criteria

As with each chapter on techniques, network analysis is assessed using selection criteria relating to resource requirements, applications, and outputs for the technique. To compare network analysis with other techniques, review Table II.1.

Resource Requirements

The *cost* of network analysis depends largely on whether the networks are already developed for the project. If so or if only modest modifications are required, then extensive labor can be saved because only the risks inherent in the relationships must be examined.

The *proper facilities and equipment* requirement should include computers loaded with current project management software and ideally, large-form printers or plotters. Without the printers, some network analyses bog down as massive cut-and-paste operations with team members developing giant networks by taping together dozens of small sheets of paper. Some teams use erasable boards and "stickie" notes to develop the initial draft of the network diagram. The key is to capture the outputs from such analyses before the information is damaged or destroyed. A digital camera may be used to retain those data for later inputs into a computer model.

The *time needed to implement* the technique can be extensive depending upon the complexity of the network and the number of participants. A small network that three or four team members have developed may be completed in a couple of hours. In contrast, a multilayered network of 1,000 activities that 10 or more team leaders have coordinated may take days to develop.

Network analysis can be challenging and thus does not score well in terms of *ease of use* because the processes of building the networks, capturing expert judgment, and understanding the software are not inherently easy to master. Ease of use increases significantly with greater process familiarity.

Although the project manager's *time commitment* is slight to moderate, the project team must be educated on the process and the project manager must support changes to the networks over the long term. Networks that are changed frequently may increase the level of time required of the project manager.

Applications

As discussed earlier in this chapter, networks have a high degree of utility. Therefore, all applications listed are relevant.

Network analysis clearly supports *project status reporting* because, as the project progresses, changes in the duration of activities may drive changes in the project critical path.

Major planning decisions should include a review of the network diagrams and network risks. Even modest changes in the network can have significant implications, so all major planning decisions should be reviewed in the context of a thorough network analysis.

Network analysis supports *contract strategy selection* because the flexibility of the schedule may make certain types of clauses (especially liquidated damages) either more or less acceptable.

Because milestones often become focal points in a network, network analysis becomes a critical input to *milestone preparation*.

For *design guidance*, network analysis serves a role in clarifying schedule risks and the overall implications of switching from one design to another.

Scheduling considerations may in part drive *source selection*. Thus, network analysis is important here as well.

Budget submittal is probably the least applicable category for network analysis, although resource loading often drives budgets. If the resources are assigned across a longer period of time, then budgets will inherently be higher. Thus, there is a modest relationship between budget submittals and network analyses.

Outputs

With respect to outputs, the accuracy of the analysis is a function of the validity of the network itself and the levels of effort generated for each activity.

The *accuracy* of the analysis is a direct function of the validity of the network itself and the level of effort generated for each activity. If there is a significant (perhaps disproportionate) level of effort in a single activity, then the accuracy of the network can be diminished. If, however, the work packages are developed in a relatively uniform fashion (similar sizes, similar costs, similar durations), then there is a higher probability of accuracy.

In many cases, management or the project manager determines the *level of detail*, which can be low, medium, or high. Because different project managers use network analysis to achieve different perspectives, the level of detail is a function of how much detail is desired.

The *utility* of the networks generally is high if only because managers are forced to fuse detail into their plans before project implementation.

Summary

Network analyses are critical to risk management, given their role in ensuring that schedule objectives are met. These analyses focus attention on the relationships of activities and the interrelationships of risk among those activities. Although network analysis models sometimes fail to give cost risk its due, they are invaluable early in the project when schedule risk is at its greatest. As with most tools, these are not the only tools required to evaluate or mitigate risk comprehensively. However, when used in conjunction with other tools and techniques, network analyses are invaluable to the risk manager.

23
PERT

The Program Evaluation and Review Technique (PERT) is considered a project management classic. Besides being one of the original scheduling techniques,* PERT was the first significant project-oriented risk analysis tool. PERT's objectives included managing schedule risk by establishing the shortest development schedule, monitoring project progress, and funding or applying necessary resources to maintain the schedule. Despite its age (relative to other project risk techniques), PERT has worn well the test of time.

Technique Description

PERT is based on a set of mathematical equations known as Runge–Kutta. Best- and worst-case scenarios are established and weighted against the most likely set of occurrences. Task PERT mean and standard deviations and the project PERT duration and standard deviations are established, which allow the project manager to evaluate the likelihood of achieving specific schedule targets based on the network and PERT durations.

When Applicable

PERT is particularly applicable when historical schedule data are limited. In many projects, information is insufficient to ascertain precisely how long a given task might take; or sometimes team members are reticent about sharing planned duration for activities they have never performed. By allowing or encouraging each team member to provide a best-case duration, a worst-case duration, and a most probable duration for each activity, team members have the opportunity

---

* PERT was originally developed during the Polaris submarine program in the late 1950s.

to share information they might not otherwise have considered (in a single data-point estimate). Consequently, PERT is normally applied early in a project when uncertainty is high.

Inputs and Outputs

Inputs for PERT include the multiple duration data points for each activity and the basic network of activities (see Chapter 22). Gathering this information may require a significant level of effort, but it is normally tracked with the work packages in the project management software. Most project management software packages incorporate PERT fields in their databases.

Outputs from PERT are mean durations for the project's critical path, as well as normal distribution curves to establish the likelihood of meeting various schedule targets. These outputs are normally more pessimistic than the duration derived from critical path method (CPM) analysis because they take into account best and worst cases (and worst-case scenarios tend to diverge further from the most likely duration than do best-case scenarios). Thus, PERT duration reflects more risks inherent in the network and the project as a whole.

Major Steps in Applying the Technique

PERT is applied in two general phases, first at the task level and again at the project level.

At the task level, there are three steps that must be conducted for each task:

Gather the task duration information. As mentioned earlier, this will consist of establishing best-case, worst-case, and most likely durations for each task in the network. This information is normally extracted from individual team members performing the task.

Calculate the PERT mean and standard deviation for each task. This is frequently done by using computer tools, although it can be calculated manually. For the PERT mean, the following formula is applied:

$$\frac{(Optimistic + (4 \times Most\ Likely) + Pessimistic)}{6}$$

To establish the PERT standard deviation, some of the same information is used:

$$\frac{Pessimistic - Optimistic}{6}$$

Catalog the information. Storing the information for easy retrieval is important because PERT data at the task level have limited utility. That may be helpful for establishing the basic duration of a task, but to apply the robust nature of the PERT process, the entire network must be considered.

At the project level, there are three steps that must be conducted after PERT information is available for each task:

Establish the PERT critical path. The project manager must calculate the critical path based on PERT durations rather than the conventional, most probable durations. Because PERT durations frequently differ from their most likely counterparts, there is the distinct possibility that the PERT critical path will represent a different set of activities than the conventional critical path. The duration of this path therefore becomes the PERT mean for the project.

Establish the standard deviation for the PERT critical path. This tends to be one of the most confusing steps in the process because it involves calculating the square root of the sum of the squares of the task-developed standard deviations. The process (again, frequently performed by computers rather than people) is not as onerous as it may sound. First, square each of the individual task standard deviations. Then add those squares together. Finally, calculate the square root of their sum. The formula looks like this:

$$\sqrt{SD_1^2 + SD_2^2 + SD_3^2 + SD_4^2 + SD_5^2 + \ldots}$$

That number provides the standard deviation for the PERT duration of the project as a whole. It is noteworthy that this number is significantly smaller than the sum of the standard deviations for the project's PERT estimates. That is because it factors in the reality that not all activities will occur in their worst case on the same project. It also acknowledges that, although some activities may be delayed, that will probably not be the case for the entire network.

Plot the PERT mean and standard deviation into a distribution. There are two fundamental approaches to assessing the distribution of activities under a PERT mean. The first is the classic approach to normal distributions with a curve like the one in Figure 23.1.

In this scenario, the assumption is that there is a 68.26 percent chance that the duration of the project will occur within one standard deviation of the PERT mean. There is a 95.4 percent chance the duration will be within two standard deviations. Moreover, there is a 99.7 percent chance that the

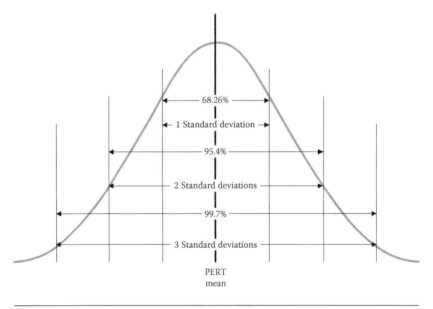

Figure 23.1 Normal distribution.

duration will be within three standard deviations. Normal distribution is discussed in greater depth in Appendix C, "Basic Probability Concepts."

Another assumption set may be applied that actually works more in the project manager's favor. In many organizations, any performance to the left of the mean is wholly acceptable. In other words, there is no such thing as too early. Thus, all the points to the left of the mean (which account for 50 percent of the outcomes) are acceptable. In a single standard deviation assessment (68.26 percent), roughly half of the values (34 percent) are to the left of the mean and half are to the right. However, if *everything* left of the mean is acceptable, then the single standard deviation assessment encompasses 84 percent of the total population (50 percent, on the left, added to 34 percent, on the right), rather than 68 percent. The difference is substantial. In a diagram similar to the one above, the difference would be as displayed in Figure 23.2.

The second approach has a far more positive perspective on the project, as it does not penalize for early performance. The final outputs are

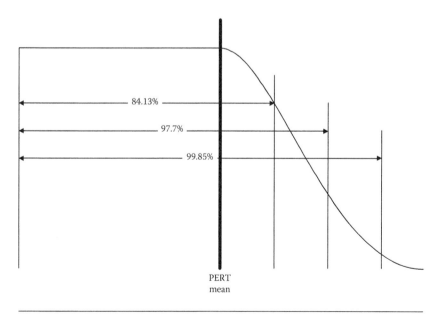

Figure 23.2 Normal distribution accounting only for late outcomes.

normal distributions of the potential project duration, which afford the project manager the ability to objectively predict or declare confidence with a given duration.

Use of Results

PERT outputs are normally used in discussions on the potential for achieving project schedule targets. By expressing a clear level of confidence, the project manager can indicate the potential for achieving any given project schedule target for the mean or higher. Using the assumptions associated with Figure 23.2, the PERT mean represents 50 percent confidence. That indicates that half the time this project is conducted that duration or less will be achieved. That is an important distinction. Many project managers believe the PERT mean duration to be a reasonable and realistic target to hit, when in fact it will be achieved only half the time. In most organizational cultures, 50 percent schedule confidence is not deemed acceptable. If the project manager includes one standard deviation later than the mean, however, then the duration identified will be achieved 84 percent of the time. This 84 percent confidence is frequently considered sufficient to establish accurate estimates.

Resource Requirements

Someone skilled in drawing out multiple duration data points is the best candidate to conduct the PERT process. That, in itself, is the most daunting single resource requirement for the practice. In addition, computer tools should support the process. Most current project management software packages will support PERT analysis and will facilitate both data entry and calculation.

Reliability

As projects have more work packages, PERT becomes more reliable. A project of 10 or 15 work packages will still have high levels of schedule variability even if PERT is applied. However, if a project has more work packages, including many occurring concurrently, then PERT will balance out some of the natural incongruities and inaccuracies. PERT is also *perceived* as being more reliable when standard deviations are calculated and then applied as schedule targets. A project manager is far more likely to achieve schedule duration of one or two standard deviations from the mean than he or she is to realize a PERT mean as the project duration.

Selection Criteria

As with each chapter on techniques, PERT is assessed using selection criteria relating to resource requirements, applications, and outputs for the technique. To compare PERT with other techniques, review Table II.1 in Part II.

Resource Requirements

The *cost* of PERT is relatively low, as most information-gathering processes that are associated with PERT will be conducted in one form or another with or without the tool. Because duration must be determined for each activity, it is not excessively time-consuming to gather additional data for optimistic and pessimistic duration. However, because PERT calculations are normally embedded in project management software, investment in additional software is normally unnecessary.

Proper facilities and equipment for PERT consist of a computer loaded with PERT-supporting project management software.

The *time needed to implement* PERT is associated more with data gathering than with actual PERT calculations. Interviewing task leaders and team members to establish optimistic, pessimistic, and most likely durations is the single most time-consuming effort and varies with the number of tasks associated with the project.

PERT's *ease of use* is high if the project management software package being applied has built-in PERT capability. Because data fields for data entry and built-in calculators to perform the mean and standard deviation calculations already exist, most of the time and effort in actual calculation of PERT is in validating the outputs.

The project manager's *time commitment* ties directly to his or her role in gathering PERT data. Because that is the single most time-consuming effort associated with this technique, the project manager's role in that process is crucial in terms of establishing how much time is truly required.

Applications

Because many organizations live and die by their project schedules, accurate scheduling is a core competency that cannot be ignored. PERT affords more realistic schedules by taking more factors into account in establishing the duration for each project activity.

- PERT supports *project status reporting* because it can provide a sense of likelihood of achieving schedule targets. Because many status reports include requests for information on the probability of schedule success and estimated time to complete, PERT has a high level of utility here.
- PERT also supports *major planning decisions* for many of the same reasons. Planning decisions and approaches are frequently resolved by opting for the approach that best meets customer requirements and schedule deadlines. Because PERT affords clarity on the probability of meeting deadlines, it can plan a major role in planning decisions.
- PERT does not strongly support *contract strategy selection*. Even though scheduling considerations may play a role in contract options, the relationship here is weak. The only exception would be in determining the organization's exposure to late penalties or liquidated damage payments.
- PERT can be key in *milestone preparation* because milestones are a function of the schedule (and vice versa). PERT is easily applied to determine the likelihood of achieving certain milestones or to determine milestone realism.
- *Design guidance* is not normally a function of PERT. Although PERT supports the schedule, it does not facilitate understanding of given designs. In terms of the three sides of the triple constraint, PERT is somewhat one-sided with an emphasis on schedule.

PERT does not support *source selection* unless external vendors will play a key role in determining the organization's success at achieving schedule targets. The only relationship between PERT and source selection stems from potential schedule inputs that vendors might have to support the process.

Budget submittal is a cost issue; PERT is a scheduling tool. Although schedule and cost are inextricably wed, the link is not so great as to make PERT a viable support tool here.

Outputs

The *accuracy* of PERT is high. Compared to conventional precedence diagramming or CPM analysis, PERT's accuracy is much higher because multiple data points are established for each of the project's activities. This additional consideration for each activity affects the level of accuracy by increasing both the time invested in considering project duration and by ensuring that the full range of potential task outcomes has been considered.

PERT's *level of detail* is relatively low because it focuses on one issue and one issue alone: duration. It does not provide specificity on types of risks, risk issues, categories, or symptoms. Rather, it affords only information on the schedule and potential schedule outcomes.

The overall *utility* of PERT is high in that it provides the means to establish a fair, reasonable schedule with risk factored in and with a nominal level of additional effort.

Summary

PERT has been available to project managers for decades but still enjoys only limited use because of what has been perceived as the onerous level of effort associated with data gathering and calculation. Due to its incorporation into most project management software practices, coupled with executive management calling for ever increasing schedule accuracy, PERT currently is becoming more popular and better understood.

24
OTHER DIAGRAMMING TECHNIQUES

In addition to PERT and network diagrams, there are a variety of other diagramming techniques that have broad application in a project risk environment. Flowcharts and probabilistic analysis tools, such as GERT (Graphical Evaluation and Review Technique) and VERT (Venture Evaluation and Review Technique), open the doors to other opportunities for risk examination and understanding. Similarly, force field charts and Ishikawa's cause-and-effect diagrams also have risk applications.

Technique Description

All diagramming techniques have one element in common. They provide visual cues for risk issues that might go unnoticed or unattended in a text-based or mathematically derived tool—that is, information that could be lost.

Flowcharts and GERT and VERT tools provide project analyses that depict project processes as flows, cycles, inputs, and outputs. Whereas flowcharts function without calculation, GERT and VERT analyses incorporate probabilities of occurrence for particular paths and may also incorporate the potential costs for each of these cycles.

Ishikawa's cause-and-effect (or fishbone) diagrams depict the general concern associated with a negative outcome and allow for exploration of that consideration in the context of its numerous causes (and, in turn, the causes' causes). Such diagrams serve as idea-generation tools and are particularly supportive in establishing multiple risk sources and root causes.

In contrast, force field charts are single-issue risk diagrams that highlight or illustrate potential pressures on a project or on a project issue.

Although these diagramming techniques vary widely in design, application, and use, they share the commonality of a visual display of risk information.

When Applicable

As visual tools, these techniques are most applicable when displayed well and when their display successfully provides the organization more risk information or team awareness and project understanding. They should not be perceived as tools for rigorous individual analysis but, instead, as opportunities to share information and gather the interpretations of others on a given set of data.

Inputs and Outputs

Flowcharts, GERT, and VERT. For these three tools, the key input is process. They all depict the project process in minute detail, including any potential reverse loops that might be required to work through the project as a whole. Inputs normally include a list of all process steps, together with an analysis of the relationships among those steps. Decision points, acknowledging when and where the project process may take different directions, are crucial as well. When using GERT and VERT, the only key supplemental inputs would be probabilities associated with each major junction in the workflow. GERT and VERT take into account the likelihood of repeated loops through the process and account for them in their analyses. These probabilistic flowcharts provide a sense of how the iterative cycles may have an impact on time and cost.

Outputs for these tools are detailed process diagrams for the project, which provide greater clarity on the potential process flows the project may follow. VERT also provides extensive data based on simulations of the project.

Fishbone diagrams. With fishbone diagrams, the key input is the effect that will undergo scrutiny. Then, as the analysis is conducted, the inputs become the causes of that effect, and their causes and their causes. The effort continues until all root causes (including some that critics might deem minutiae) are developed.

Outputs are lists of causes linked to the resulting effects that they cause. If there are repeating causal themes within the fishbone diagram, it may indicate a potential root cause of the risks in the effort.

Force field charts. In a force field chart, single-influence issues are balanced pro and con against the project as a whole. The inputs are the key issues that may have, one at a time, either a positive or detrimental effect on the project as a whole.

Outputs from this process are diagrams that allow for at-a-glance analysis of the positive and negative pressures that may affect this project.

Major Steps in Applying These Techniques

Flowcharts

Determine the process relationships. The first and most daunting step in any flowcharting process is to determine and map out the process relationships. This can be done either by using a computerized tool or by using traditional facilitation techniques on an erasable board or flip chart. The key is to identify all steps in the project process and then to ascertain how they interrelate. Unlike precedence diagramming where all processes flow forward, flowcharts allow for iterative flows and cyclical processes, which, in some instances, may more accurately reflect the project environment.

Review the relationships for risk. Any time a process step is completed and another begins, there is a modest amount of risk. In some processes, however, the risk is significantly greater than others. All risks identified should be documented and preserved for qualification and quantification, as well as the remaining steps in the risk management process. Because there are iterative cycles in flowcharts, some processes should be examined for their probability of recurrence. When using specialized flowchart-compatible tools like GERT and VERT, these probabilities are important and significant inputs. They represent the true risk associated with the process and the cycles thereof. If those tools are to be applied, then it will be important to establish cost targets and probabilities for each of the iterations.

Ishikawa (Fishbone) Diagrams

> *Establish the premise for analysis.* In Ishikawa diagrams, it is important to focus on a single issue to be addressed as the net effect of all causes in the cause-and-effect diagram. The broader the premise, the more likely there will be countless fishbones supporting it. Conversely, a narrower premise will yield a more directed analysis of the causes.
>
> *Build the basic diagram structure.* The basic structure is consistent in most cause-and-effect analyses, similar to the one in Figure 24.1.

The basic structure includes causes related to personnel, equipment, methods, and materials. Although organizations may have broadly different risk issues and concerns, these remain the four classic elements of the structure.

> *Identify the causes and their causes.* The key in this diagram is to identify root causes for significant concerns. As new causes are identified, the question should be asked, "What caused that cause?" This inquiry continues until all causes associated with the effect have been exhausted. As discussed earlier in "Root Cause Identification and Analysis" (Chapter 16), it may be important to ask the question "Why are we having this effect?" at least five times for each major causal area to truly uncover all the causes of the causes.

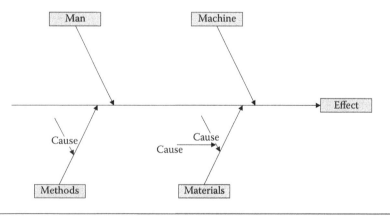

Figure 24.1   Ishikawa (fishbone) diagram.

Force Field Diagrams

Establish the desired condition. The key to successful force field diagramming is a clear definition of the desired condition for the project or issue at hand. The fundamental premise is that anything that will draw the organization closer to its ideal is good. On the other hand, anything that distracts from achieving that goal is bad. Thus, clearly establishing the desired (ideal) state to be examined is important because all analysis will be conducted in that context.

Identify positive influences. Project team members should conduct an environmental scan (that is, an analysis of the world around them) to determine what external forces could expedite arriving at the desired state, make the journey less expensive, or otherwise positively influence their ability to achieve or maintain the desired state. Every force—no matter how seemingly inconsequential—should be incorporated in the analysis.

Identify negative influences. Similarly, the situation must be reviewed to ascertain the external forces that could have a negative impact on our ability to achieve the desired state. Those forces that would slow the journey to that state or that would make it either more expensive or challenging to achieve should be documented.

Map the insights on a force field chart. Outcomes of the discussions on positive and negative influences are ultimately documented on a force field chart. Positive influences are arrayed on top of the desired state and the negative influences are documented in Figure 24.2.

Use of Results

The results of these three diagramming techniques can vary widely yet follow a common theme. Data are used for alternative interpretations of risk information. However, all three techniques may point to the same issues. A risk identified along a process line in the flowchart may also be in evidence as a cause toward the negative effects in question on the Ishikawa diagram. That same risk may also be seen as a

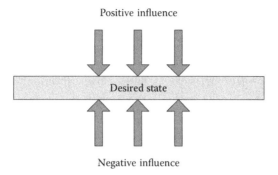

Positive influence

Desired state

Negative influence

Figure 24.2 Force field analysis.

negative influence on the bottom half of the force field chart. Because people may interpret information in different ways, the solution is to ensure that everyone has the opportunity to review the information in a fashion in which he or she can put it to use.

Still, with all diagramming techniques, one key use is to post the diagrams for better project risk communication. This will serve both as a reminder and for future analysis of the information embedded therein.

Resource Requirements

Even though there are specific computer tools that will develop these diagrams, any good graphics application software package is normally sufficient to present the information effectively. In terms of resource effort, the requirements for flowcharts, GERT, and VERT will be significantly higher than those for the other applications presented here. Flowcharts require far more research and in-depth analysis because they must accurately depict the processes that myriad team members perform over an extended period of time. The resource requirements for force field analysis and cause-and-effect diagrams are extremely limited.

Reliability

Of all the diagramming techniques discussed here, flowcharts have the highest level of detail and, therefore, generally have the highest perceived level of reliability. The issue, however, is that once again outputs of the process must be measured against who develops inputs. The more qualified the individuals conducting the process flow reviews are, then the more reliable the flowchart will be.

Although the other two diagramming techniques are broader in scope, they are not inherently less reliable. Rather, they are inherently less detailed.

Selection Criteria

As with each chapter on techniques, the diagramming techniques in this chapter are assessed using selection criteria relating to resource requirements, applications, and outputs for the technique. To compare these diagramming techniques with other techniques, review Table II.1.

Resource Requirements

What resources a technique requires is often the dominant consideration in the selection process. Diagramming techniques require someone literate in the techniques themselves, as well as someone well versed in using the computer applications to capture and document the outputs.

> *Cost* for diagramming techniques depends upon the technique applied. Fishbone diagrams and force field analyses are relatively inexpensive, broad tools. They usually do not take long to develop (1 or 2 days) unless there are extraordinary project needs or an unusual level of depth is pursued. However, flowcharting a process and documenting sundry costs, issues, and risks associated with the iterations in the project can be a time-consuming endeavor. Whereas applying some of the more advanced approaches (such as GERT) should not span more than a few weeks, the analysis alone may take as much as a week to complete.
>
> *Proper facilities and equipment* for diagramming techniques include sufficient wall space or art space to allow them to grow to their natural size. Some flowcharts in development

may require as much as 20 feet (approximately 6 meters) of open wall space. Although the information ultimately must be captured in a computer tool, the original diagram development is normally done in an open, facilitated setting, thereby requiring adequate space to allow the charts to develop. Some advanced diagramming processes like GERT and VERT will require either custom software or software specific to the task, which most organizations do not possess.

The *time needed to implement* the diagrams, as stated under "Cost," normally is nominal. If resources and facilities are available, then the time should not be extensive.

Ease of use is one of the most attractive elements of the diagramming techniques as they do not require any formal or extensive training to apply (unless using advanced techniques). Even though a flowchart may require a good facilitator, once the ground rules for processing information have been established, most participants will not be concerned about any challenges associated with applying the tool. Moreover, although flowcharting and VERT and GERT are the most complex of the diagramming processes discussed here, the most challenging aspect is gathering the baseline data for tool inputs.

The project manager's *time commitment* is sometimes based on the skill levels of the project manager. However, if the project manager is familiar with facilitating process discussions and knows how to ensure the best possible outcome in a reasonable period of time, then the effort may go very quickly. Project managers who are not effective in marshaling insights from a variety of resources may find themselves taking more time than anticipated in developing both tool inputs and outputs.

Applications

The advantage to diagramming techniques is that, once built, their outputs are very easily interpreted. No training is required. Interpretation becomes a function of the individual's level of expertise and understanding of the organization and project together with their processes.

Diagramming techniques generally do not support *project status reporting*. Although status reports normally reflect schedules (and, to a lesser degree, processes), the diagramming techniques described here are not designed to address these concerns in a reporting format.

Major planning decisions may rely in some measure on how these techniques are deployed. Whereas the diagrams do not drive major planning decisions, they do present information that can be perceived as valuable in such settings. The connection here is moderate.

Contract strategy selection is not normally a function of diagrams or their outputs.

Although some of the other diagramming techniques from other chapters may support *milestone preparation*, the connection here is extremely indirect. As such, diagrams play only a minor supporting role in developing milestones.

Flowcharts can strongly support *design guidance*. Because many service projects (or even product-oriented projects) require a service element and extensive customer interface, some of these diagramming techniques can be invaluable in establishing how the relationships should ultimately be designed and defined.

Source selection is not a prime application for these diagramming techniques. Inasmuch as the techniques can illustrate the concerns associated with particular vendors or highlight the vendors' role in the overall process, the connection is largely tangential.

Even though these diagrams may indirectly support *budget submittal*, the relationship is extremely indirect. Although project managers may use the diagrams to defend a particular budget position, they provide no true budgetary information.

The diagrams described herein serve other applications as well. They provide insight on potential approaches to projects. They focus attention on particular issues and causes. They encourage open discussion on environmental pressures. And most importantly, they provide visual cues on how to interpret what is frequently vague information.

Outputs

Outputs of the diagramming techniques are in the form of their respective diagrams, which are normally used for display purposes to highlight and illustrate issues and concerns.

> The *accuracy* of diagramming techniques relies on their inputs, but the accuracy is generally perceived as high. Because the diagrams depict processes, causes, or environmental conditions, a high probability of significant error does not exist, unless those processes, causes, and conditions are broadly misunderstood.
>
> The *level of detail* associated with diagrams can be extremely high because process diagrams (like GERT and flowcharts) generally dissect processes to a very fine level of granularity. Although some organizations may apply top-down flowcharts or keep their analyses at a high level, flowcharting is respected as a tool that leads to a rather exhaustive level of detail.
>
> *Utility* of diagrams is dependent on the particular diagram and the audience. If the audience can take advantage of the information being presented, then the utility is high. If, on the other hand, the diagrams are generated only for their own sake and have no specific or intended audience, then their utility may be reduced. For the most part, however, the outputs have a relatively high level of utility.

Summary

Diagramming techniques are valuable tools for sharing information in a group setting that otherwise may be somewhat challenging to share. Process flows, environmental forces, and cause-and-effect linkages can be difficult to explain and even more difficult to document without clean, clear diagrams. Diagrams also afford opportunities to build the project team by encouraging open discussion of issues and concerns in a group setting.

25
RATING SCHEMES

Every risk event has both probability and impact. In most organizations, those values are established qualitatively rather than quantitatively. That creates problems because perceptions frequently differ as to what constitutes a "high" probability or a "moderate" impact. Driving those differences in perception is, in part, the lack of organizational standards or schemes to determine those values.

Technique Description

Rating schemes are standardized and are applied on either a project-wide or (ideally) an organization-wide basis to clarify the relative magnitude in terms of impact and probability for a given risk. They define terms like "high," "medium," and "low" for those risk considerations. Clear definitions and the means to test individual risks for their compliance with those definitions support the terms.

When Applicable

Rating schemes are applicable any time a qualitative analysis will be conducted. Because qualitative analysis prompts a review of the probability and impact of risk, schemes should be applied any time the risks are undergoing qualitative review. The schemes are applicable only after they have been developed and after there is general concurrence among team members or the project organization that they are truly applicable in the environment in question.

Inputs and Outputs

Inputs to *develop* rating schemes will be evaluations from the organization's most veteran project managers on the relative values for both probability and impact. However, inputs to *apply* rating schemes will be the actual schemes themselves, along with support and evaluation of the team members' project risks in question.

Outputs from *developing* rating schemes will be clear definitions of terms and values for high, medium, low, and extreme probabilities, as well as unambiguous definitions of impact values for such issues as cost, schedule, performance, and other areas of importance within the organization. Outputs from *applying* rating schemes will be probability and impact assignments for each project risk.

Major Steps in Applying the Technique

Unlike other risk management techniques, there are actually two major areas of focus here. The first is in developing the schemes; the second is in applying them.

Scheme Development

Identify basic probability values. Using a numeric scale and/or value statements, a core group of project office, senior management, or project team members should establish the basic probability values to be applied across the project (or ideally, across all projects). These values should be designed to minimize confusion or misinterpretation of probability assignments, which risk impact often inappropriately sways. The values should be set to reflect the organization's tolerance for frequency of risk occurrence. Thus, organizations with a high tolerance for risk in general (such as research and development operations) may classify the *low* value using phrases like "won't normally happen," or they may set it numerically at 30 to 40 percent. On the contrary, organizations with a low tolerance for risk (such as medical product developers) may categorize their *high* value using phrases like "could reasonably happen," or they may set it numerically at 15 to 20 percent. Difference in organizational concerns will influence what constitutes a low, a medium, or a high probability.

Publish probability values. Probability values should be documented and distributed to all team members so that they are aware of perceptions on the potential frequency of occurrence and the organizational culture for probability. Such publication may simply be a memorandum including guidance on probability application. The guidance need not be minutely detailed; but it should provide a sense of the application of terms and the interpretation of frequency versus probability within the organization or on the project team, as is depicted in Figure 25.1.

Note that the probability values are assigned as fixed numbers rather than ranges. This affords the project team consistency if other practices (such as expected monetary value) are applied using the probability values. Although probabilities cannot be predicted with accuracy (and probably are more accurately reflected in a range), establishing a single data point to represent high, medium, and low probability opens the door to more consistent interpretation of risk and risk values.

EXAMPLE

To: *Project Team*

From: *Project Manager*

Re: *Probability Guidance*

In all project reviews and risk analyses, please use the following standard to establish values for probability of occurrence and for communicating probability:

- *High (80 percent)*—This risk has occurred in past projects, and the current project has environmental conditions that make it likely to recur.
- *Medium (50 percent)*—Even though this risk may not have occurred in the past, environmental conditions make it a very real possibility. Or: This risk has occurred in the past, and although environmental conditions are different, it is still a very real possibility.
- *Low (10 percent)*—This risk may not have occurred in the past, but it cannot be dismissed, even though environmental conditions make it somewhat less likely. It remains a distinct possibility.
- *Extreme (<1 percent)*—This risk will likely *not* come to pass, but its occurrence is not completely outside the realm of possibility.

Please apply these values in all discussions of probability in project correspondence.

Figure 25.1 Sample probability guidance.

Identify impact areas. There should be basic areas of concern when it comes to risk impact. Although they will not cover the breadth of possible project risk, they should encompass as many different areas as possible. The classic, basic areas are schedule, cost, and performance (or requirements). Other impact areas may include organizational politics, public relations, shareholder value, team member retention, and so on. The most significant impact areas will be those that the organization prizes most highly on its projects and those that cover the greatest range of organizational concerns.

Establish impact values. This is frequently done on a project basis, as well as organizationally. The effort establishes what constitutes low, medium, and high impact within each impact area identified in the previous step. This process tends to be somewhat more complex than establishing probability values because impact values can vary widely from project to project, as well as from organization to organization. As such, careful consideration must be made to ensure that either the impact values are set to apply to all projects or guidance is provided to support project managers as they modify them for project application.

Impact values may be established by setting the high value as the point when the full time and attention of the project team (or senior management or a task force) would be mobilized to deal with the impact of the risk. High values often represent an organization's "threshold of pain." Low values can be defined as those times when the risk is still of some note (if only for documentation or historic purposes) but will not impede project completion or the organization's stated objectives. Medium impact risks are those that fall between those two points. Different impact statements will be established to clarify the range of impacts for cost, schedule, quality, and other risk areas.

Publish impact values. Impact values should be documented and distributed to all team members so that they are aware of the perceptions regarding the potential magnitude of risk impact. Such a document may simply be a memorandum including guidance on impact value application. The guidance need not be excessive in its detail, but it should provide a sense of the application of terms and the interpretation of risk impact, as in Figure 25.2.

EXAMPLE

To: *Project Team*
From: *Project Manager*
Re: *Impact Guidance*

In all project reviews and risk analyses, please use the following standards to establish values for the potential impact of risks if they come to pass and for communicating risk impact:

Cost
  * *High*—More than 25 percent of remaining contingency budget
  * *Medium*—5 percent to 25 percent of remaining contingency budget
  * *Low*—Less than 5 percent of remaining contingency budget

Schedule
  * *High*—Would delay one or more tasks on the critical path
  * *Medium*—Would delay tasks within their available total float
  * *Low*—Would delay tasks within their available free float

Requirements
  * *High*—Would cause deviation from the requirement or specification, which the customer and end user would clearly discern
  * *Medium*—Would cause deviation from the requirement or specification, which would not be visible to the customer or end user but would still constitute a clear deviation from specifications/requirements
  * *Low*—Would modify the existing approach to requirements but would not constitute deviation from specifications/requirements

Politics
  * *High*—Would prompt issue escalation to senior management
  * *Medium*—Would prompt issue escalation to functional manager
  * *Low*—Would prompt issue escalation to project manager

Please apply these values in all discussions of impact in project correspondence.

Figure 25.2 Sample impact guidance.

The impact values above are samples only and should not be construed as true and actual. Each organization (or in some cases, project) will have a clear set of risk impact values, which should reflect their culture and project management approach.

When publishing impact values, stress the importance of consistent application. It is also important to emphasize that a risk should be considered "high impact" whenever any of the impact values are high.

A risk with a high requirements impact but a low impact value for all the other scales would still be considered a high-impact risk.

In some organizations, a third dimension— frequency— has been added to these schemes. Frequency differs from probability and impact in that some risks may have a significant probability but a low impact and still occur with sufficient frequency that they can become a major project nuisance. Similarly, some high-impact risks with a high probability may be completely survivable if they happen just one time. More than one occurrence, however, could spell disaster to the project.

As with the other approaches, rating risk impacts is a process of establishing terms and ensuring open communication about them.

> *Identify frequency values.* This can be done on an organizational basis in terms of establishing continuity for terminology like "highly repetitive," "intermittent," and/or "one-time." Frequency values should be accompanied by some clarification on how they will be applied (most often as a clarifying factor for probability and/or impact).
>
> Frequency values may be established by providing examples of events or impacts that represent the terms and then obtaining concurrence that whatever occurs with that frequency shall be judged according to those terms.
>
> *Publish frequency values.* Frequency values should be documented and distributed to all team members so that they are aware of perceptions about the recurrence of risks and how (or if) that level of recurrence was used to establish probability and impact.
>
> The guidance need not be excessive in its detail, but it should provide a sense of the application of the terms and the interpretation of the risk impact, as in Figure 25.3.

Scheme Application

> *Review identified risks for probability.* For each risk identified, the expected likelihood of risk occurrence is based on the metrics developed for probability under the rating scheme. Catalog or mark the risk as high, medium, or low probability. Ideally, multiple team members should participate in the ranking

EXAMPLE

To: *Project Team*
From: *Project Manager*
Re: *Frequency Guidance*

In all project reviews and risk analyses, please use the following standards, as appropriate, to establish values for the risk frequency that was applied in considering the probability and impact for the risk event:

Frequency
- *High*—Assumes repeated occurrences (with no maximum) at regular intervals throughout the project
- *Medium*—Assumes repeated occurrences (with a maximum of four or five occurrences) at intermittent intervals throughout the project
- *Low*—Assumes a one-time occurrence on the project

Please note that these rates of frequency will not aect probability and impact guidance but rather should work the other way around. For example, a risk with low frequency but high probability and high impact indicates a risk of sufficient magnitude that a single occurrence would be drastic and dramatic.

Figure 25.3 Sample frequency guidance.

process to ensure that a single individual's personal experiences do not bias the value. Remember, for each risk that the question is the same: "What is the likelihood that the risk event will come to pass?"

Review risks for impact. For each risk event, the team members should now use the rating scheme to establish a high, medium, or low impact. Because impact values will exist for multiple areas (such as cost, schedule, frustration level), it is important that those risks marked as low impact in one area are reviewed for their potential impact in other areas. The highest value becomes the risk event's impact value. A risk that has a low cost and schedule impact but a high impact in terms of organizational politics is a high-impact risk.

(Optional) Review probabilities and impacts applied for frequency. How many occurrences were assumed when making the

evaluations? If frequency will dramatically affect any of the risk events, then it may be productive to break down the one risk into two or more risks. For example, although one risk with a moderate probability may have a low impact at low frequency, it may have a remote probability of occurrence and produce extreme impact at high frequency.

Use of Results

Risk rating schemes can be used in various ways to support qualitative analysis. They provide support for organizations attempting to establish a common risk language for probability and impact. They afford team members the ability to share information consistently on a given project and to conduct comparative risk analyses among multiple projects by virtue of their consistency.

They also provide support in terms of how the risk can be quantitatively evaluated for both expected value and risk models. Because ratings schemes may establish congruous probability or impact values, they can facilitate consistent prioritization of risk, as well as concordant assessment of risk prior to response strategy development.

The values that risk rating schemes establish are used in lieu of quantitative values when quantitative analysis is either unavailable or excessively expensive to apply.

Resource Requirements

Resource requirements essential for developing a rating scheme are much more significant than those needed to apply it. Rating scheme development generally requires the participation of senior-level project management (or organizational management). This may take the form of representation from the project office or the participation of program managers with extensive organizational experience. Management participation is integral if the rating scheme is to be applied and accepted universally.

To apply a rating scheme, however, the resource requirements are minimal. After the scheme is in place, its application on a project-by-project basis becomes an issue of basic project cognizance. Anyone with a clear understanding of the project's nature and environment can apply a well-crafted scheme.

Reliability

Reliability is a function of use. Over time, rating schemes are adjusted to accommodate changing environments and changing needs. As a rating scheme is tested and proved, it becomes progressively more reliable. Moreover, because rating schemes ultimately reflect the organization's posture on risk impact and probability, absolute values are not nearly as important as the organization's ability to assess the relative risks of one project over another. Over time, reliability becomes high.

Selection Criteria

As with each chapter on techniques, rating schemes are assessed using selection criteria relating to resource requirements, applications, and outputs for the technique. To compare rating schemes with other techniques, review Table II.1.

Resource Requirements

> The *cost* of rating schemes is low as it actually reduces cost in the risk qualification process by minimizing the need for data gathering. By providing common metrics and terms, the cost associated with risk assessment is actually reduced.
>
> *Proper facilities and equipment* for rating schemes consist of the schemes themselves and a conference room sufficient to conduct a review of risk based on those schemes. The information should then be ultimately stored in an organizational database.
>
> The *time needed to implement* rating schemes is low. As with cost, this approach actually reduces the time commitment required to conduct a thorough risk assessment. With the schemes in place, any risk assessment becomes a relatively cursory review of the nature of each risk and the application of the scheme.

The *ease of use* associated with rating schemes is high. If the scheme is well written, then virtually any team member with project familiarity can apply the scheme.

The project manager's *time commitment* is actually a function of scheme development rather than application. During scheme development, the project manager's time commitment is significant because time and effort must be committed to building organizational and executive buy-in. After the scheme is actually constructed, however, the project manager's time commitment is minimal inasmuch as the responsibility to apply the scheme can readily be delegated.

Applications

The primary application of rating schemes is to provide a consistent understanding of the probability and impact of each risk in the project. Because those terms are somewhat imprecise, the development of metrics to generate consistency allows organizations to build contingency policies, management strategies, or organizational dicta on how risk should be managed. The metrics also allow for the simple ranking of project risk, a critical endeavor for any project.

Rating schemes support *project status reporting* only if risk status is an element of such reports. If the reports include notification of major project risks together with the status of those risks, then the rating schemes are invaluable because they provide common terminology and understanding of the criticality of a given risk.

For the same reasons, rating schemes also support *major planning decisions*. Because major planning decisions depend on an understanding of risk in the organizational context, the common terminology that the schemes afford engenders a clearer understanding of the nature of any concerns associated with the decisions.

The schemes can support *contract strategy selection* if the selection process is directly tied to the volume and nature of the project risks. However, because very few contract organizations are structured to consider these issues, the relationship here is generally weak.

Rating schemes serve no useful function in *milestone preparation* because milestones are a function of the schedule, and the schemes themselves have no direct effect on the schedule.

Design guidance is not a strength of rating schemes, save for the comparative analysis of one design versus another in a consistent fashion.

The schemes could support *source selection* in the case where risk is a critical deciding factor in the process. Otherwise, they do not provide extensive support.

Budget submittal may or may not incorporate contingencies. If the budget in question does not incorporate contingency funding, then rating schemes serve no useful function. However, if the budget will include contingency funds, then the rating schemes play a pivotal role in ensuring that funding levels are appropriate and are in keeping with the organization's perspective on probability and impact.

Outputs

The *accuracy* of rating schemes is moderate. Because they are qualitative tools, they lack the precision that is sometimes desirable in a thorough risk analysis. But precision is not the same as accuracy. Accuracy is a reflection of how well the tools actually establish the probability and impact of given risks. Because different team members may have diverse perceptions on the severity of risk, the schemes lend a degree of accuracy that would be unattainable without them.

The *level of detail* is relatively high as rating schemes provide a means to conduct a risk-by-risk analysis of probability and impact. Rating schemes raise risk analysis to a very detailed level and make it a type of analysis that some would abandon if a means did not exist to facilitate the effort. In essence, that is the role of the schemes.

The overall *utility* of rating schemes is high in that they provide metrics where metrics would otherwise not exist. They facilitate a thorough, consistent assessment of probability and impact, yet without the significant investment associated with many of the more quantitative approaches.

Summary

Rating schemes require an up-front investment of time and management energy to establish consistent measures for probability and impact, which is enough to dissuade some organizations from the investment. However, once in place, the measures make risk qualification simple, consistent, and clear from team to team and from project to project. Even though they do not generate hard numbers with which to work, they do generate a clear sense of risk relative to other projects and other organizational risks. Furthermore, they encourage a common risk vocabulary within the organization so that all parties involved know how high "high" is.

26
URGENCY ASSESSMENT

In a variety of situations, the question is not whether a particular risk must be addressed but rather whether it must be addressed *now*. Although a critical criterion for assessing risks, urgency normally falls into an analysis process *after* the assessment of probability and impact. However, because urgent, low-threat risks generally do not receive a great deal of attention in a high-pressure environment, they are not typically the subject of an urgency assessment. By contrast, high-probability, high-impact threats may need to be assessed for urgency to determine which threat events should be dealt with first. As a consequence, an urgency assessment is customarily based on the immediacy of the threat plus the effect that a timely response will have on strategy efficacy.

Technique Description

An urgency assessment is captured in a form or template to document criteria that constitute high, medium, or low urgency. Documented in the form of a checklist or fill-in-the-blank template, an urgency assessment allows the organization to determine which environment(s) generate and warrant a true need for immediate or near-immediate action versus those where a wait-and-see attitude may be a more intelligent response. The technique involves assessing only those risk events deemed "high" overall, as there is no real need to filter lower risks by urgency.

When Applicable

Urgency assessments are applicable only when there are sufficient high risks (normally high probability, high impact or moderate probability, high impact), such that no possibility exists for the project team to effectively deal with them all—at least not in a timely fashion. Thus, the urgency assessment is appropriate as a tool to define which high risks merit immediate attention in a resource-limited environment.

Inputs and Outputs

Because an urgency assessment is predicated on an organizational template, two sets of inputs must be considered. The first consists of inputs to create the template or checklist itself, and the second comprises inputs to populate the template or checklist.

Inputs to create the template include information regarding what environmental conditions create true urgency regarding a risk event. In mountain rescue environments (one of the most common environments for application of an urgency assessment), the templates incorporate information about the age, fitness, clothing, experience, and conditions pertaining to a lost hiker. For example, a young hiker in shirtsleeves is definitely a more urgent case than a veteran hiker with a full pack. In project management, urgency may tie together such issues as project deadlines and milestones, customer sensitivity, team member expertise, and project complexity. The form should incorporate those components that render risk events more urgent and should provide the ability to ascertain relative levels of urgency among risks.

The output from the urgency assessment template creation will be the template itself. The template either may take the form of a checklist or may provide a scoring metric to generate the relative level of urgency for the risk events in question, as shown in Figure 26.1.

Although the criteria and their relative weights will vary by organization, the template nevertheless affords the organization an opportunity to build a measure of consistency into their application of risk management as it applies to urgency assessment.

After identification, inputs into the template merely consist of the values in the scoring column(s) as driven by the answers to the questions in the template. Any assumptions made in developing those answers should be documented with the form to ensure they are captured for consistency's sake in the evaluation. However, different assumptions may drive diverse answers to the questions and thus may generate altogether different outcomes in terms of which risks are most urgent.

The outputs from the templates will be urgency scores for the individual risk events. This allows filtering of the various risk events based

Project Name			Risk Event		
Urgency Assessment					
Evaluation Criterion	1	2	3	4	Score
Experience of the project team in dealing with this type of risk	Known competence in workarounds and ad hoc solutions for this type	Some experience in dealing with risks of this type	One or two team members with some experience in risks of this type	No team experience in risks of this type	
Probability risk will occur *prior* to the next stage gate	Probability is higher later in the project and not prior to the next review	Probability is just as high later in the project as prior to the next review	Probability is high prior to the next review	Probability is at its highest in the next two time periods (for example, weeks, months)	
Customer sensitivity	Customer has no expectations regarding this risk and would assume we would resolve it	Customer would expect this type of risk to be resolved without delay	Customer would expect prior notice if this risk became imminent	Customer would never expect this risk to occur	
Project complexity/ integration	This risk event affects only one module of the project and that module can be dealt with independently	This risk event affects the entire project but is integrated toward the end of the project life cycle	This risk event affects multiple modules and is integrated early in the project	This risk event affects multiple modules and they are all highly dependent on it	
Visibility	The risk event can easily be identified in advance of its occurrence, allowing for last-minute action/resolution	The risk event has some detectable cues that may allow for early identification	The risk event is only detectable when it is actually beginning to occur	The risk event is only detectable *after* it occurs	
Total					

Figure 26.1   Sample urgency assessment template.

on urgency as well as the organization's resource capacity to deal with risk. Those risks that fall into the high-risk category by virtue of their probability and impact can then be screened for urgency, thus permitting the project team to work toward resolving the high-urgency, high-threat risks first. Other risk events, though not ignored, may be relegated to a later resolution, as they do not have the high level of urgency associated with those risks that scored highest in the template.

Major Steps in Applying the Technique

The first step in building an urgency assessment template is to determine the criteria that render one risk event more urgent than another.

Developing those criteria involves consultation with experienced project personnel who recognize common elements associated with risk urgency. These are normally individuals who understand the organizational environment well enough to know what must be considered so as to determine whether a risk event will be imminent. (In the aforementioned mountain rescue example, the analogous equivalent would be an expert climber familiar with the terrain in question.) These individuals should evaluate those criteria within the organization that are most consistently indicative of an imminent risk, regardless of the impact level. As long as those criteria can be properly identified, metrics can then be established within the criteria to determine the degree to which conditions favorable for urgency exist.

Identify the criteria. Criteria that create conditions indicating that risk events may be imminent need to be identified and cataloged.

Identify a gradient scale. For each criterion, identify a numerically gradient scale indicating the level of influence toward urgency, ranging from a high number (a high level on urgency) to a low number (a low level of influence on urgency). Adjust the scale as necessary, based on the relative levels of influence on urgency, to attempt to make the final outputs evenly weighted.

Validate the template. Validation is performed by testing a variety of known urgent and non-urgent risks against the criteria. The template should reflect the historic level of urgency associated with those risks. However, if it does not, then the scoring metrics may need to be adjusted to more accurately reflect the relative levels of urgency.

Evaluate all significant risks. After the template has been validated, all significant (high-probability, high-impact; and moderate-probability, high-impact) risks should be evaluated within the template to determine their relative levels of urgency.

Prioritize risk events. High-risk, urgent events should be given priority in response development.

After performing the urgency assessment, the risk events should be cataloged in the risk register (see Chapter 17, "Risk Registers/

Tables"). As with any evaluation process, urgency assessment should be conducted whenever there is a reassessment of risk.

Use of Results

The urgency assessment's primary application is in determining the highest priority risks. Although other assessment processes may generate a pool of the highest risks, urgency assessment serves as a triage process for establishing those risks that must be dealt with first. Moreover, viewing them from an historical perspective, the results are also used on post-project reviews to determine whether those risks initially deemed "high" and "urgent" actually were.

Resource Requirements

The resources for the urgency assessment include senior-level experts who can identify criteria to establish relative urgency. The templates that they develop ultimately become organizational assets for comparison in future risk assessments.

Reliability

The urgency assessment is reliable in applying a consistent method to determine the most urgent risks. Its reliability also lies in developing a triage process for dealing with the most urgent risks first. As long as the criteria accurately reflect the environment that drives urgency, the technique is highly reliable.

Selection Criteria

As with each chapter on techniques, the urgency assessment is assessed using selection criteria relating to resource requirements, applications, and outputs for the technique. To compare urgency assessment with other techniques, review Table II.1.

Resource Requirements

> The *cost* of implementing the urgency assessment can be moderate. Because the technique requires resources who have deep experience and knowledge of the organization, the resources

may be among the more expensive personnel resources avail-able to a project. After the template is constructed, however, the cost drops to low.

In terms of *proper facilities and equipment*, there are no special equipment needs for this technique.

The *time needed to implement* the urgency assessment is high at the outset; but again, after the template has been constructed and is in place, the time requirement is much lower.

The urgency assessment has high *ease of use* after the template has been constructed. As it is primarily a data assessment function, the ease of use is very high.

The project manager's *time commitment* to the urgency assessment is high if the project manager is responsible for building the template. If, however, the experts building the template do not include the PM, then the project manager's commitment is low.

Applications

The urgency assessment supports some application categories in Table II.1.

For *project status reporting*, the urgency assessment has limited utility because urgency assessments are not conventionally part of the status report.

Major planning decisions may hinge in part on an understanding of near-term risks, which are best identified by an effective urgency assessment.

The urgency assessment does not directly support *contract strategy selection*.

The urgency assessment may support *milestone preparation* in that it may indicate when certain milestones represent points at which certain levels of urgency have passed.

The urgency assessment can support *design guidance* if the design can be changed to modify the relative urgency of certain risks.

The urgency assessment generally does not support *source selection* unless the vendors directly influence the relative risk urgency.

The urgency assessment may support *budget submittal* by identifying when and how contingency must be applied (either long-term or short-term).

Outputs

The output from the urgency assessment is a form or template that is completed for each "high" risk and that indicates a relative urgency score to determine which risk events are the most urgent.

> *Accuracy* of the urgency assessment is high, in that it establishes a relative level of urgency for the most significant project risks.
> The *level of detail* in the urgency assessment is low because it only addresses the criteria established on the urgency assessment form.
> The *utility* of the urgency assessment is high in projects where there are a significant number of high risks and limited resources to deal with them all.

Summary

The urgency assessment provides one more filter for environments where a significant body of high risks exists. The need for supplemental filters in such environments is often driven by the sheer volume of risks and the team's inability to deal with all of them. The urgency assessment affords the ability to evaluate risks that must be handled first. It presents a clear understanding of what *must* be managed now as opposed to eventually.

27
FUTURES THINKING

Whether in risk identification, qualification, quantification or response development, the exercise of risk management is largely one of clairvoyance. It is a function of being able to look into the future and identify the various possible states that may exist. Futures thinking is the art and science of identifying those future states of nature, selecting the most desirable state, and working toward that reality as a goal. The key risk components of futures thinking are those of identifying the impediments to that future state and how those impediments can be avoided. Futures thinking also takes into account the anticipated reaction to alternative (less desirable) future states and how that reaction will manifest itself.

Technique Description

Futures thinking is a team analysis of a future environment (against a specific target time-frame) in terms of how not only the project will be/function/apply, but also how the environment will respond to the implementation of the project and how the world will look different as a result. Once the initial desired state is established, there is a quest for drivers of the ideal state (as well as the drivers of all of the various possible outcomes), followed by an examination of the various alternative states that may exist. Ultimately, the analysis concludes with an assessment of what efforts and strategies must be in place to achieve the desired outcome.

When Applicable

Futures thinking is most applicable when there is a need for a uniform vision of the desired outcome, as well as a clear understanding of the environment necessary to achieve that outcome. The process applies when project value propositions are in question and when there is widespread concern that the outcomes may not serve the organization or the environment favorably.

Inputs and Outputs

There are several key inputs into futures thinking. They include the—

Initial question
Time frame for the analysis
Environmental scan
Outcomes evaluation
Strategic proposal

Futures thinking is largely a cyclical process, and each step in the cycle relies heavily on the one before it. In determining what future is under consideration, it's vital to ascertain not only the goal of the assessment, but also the target time for the assessment. The processes for environmental scanning, outcome evaluation and strategic assessments should be in place, but the answers should not be predisposed.

The outputs from futures thinking are the determinations as to what approaches make the most sense in terms of the organization, the desired outcome and its risk environment.

Major Steps in Applying the Technique

Frame the original question. The key in establishing the original question is to determine what aspect of the future is under consideration and what the desired information output from the process will be. A poorly framed question can lead to data that has no real value for the remainder of the analysis. The question may include the time-frame, the goal of the analysis, and an acknowledgment that different outcomes are possible (e.g., "Three years from now, if this project is implemented and completed, how will the organization and its customer relationships look different?"). The original question will create the future environment to be evaluated in the risk context.

Affirm the time-frame. Because time is a critical risk driver, it's important to clarify the point in time for which the evaluation is being conducted. The outcome of a project in two years (when it's fresh and new) is radically different from the outcome of a project nearing its decommissioning. Generally, the time frame is selected based on the prevailing management strategic window. If management tends to evaluate process and progress in annual increments, then a year or two may be appropriate. If management's strategies are based on 5- or 10-year outcomes, a one-decade target makes more sense.

Conduct an environmental scan. Asking what's going to contribute to the outcome or hinder it is crucial to futures thinking. Assessing projects will rely heavily on the environment under consideration. Seaside construction is not the same as building in a desert. Software development for portable apps is not the same environment as mainframe code authorship.

Ask what outcomes are possible. Rather than trying to identify what problems may arise in development, futures thinking goes to the end of the process and attempts to identify what various outcomes may happen. There will always be at least one desired outcome, but the other outcomes are considered critical to the analysis, as some of them may not be the most desirable, but may be acceptable. This step is also important in identifying if any outcomes are completely unacceptable, so that those outcomes may be planned for and avoided. By documenting the range of possibilities, it becomes possible to track the trajectory of the project toward or away from any of the given set of possible outcomes.

Determine the strategic approach. Once the various outcomes have been determined, the next critical step is to define the strategy(ies) that will best achieve the desired outcome. Such strategies may involve careful project planning to align with the desired outcome or risk responses to preclude or minimize the possibility of alternative outcomes. The approach should take into account the project environment established in the environmental scan, as those assumptions will frequently determine the likelihood of possible outcomes. In assessing the strategic approach's potential efficacy, it should be evaluated in terms of the organization's capacity to carry it out, the risk appetite of the organization for such an approach, and the history of similar implementations. Strategic approaches with a history of success, a supportive organization, and adequate resources are far more likely to succeed than those that meet none of those criteria.

Document and communicate the approach. As early as practicable, the strategy should be communicated to the team, supporting management, the sponsor, and the client (where applicable). Any time there are significant shifts in the approach or in the likelihood of achieving the desired outcome, those shifts should be communicated to the same parties.

Use of Results

Futures thinking is used to take an alternative "reverse engineering" approach to risk management. Rather than identifying the risks and stepping through the conventional process, the first output is the likely outcome. From that point, assessments are done in reverse, asking what strategies will lead to that outcome and what risks may impact those strategies. Futures thinking is particularly effective in taking management and team members out of the details of the process, and instead getting them to focus on the end of the effort. It is particularly useful when process discussions cause relationships to bog down and inhibit discussion.

Resource Requirements

Resources for a futures thinking analysis will include analysts who step beyond process and envision the future state of the project's outcomes. These individuals need the ability to not only envision the desired state, but also the other possible outcomes that may eventuate from the project. From those perspectives, they should then have the ability to identify the environments and the processes that would likely lead to the outcomes described.

Reliability

Futures thinking reliability hinges almost exclusively on the quality of the analysts. The greater their ability to serve as futurists, looking into the proverbial crystal ball, the higher the reliability. Reliability increases when the analysts are allowed to explore the full range of possible outcomes without criticism, as premature critiques may lead to reluctance to explore the more seemingly unusual outcomes (despite the fact that such outcomes may prove to be likely).

Selection Criteria

As with each chapter on techniques, futures thinking is assessed using selection criteria relating to resource requirements, applications, and outputs for the technique. To compare futures thinking with other techniques, review Table II.1.

Resource Requirements

The *cost* of implementing futures thinking can be low to moderate. Because the technique requires resources having only familiarity with the history of the organization and the nature of the project, it may include the personnel resources from a variety of backgrounds. This range of options in personnel opens the door to cost containment.

Because the technique is largely rooted in brainstorming and discussion, there are no significant *proper facilities and equipment* required for this technique.

The *time needed to implement* futures thinking is moderate and is dependent on the magnitude of the project, the history of implementation, and the breadth of possible outcomes. If there are only a handful of possible outcomes, the time needed is very limited. In most situations, the time needed is moderate as most undertakings can lead to a broad range of outcomes.

Futures thinking has high *ease of use* in that the background and educational requirements essential to apply the tool are limited.

The project manager's *time commitment* to futures thinking is moderate if the project manager is responsible for conducting the assessment. If, however, the experts responsible for the assessment do not include the PM, then the project manager's commitment is low.

Applications

Futures thinking supports some application categories in Table II.1.

For *project status reporting*, futures thinking has moderate utility, as the desired outcome becomes a critical consideration in the baseline evaluations of the project.

Major planning decisions may hinge in large part on an understanding of a desired outcome.

Futures thinking may directly support *contract strategy selection*. Since the contract will lead to the outcomes, and since the outcomes spelled out in the contract may be determined by futures thinking, there is a direct correlation.

Futures thinking has high support for *milestone preparation* in that the status of the potential outcomes needs to be established at critical decision points. By selecting milestones that represent turning points in the decision-making process, futures thinking is a vital input.

If the design or an element thereof is the subject of the futures thinking outcome, then futures thinking can support *design guidance*.

Futures thinking supports *source selection* in that vendors may be required to model their services against the desired outcome.

Futures thinking does not directly support *budget submittal*.

Outputs

The outputs from futures thinking include a report indicating the range and likelihood of possible outcomes, the desired outcome, and the strategies that will lead to that outcome.

Accuracy of futures thinking is moderate because it relies on the quality of the analysts.

The *level of detail* in futures thinking is high, as it provides in-depth scrutiny of the possible outcomes associated with a given hypothesis.

The *utility* of futures thinking is moderate, in that it addresses a broad range of risks in a project based on a range of possible outcomes.

Summary

Futures thinking provides a wide-ranging analysis of possible outcomes for a project. Rather than assuming only the desired outcome will be achieved, futures thinking acknowledges the reality that many projects don't precisely hit their targets, but still have high utility *if* the various outcomes are considered early enough in the planning stages. Although futures thinking does not apply to the breadth of risks that may potentially plague a project, it does, however, afford a clear understanding of risk's influence on the ultimate outcome.

28
RISK MODELING

Risk models are developed so that project managers will be able to better identify high-risk or high-opportunity projects consistently. That drive for consistency is actually closely aligned with the discussion on rating schemes (see Chapter 25). The problem that many organizations encounter is their own inability to measure projects for risk. Although they will have predictive tools for cost and schedule, there are very few tools specific to the notion of risk. The risk model seeks to fill that void by encouraging the consistent evaluation of projects for issues that put the organization at risk, as well as concerns that afford the organization the highest probability of success.

Technique Description

The technique consists of constructing a set of questions that, when answered candidly, will provide a metric value as to the overall risk and opportunity associated with a project. The questions should span the organization's experiences and concerns and should reflect the organization's risk tolerances. Because this involves a clear understanding of what risk tolerances exist within an organization, it is prudent to develop rating schemes prior to attempting to build an organizational risk model.

When Applicable

Project risk models are normally built only after an organization encounters a series of significant project risks or failures and then wants to ascertain how they can avoid these concerns in the future. Once built, the models should be applied in much the same fashion as any major evaluation. They should be applied during the go/no-go decision process and again at any major evaluation and decision points.

Inputs and Outputs

Model Development

Inputs into risk model development include a list of critical risk issues and tolerances for the organization, as well as a list of what the organization perceives as its strengths and opportunity generators. Those inputs will be crucial in constructing the model, as they will provide the baseline against which all projects are judged. Other inputs will be concurrent among senior management staff as to the relative weights of the individual risk and opportunity issues and the objective metrics by which the likelihood of occurrence can be measured.

The outputs of risk model development are the models themselves. This is most effectively built into a spreadsheet or database program that allows the information to be plotted against a chart, graph, or other display to illustrate the relative level of risk on the project or aspect of a project under consideration.

Model Application

The inputs for applying risk models are information germane to the questions asked within the model. Project managers and team members are charged with answering the questions objectively and applying the measures identified in the model.

The outputs from the risk model are normally a grid, graph, or display that highlights the position of the project (from a risk perspective) relative to other risks within the organization. This example plots risk using a graph like the one shown in Figure 28.1.

A straight line across the top is indicative of a low-risk, high-opportunity project. An oblique line from lower left to top right highlights a high-opportunity, high-risk project.

Major Steps in Applying the Technique

As with rating schemes, there are really two major applications here. The first is in building the risk model; the second is in applying it.

Decision scale

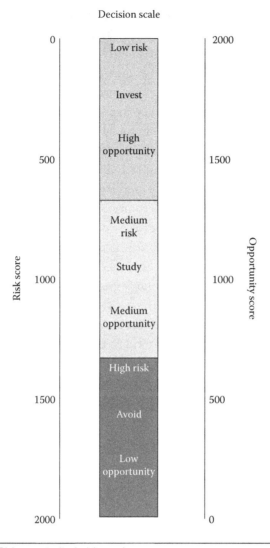

Figure 28.1   Risk–opportunity decision scale.

Model Development

Building a risk model requires time and energy on the part of senior management or senior project management to clearly establish the metrics by which all projects will be judged (from a risk perspective). They should be parties to all the steps in this process.

   Identify critical risk and opportunity areas. The identification of threats and opportunities within an organization is normally not a challenging effort; however, the identification of critical threats and opportunities is. Senior managers participating in this process will frequently have many years or even decades of experience within the organization. As such, their insight is invaluable. It is also possible that as a result they will have somewhat skewed perspectives as to what issues are likely to be critical to the organization. Thus, this approach is more effective when the senior managers involved first share their perspectives on all threat and opportunity areas they can identify rather than simply identifying those that are critical. After all threat and opportunity areas have been identified, then a sorting or filtering process can begin.

Note that these are opportunity and threat *areas* rather than simply opportunities and threats. They can be synonymous with categories or terms like "repeat offenders." These threat areas are spheres of concern that strike the organization with sufficient regularity to warrant attention and redress. In contrast, opportunity areas are those that the organization most consistently acknowledges as positive or rewards.

These threat and opportunity areas should be sufficiently well defined that developers can build metrics to characterize the probability of their occurrence later in the model building effort.

EXAMPLE 1

Risk area: Technological novelty

"In our organization, projects that apply new technology inherently promote greater risk."

Opportunity area: Trade press

"The trade press is generally very favorably disposed to us. Projects that attract trade press increase opportunity for us."

Assign impact weights or values to threat and opportunity areas. Weights are numerically assigned and should be established on a scale with the highest values being assigned to risk areas of greatest concern and to opportunities of greatest value. If some risk areas pose dramatically greater concern, then they should be assigned a significantly higher value than those of lesser concern. If, however, the differences are marginal, then the differences in values should be marginal as well. Thus, because of the need for fine-tuning on such models, scales frequently range from 1 to 5 or 1 to 10 to allow for modest adjustments. A model with a range of 1 to 3 does not allow for fine adjustments.

EXAMPLE 2

Risk area: Technological novelty

"This issue is not as important as multivendor integration (on our scale) but is more important than potential employee loss (on our scale). We will weigh technological novelty as a 4"

Opportunity area: Trade press

"This issue presents an opportunity for us but not to the degree of potential profit (a) or shareholder value (a). We will weigh trade press as a 3."

Establish the probability scale. Probability scales in risk models are not the same as probability rating schemes as defined in Chapter 25. In risk models, the probability scale is a ranking (normally set at 1 to 3 or 1 to 4) of the likelihood that conditions will be ripe for a threat or opportunity area to become a significant issue in the project. Scales of probability for each area will be mapped to metrics to allow for consistent evaluation of their probability of occurrence.

EXAMPLE 3

"For all risks, we will assess probability as low, medium, or high, and rank them as 1, 2, and 3 respectively."

Develop metrics to assess probability of occurrence. This, in many ways, is the single most arduous step in the process. For each threat and opportunity area, clear, objective measures need to be established to identify when conditions for the risk area are likely to exist and when they are highly unlikely to exist. For each area, the first question to consider is "How does one know when conditions are ripe for this area?" Afterward, objective statements must be established to clarify whether they fit on the scale established in the previous step. This process takes time because each risk area must be examined and analyzed to ensure that objective measures accurately reflect the threat or opportunity area in question.

EXAMPLE 4

Risk area: Technological novelty.

1. The technology is well established and familiar.
2. The technology is new to our organization but well established in the market-place.
3. The technology is new, but we participated in developing it.
4. The technology is new and was developed outside our organization.

Opportunity area: Trade Press

1. The project is internal and does not involve any new approaches or technology to interest the trade media.
2. The project is external and does not involve any new approaches or technology to interest the trade media.
3. The project involves new approaches to existing technology and may have modest interest for the trade press.
4. The project is a breakthrough effort that will draw the attention of clients, media, and competitors.

Determine the range of scores for the outputs. Each impact value should be multiplied by the lowest probability value to establish the lowest possible score for each threat and opportunity area. All low-threat scores should be summed to establish the lowest possible threat score. All low opportunity scores should be summed to establish the lowest possible opportunity score. Thereafter, each impact value should be multiplied by its highest probability value to establish the highest possible score for each threat and opportunity area. All high-threat scores should be summed to establish the highest possible threat score. All high-opportunity scores should be summed to establish the highest possible opportunity score.

EXAMPLE 5

Risk area: Technological novelty   *Opportunity area*: Trade press
Impact weight: 4   Impact weight: 3
Low score: 1   Low score: 1
Risk score (Low): $4 \times 1 = 4$ Opportunity score (low): $3 \times 1 = 3$
High score: 4   High score: 4
Risk score (high): $4 \times 4 = 16$ Opportunity score (high): $3 \times 4 = 12$

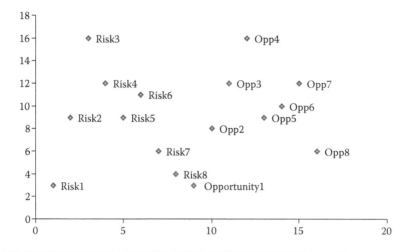

Figure 28.2   Scatter diagram example.

Create a graphic display for the outputs. The risk model can be mapped to a variety of graphic displays, ranging from the model in Figure 28.1 to a simple grid to a scatter diagram (see Figure 28.2). (A scatter diagram is appropriate if all individual threat and opportunity answers are to be displayed on the grid rather than merely the summed score.)

Test the model. After all impact values and probability metrics have been established, the model can best be tested on old projects perceived as high threat–high opportunity, high threat–low opportunity, low threat–high opportunity, and low threat–low opportunity. The model's questions should be completed based on the perceptions for the project when it began rather than after completion. If built properly, then the model should accurately reflect the levels of opportunity and threat as established after the project was completed.

Model Application

Apply the tested model to new projects. When a project is conceived, project team members should host a meeting to evaluate the new project in the context of the questions in the model. They should mark each of the correct objective statements and score the project in the model accordingly.

Score the project. Based on the scoring practices created for the model, the new project should be scored for total threat and total opportunity scores. The scores should then be mapped into the model's graphic.

Communicate the score. As risk models are frequently a component of go/no-go decisions, the information developed should be sent to the key decision makers on the project to facilitate their efforts in deciding whether the project is viable. The entire score sheet should be retained for historic purposes in determining long-term model accuracy and the need for adjustment.

Use of Results

Risk models can be used to—

Communicate relative levels of risk to senior management and project decision makers

Establish or defend the need for contingency funding on a given project based on its overall threat and opportunity scores

Challenge assumptions as to the relative levels of threat and opportunity that marketing or technical personnel may make

Present an argument for certain levels of support or reward based on project complexity, opportunity, and threat

The models' applications are as varied as the organizations that use them. However, their primary use is simply to create a situation where risks can be consistently evaluated within a given organizational climate. In the nascent days of a project, risk is all too frequently assessed according to the individual perception of the most effective negotiator. The model is designed to mitigate some personality issues associated with risk and to encourage a significantly higher level of consistency.

Resource Requirements

The resource requirements to develop the risk model are significantly greater than those required merely to apply the model. Although model development requires inputs from senior project personnel and senior management personnel, model application generally requires inputs only from those individuals who understand the nature of the project in question. Apart from personnel needs, the only other requirement for both applications are database capabilities to store and maintain outputs from the model.

Reliability

Risk models have reliability only when applied consistently within the organization. The challenge in many organizations is that individuals attempt to modify the metrics to color the perspective on their individual project. That defeats the purpose of the model as well as its ability to interpret the information accurately. However, when applied properly and consistently over an extended period of time for multiple projects, the model has increasing reliability.

Selection Criteria

As with each chapter on techniques, risk modeling is assessed using selection criteria relating to resource requirements, applications, and outputs for the technique. To compare risk models with other techniques, review Table II.1.

Resource Requirements

> The *cost* associated with implementing risk models is extremely limited. The resource time commitment consists of the time required to review the project in the context of the risk model.
>
> There are no special equipment needs for this technique because it is primarily a small administrative burden. For *proper facilities and equipment*, the only requirement is to locate the files, databases, or shelves housing the information to support the model and store its outputs.
>
> The *time needed to implement* risk models is very short. Very little time is involved beyond ensuring that the information required to assess the project against the objective metrics is available.

Risk models have extremely high *ease of use*. The intent is to provide a quick snapshot of the project in terms of both risk and opportunity.

The project manager's *time commitment* to the models is extremely low because developing responses to the objective statements is generally quick, easy, and readily completed.

Applications

Project risk models can be used in some application categories in Table II.1. In some of the applications, risk models are effective only if they are applied on a regular basis in project reviews and midterm assessments, as well as at the beginning of the project.

For *project status reporting*, project managers may find risk models very effective in determining the relative status of a project's risks and opportunities when compared to earlier assessments.

Major planning decisions can definitely hinge on outputs from risk models. Risk models can be applied to establish go/no-go decisions, set up contingency funds, or determine appropriate courses of action to improve relative threat and opportunity scores.

Contract strategy selection may also be tied to the risk model. Firm-fixed-price contracts can be used with those projects that have lower risk and higher opportunity, whereas cost-plus contracts may be more appropriate for those where the organization must assume higher threats and less opportunity. The model can provide early indicators of which tendencies the project may display.

Risk models do not support *milestone preparation*.

In terms of *design guidance*, risk models have very limited utility, unless multiple risk and opportunity questions are directly focused on design.

Risk models do not directly support *source selection*.

Risk models may support budget submittal. If the risk model is used to establish levels of a contingency fund by percentage or score, then the risk model can be crucial to proper *budget submittal*.

Outputs

Outputs from a risk model are the completed model questionnaire and the graphical outputs thereof. Some organizations maintain risk questionnaire responses as a means to discern what areas of risk exist in a project (rather than simply relying on the overall score).

> *Accuracy* of the risk model is high if the model is well established and has historically been applied to a variety of projects.
>
> The *level of detail* obtained through risk models is low. Although the risk model analyzes a variety of categories, it does not explore the detail associated with a particular project. Instead, it consistently examines risk areas across projects. And although that focus has value and can be highly indicative of relative risk levels, the level of detail is slight.
>
> The *utility* of risk models rests in their consistent application. If they are used consistently across the organization and are used to evaluate relative levels of risk or capability, then the utility is high.

Summary

The keys to project risk models are consistent application and a clear understanding of the tool's role. The risk model will not develop detailed lists of highly project-specific risks. Instead, the risk model will provide a scoring system and a metric that can be applied effectively to make go/no-go decisions, establish appropriate contingency reserves, and ascertain areas of heightened concern or interest. Consequently, it is a general evaluation tool and should be treated as such.

29
SENSITIVITY ANALYSIS

Sensitivity analyses answer one simple question: What would happen if a single parameter in the project environment were changed? The thrust behind an effective sensitivity analysis is to examine the potential influence of one alteration to the project in terms of the risk context. The parameter being changed can be almost anything, ranging from a single change in the project's environment to a change of one of its constraints. The key, however, is to modify one parameter early enough to determine the degree of influence the change would have on the situation.

Technique Description

Sensitivity analyses can take a number of forms, including qualitative and quantitative assessments of the change in a given parameter. In qualitative assessments, expert authority is used to divine what the outcome of a modification to a single parameter would be. Conversely, in quantitative environments, one change is made to the parameters of the assessment (frequently in a Monte Carlo analysis), and simulations are conducted to determine the relative level of the change's influence.

When Applicable

Sensitivity analysis is normally applied when a significant project change is under consideration and some disagreement exists as to the potential influence of that modification. Sensitivity analysis permits a before-and-after comparison of the predicted project states to determine whether the change proposed is viable and appropriate.

Inputs and Outputs

Because sensitivity analysis can be used to assess virtually any change proposed, the key input is the detailed information (assumptions, background, rationale, approach, and so on) associated with the modification. Other key inputs are the remaining information regarding the project. For a subjective (qualitative) assessment, such information would include background data on the project's objectives, approach, project plan, and other information germane to the assessment. For a qualitative assessment, the information would align with much of the data established for Futures Thinking (discussed in depth in Chapter 27). For a quantitative assessment, such information consists of the data input into a project planning tool supported by Monte Carlo simulations. That data would include the distributions of outcomes for individual tasks, resource data, and other information as discussed in depth in Chapter 30, "Monte Carlo Simulations."

Outputs from a sensitivity analysis consist of comparisons of the original predicted state of the project environment prior to change and the estimated state of the project environment after modification. These two sets of information can then be analyzed to determine whether project performance projections under the proposed change fall within acceptable parameters. For quantitative analyses, these projections take the form of cost and schedule curves; and for qualitative analyses, these estimates are captured as narrative derived from expert assessments of the project's direction.

The criterion being assessed will vary from analysis to analysis, but the potential criteria that *could* be assessed are as different as the number and types of project tasks. That is why sensitivity analysis is normally limited to a single parameter. Otherwise, the range of possible variables would be so great as to render moot the analysis of any single data point's influence.

Major Steps in Applying the Technique

The first step in conducting a sensitivity analysis is to ensure that all background information required for the assessment will be readily available to the experts responsible for the analysis. This means that information regarding project planned performance, environment, and assumptions is documented and available in a single repository. Without that information, no baseline exists for comparison when parameters are changed.

Document background information. Establish and document the background information, current state of the project, and current assessment of projected project performance.

Determine the parameter to be evaluated during the sensitivity analysis. If more than one parameter will change, then multiple sensitivity analyses must be conducted to capture the impact of each alteration. An effective sensitivity analysis will evaluate *only* one parameter for each evaluation. This allows for comparison of the state of the project environment before and after the change has been implemented.

Conduct either a qualitative or quantitative analysis. If a qualitative analysis is being conducted using authoritative resources, then ask the resource to describe the state of the project after the parameter has been changed. Explore all three aspects of the triple constraint (time, cost, and requirements) and other areas (such as politics, culture, team retention, public relations, and so on) as appropriate. Document the responses and prepare a report comparing the two states (projected performance with and without the change). However, if a quantitative analysis is being conducted, then run an analysis of the project performance using the quantitative tools available. This may include a simple project report from project management software, or it may be as complex as a Monte Carlo analysis (as described in Chapter 30). Preserve a copy of the project file as it currently estimates the project outcomes. Change the parameter in the tool. Run an analysis of the project performance with the change in place.

Compare and contrast the outcomes. Note differences in terms of project performance and any related impact to the project or organizational environment.

Any decisions resulting from the analysis should be accompanied by copies of the files (or support documentation) that led to the conclusion.

Use of Results

The primary application of sensitivity analysis is in evaluating limited project modifications that may have significant implications. It provides a clear comparison of the assessed state of the project before and after a given parameter has been altered. The concept is to ensure that implications of change are clear, well considered, and understood by those parties who will either make the decision or live with the outcomes.

Resource Requirements

The resources for sensitivity analysis vary depending upon the type of analysis being conducted. If a subjective or qualitative analysis is being performed, then the resources will include authorities on the project and its future. If, on the other hand, a quantitative analysis is being performed, the resources will include whatever supporting software (including project software, spreadsheet software, Monte Carlo software, and so on) may be required to fully evaluate the change of a given parameter within the project. The resources would also include any individuals responsible for entering data into the software and running any associated simulations.

Reliability

The sensitivity analysis technique is as reliable as the information input into the analysis. Qualitatively, if an expert who truly understands the project and its projected outcomes conducts the assessment, then the reliability can be quite high. By contrast, if qualitative analyses are conducted by experts with either a vested interest in a given outcome or parameter change or by experts without a depth of project environment understanding, then the reliability will be close to useless. On the other hand, the reliability of quantitative analyses hinges purely on the quality of the data inputs: Good data entered in will result in high-quality, dependable outputs.

Selection Criteria

As with each chapter on techniques, sensitivity analysis is assessed using selection criteria relating to resource requirements, applications, and outputs for the technique. To compare sensitivity analysis with other techniques, review Table II.1.

Resource Requirements

The *cost* of implementi.ng a sensitivity analysis can be moderate. Because the technique requires resources with deep experience and knowledge of the organization, it may include the most expensive personnel resources available to a project. However, if the analysis is being conducted quantitatively, then the resource costs are those associated with data gathering and tools input.

For *proper facilities and equipment*, there are no special equipment needs for this technique beyond the software required to conduct any quantitative analysis.

The *time needed to implement* a sensitivity analysis depends largely on the scope of the parameter change. If the parameter change is significant and far-reaching, then the analysis may take several days to sift through differences in project status during the comparative analysis. If, however, the parameter change has a nominal impact, then the time needed to implement a sensitivity analysis will mainly include the setup time plus the time required for information gathering.

Sensitivity analysis has high *ease of use* for those who have access to the requisite tools and data. For a qualitative analysis, the interview process is relatively simple because there is only one parameter to evaluate and merely one fundamental question to ask ("What would change?"). Likewise, in a quantitative analysis, the ease of use is also high if the data and tools are readily available, inasmuch as the primary question is whether the parameter change rippled through the rest of the project to influence other aspects of time, cost, and/or performance.

The project manager's *time commitment* to sensitivity analysis is moderate if the project manager is also the resident expert or authority conducting the evaluation. However, if the experts evaluating relative sensitivity to a change do not include the

PM, then the project manager's commitment is low, consisting primarily of building, evaluating, and sharing the parameters to be evaluated.

Applications

Sensitivity analysis supports some application categories in Table II.1.

Sensitivity analyses are not normally applied in *project status reporting.*

Major planning decisions may rely heavily on the sensitivity analysis technique, as the analysis affords a perspective on how and why particular decisions may or may not be appropriate.

Sensitivity analysis can directly support *contract strategy selection* if the contract type is the variable being evaluated.

The sensitivity analysis technique does not directly sustain *milestone preparation.*

Sensitivity analysis often supports *design guidance* by testing diverse aspects of the design and their influence(s).

Sensitivity analysis can contribute to *source selection,* specifically if vendors are the variable under consideration.

The sensitivity analysis technique may support *budget submittal* by identifying the point(s) at which budget allocations may be so small (or large) as to potentially harm the project.

Outputs

The output from a sensitivity analysis is a document that affirms the status quo and the state of the project if the variable is changed. It is often displayed in tabular formats to reflect the contrasting aspects of the two different states of nature. This format allows for direct comparison of the environment as it exists *without* application of the changed variable against the environment as it would exist *with* application of the changed variable.

Accuracy of sensitivity analysis is dependent on the accuracy of the inputs. Generally, however, because only a single variable is changed and the level of variability is controlled, the accuracy is moderate to high.

The *level of detail* in sensitivity analysis is moderate. Although
the technique normally addresses only one variable, it still
should survey the breadth of the project parameters.

The *utility* of the sensitivity analysis technique is high, particularly in environments where small, incremental changes are a
challenge. Because sensitivity analysis examines each alteration independently, it serves a valuable function of identifying
the sometimes dramatic influences of minor change.

Summary

Sensitivity analysis opens the door for a clearer understanding of
the influence that some changes have on the project environment.
Specifically, it provides a focused examination of the impact that a
single change has on the larger project environment and allows for
comparing and contrasting two different states of nature (that is, the
"before" and the "after"). Regardless of whether performed qualitatively or quantitatively, sensitivity analysis is an effective tool to expli-
cate to management, customers, and team members the influence of a
single parameter change on the project as a whole.

30
MONTE CARLO SIMULATIONS

This technique not only considers cost and schedule risk for individual activities but also for the entire project. In many cases, there is the temptation to assume that all project risks must be accounted for in the worst case. The Monte Carlo analysis technique, however, takes a more holistic approach. As such, the total project cost risk and the total project schedule risk are usually expressed as a cumulative probability distribution of total project cost and total project schedule, respectively. Such distribution information can be used to reflect project risk by computing the probability that the project will be accomplished within particular cost or schedule targets. It can also be used to assess what level of funding or schedule would be required to virtually guarantee success.

A computer is necessary to use this technique because the analysis requires repetitive computations. Most of the software packages (for example, *Barbecana Full Monte,* and *@Risk*) conduct both cost and network analysis simultaneously, whereas some tools (*@Risk* for Excel, for example) can perform only cost analysis. Input data requirements for such models are significantly less than cost and schedule analyses.

Technique Description

The technique uses simulation analysis to establish relative levels of risk. In Monte Carlo analysis, uniform, normal, triangular, and beta distributions are used to assign risk values to cost and schedule targets for each work package within the work breakdown structure (WBS). The type of distribution applied depends on the nature of the work as well as the nature of the comprehension of that work. However, different distributions require different levels of understanding. A uniform distribution, for example, requires only that one knows what the highest and lowest possible costs and durations are. A beta distribution, on the other hand, requires a far greater depth of data and understanding.

Monte Carlo analysis uses a random-number generator to simulate the uncertainty for individual WBS elements. Some Monte Carlo tools will use Latin Hypercube sampling, rather than random number generators. In a Latin Hypercube, the analysis takes into account the outcomes of earlier analyses, rather than truly random outputs. Most analysts believe that Latin Hypercube achieves acceptable outcomes with fewer samples.

After costs and schedules are simulated for each WBS element, they are aggregated to establish a critical path, a total project duration, and a total project cost estimate. This process is repeated many times. Each time that a new set of WBS element costs and durations are developed is referred to as an *experiment*. The results of many such experiments provide a frequency distribution of total costs, reflecting the aggregate of the cost risks associated with all individual WBS elements.

When Applicable

This technique applies when the project manager needs to know the probability that a project can be completed successfully at a given funding level or within a given time frame. It is also appropriate to use when there is a need to know what funding level is required to achieve a specified probability of completing a project. To ensure that this technique can be applied, the project manager must obtain sound estimates of the cost uncertainty plus the schedule uncertainty associated with each WBS element. After cost and schedule estimates are already in place at the work package level, this becomes a relatively quick analytical procedure.

Inputs and Outputs

With Monte Carlo simulations, inputs and outputs vary depending on the models used. As an example of inputs and outputs information, *Barbecana's Full Monte* and *@Risk* (as well as Primavera's *PERTMaster*) can apply various types of cost uncertainty against each individual WBS element and then generate a variety of information types.

For each model run, three elements of data are required:

Project name
Monte Carlo sample size (number of iterations)
Decision to compute either a partial or complete analysis

For each work package, the data required become more extensive. Depending upon the type of distribution requested or required, data needs will vary widely. For instance, uniform distributions will require only the range of best- and worst-case information for cost and schedule. Triangular distributions will include the best- and worst-case as well as the most likely targets for both cost and schedule. Normal distributions may call for the mean duration as well as the standard deviations from the mean. In addition, beta distribution data will require information on the shape of the curve as well as the mean.

Some tools allow broader inputs for the work packages, thus requiring simple confidence levels (expressed as percentages) for cost and schedule. In these cases, either a uniform or normal distribution is generally applied, with the single-point cost or single-point schedule estimate as the median or the mean.

The outputs from the tools are similar to those in Figure 30.1. These outputs show that roughly 53 of the samples fall into the range near $122,388 (the mean). That type of information is used to develop the probability curve and the histogram. Each bar on the histogram represents a range of roughly $5,000. As you can tell by examining the histogram, the odds of project costs coming in at less than $115,000 are extremely low (about 10% percent).

Similarly, schedule curves can be plotted to establish ranges of probability and risk associated with given schedule targets. Figure 30.2 illustrates how schedule values can be presented in the tool.

These data can now be used to establish reasonable levels of funding and acceptable schedule targets. Based on the information in Figures 30.1 and 30.2, project funding would have to be set at more than $130,000 to achieve 95 percent confidence that the project would be funded adequately. To be 95 percent confident that schedule targets were achieved, the deliverable due date would have to be moved to November 7. That does *not* mean that the project will cost $130,000 or be done on November 7. It means, rather, that based on

Date: 8/30/09 11:08:38 a.m.
Number of samples: 100
Unique ID: 1
Name: task 1

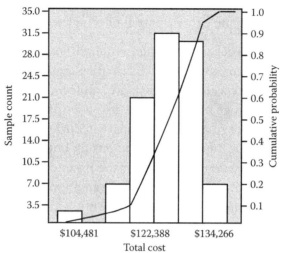

Cost standard deviation: $5,986
95% confidence interval: $1,173
Each bar represents $5,000

Cost probability table

Probability	Cost ($)	Probability	Cost ($)
0.05	111,542	0.55	123,953
0.10	114,121	0.60	124,510
0.15	115,638	0.65	125,158
0.20	117,606	0.70	126,421
0.25	118,802	0.75	126,773
0.30	119,438	0.80	127,602
0.35	120,204	0.85	128,476
0.40	120,870	0.90	129,682
0.45	121,520	0.95	130,803
0.50	122,568	1.00	134,266

Figure 30.1   Cost risk/WBS simulation model.

the simulation, there is a 95 percent probability the project can be completed within those targets.

Major Steps in Applying the Technique

The Monte Carlo simulation process assumes some baseline understanding of project computer simulation tools. Such tools are commercially available but have a significant learning curve associated

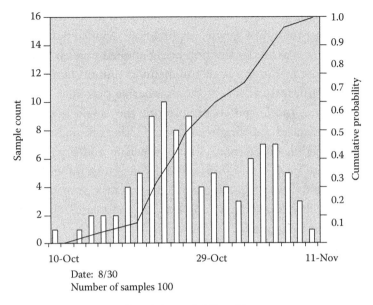

Date: 8/30
Number of samples 100

Completion probability table

Probability	Date	Probability	Date
0.05	10/17	0.55	10/28
0.10	10/21	0.60	10/30
0.15	10/22	0.65	10/31
0.20	10/23	0.70	11/01
0.25	10/23	0.75	11/04
0.30	10/24	0.80	11/05
0.35	10/24	0.85	11/06
0.40	10/25	0.90	11/06
0.45	10/25	0.95	11/07
0.50	10/26	1.00	11/11

Figure 30.2 Risk support.

with them. Although macros can be established in some project management software to achieve the same goals as a quality Monte Carlo program, the level of effort is rarely worth the investment.

Identify model input requirements. Depending on the choice of tools, the inputs required can vary widely. Some tools can take extremely simple inputs (confidence ranges or high-, medium-, or low-risk values) and use those data to generate an analysis based on predetermined values for those inputs.

Barbecana Full Monte and some other tools have this capability. Other tools, like *@Risk*, require more detailed data inputs, including type of distribution being applied to each task and data ranges. The input requirements are important as they will significantly affect the data-gathering processes.

Gather data. These two words capture the single most onerous element of applying the Monte Carlo technique for cost and schedule simulations. Data gathering and organization in Monte Carlo are significant and time-consuming. Even if only limited data are being applied, each task must be examined for its relative range of risk and in most cases, the distribution of that range.

Input the data into the tool. As tool utilization increases, facility with these processes should increase accordingly. Even so, the first-time data entry effort can be significant. If all appropriate data are in hand, then this step is generally a function of following any step-by-step instructions that the tools provide.

Establish simulation parameters. Each simulation can take on characteristics all its own. A simulation may include as few as two iterations (which would have limited utility) or 10,000 or more iterations (which borders on statistical overkill). The parameters may also change how the information is examined, whether either by classic Monte Carlo techniques or more current statistical trends (like the Latin Hypercube, a technique that supposedly takes fewer iterations to achieve statistical validity).

Run the simulation. For most simulations of any size, running the simulation can be a surprisingly time-consuming effort. A 1,000-iteration simulation running on a fast computer for a several-hundred-task project may take minutes to churn through all the data. This often comes as a surprise to novice users accustomed to computer analyses that run in the blink of an eye.

Analyze the data. The curves that the tool develops should be examined for the insights they afford. This should include identification of the mean duration, best- and worst-case scenarios, and anomalous information provided. Any trends, spikes, or outlying data elements should be reviewed to determine whether they represent anomalies or information of value.

Communicate and archive. Communicate the outputs to those who have a vested interest in or some decision-making authority on the project. Archive the results for later comparisons with project outcomes.

Review from a historical perspective. Upon project completion or at on-going major decision points, retrieve archived outputs for comparison to project outcomes. Take note of the cumulative probability assigned to the outcome(s) achieved and document them.

Use of Results

The outputs from a Monte Carlo simulation can be used to establish reasonable cost and schedule targets or to identify appropriate contingency levels. The information is used to define reasonable cost levels or to defend specific project approaches. Monte Carlo outputs from multiple simulations with modified variables can also illustrate the influence of those variables on the project as a whole.

Resource Requirements

The resource requirements for Monte Carlo are significant in that the requisite tools tend to be more expensive than conventional project management application software and because users must have specialized expertise to gather data and operate the tools.

Reliability

The mathematics and logic of the Monte Carlo simulation technique are basically sound. However, the tool is only as reliable as the inputs, and the interpretation of the outputs also influences the tool's efficacy. The technique is highly reliable at establishing cumulative probabilities of schedule and cost targets but is completely unreliable at establishing the probability of a single cost or data point. The value of the tool rests in its ability to set a range. On the other hand, Monte Carlo's greatest limitations rest in the challenges associated with obtaining sound and supportable data.

The challenges that are sometimes made against Monte Carlo are twofold. First, there is concern at times that the merge bias that naturally occurs in a Monte Carlo analysis creates a false sense of how late the project may be. Merge bias is the condition that exists when multiple project network paths converge on a single node, thereby creating a situation where the different paths may protract the schedule. In such situations, any opportunity for schedule improvements on one path is frequently sacrificed by virtue of delays in simulations on parallel paths. As a result, Monte Carlo simulation outputs tend to be pessimistic when contrasted against normal network diagramming or even against the somewhat weighted pessimism associated with PERT (Chapter 23). Merge bias, as caused by path convergence (multiple parallel paths converging on a single point), is sometimes difficult to understand, in that it seems that it strips away any potential benefits gained on a single path through careful planning and hard work. In reality, path convergence can do just that, because any situation where multiple paths occur in parallel generates the possibility that tasks on at least one of the paths will be delayed, thus negating the benefits from any parallel paths.

The second concern over Monte Carlo analyses pertains to the natural tendency of project managers and project teams to take corrective actions. Because corrections are made midproject and are based on outcomes, opponents contend that a Monte Carlo analysis reflects merely a single point in time rather than the totality of the project. In truth, such arguments against Monte Carlo analyses don't really prove valid under scrutiny because a Monte Carlo analysis is like *any* planning tool that reflects the realities of the current situation. In fact, if corrective action is required at midproject, in all likelihood it indicates that the project has been delayed in some fashion (or the budget has been overrun) and that the early schedule or underbudget possibilities cited in the Monte Carlo analysis have been negated or minimized. Thus, the need for corrective action may be an indicator that the Monte Carlo analysis's accuracy is verified.

Selection Criteria

As with each chapter on techniques, the Monte Carlo simulation model is assessed using selection criteria relating to resource requirements, applications, and outputs for the technique. To compare Monte Carlo with other techniques, review Table II.1.

Resource Requirements

  The *cost* associated with this technique includes both the one-time cost of software acquisition (which can range from several hundred to several thousand dollars) and the cost for a resource to gather data and develop the appropriate scenario to run through the computer. This resource is normally a highly skilled analyst.

  As to whether the *proper facilities and equipment* are available, the answer in many organizations is no. Although the investment is a one-time experience, some organizations feel that the information delivered through the tool represents data overkill.

  Much as with estimating relationships (Chapter 21), the *time needed to implement* after the tools and skills are in place is in proportion to the time required to gather the necessary data.

  The *ease of use* associated with this analysis method is high after a few hours of hands-on experience if the user has a basic understanding of distributions, probabilities, and the range of risk. Although available programs come with instructions, the real challenge is associated with obtaining and substantiating sound values for all cost element uncertainty information. Ideally, the best source for such information would be past experience on similar projects, but that type of information is rarely available.

  Assuming that the PM is not also the analyst, the project manager's *time commitment* is slight but necessary to ensure that team members provide information to the analyst in a timely manner.

Applications

  Project status reporting represents only a small fraction of the overall use of the technique. Only one respondent to a major survey that the Defense Systems Management College conducted identified using this technique for this purpose. Even so, as the tools become less expensive and more user-friendly, the application here could readily expand.

The Monte Carlo model is best applied when *major planning decisions* are made. The model provides insight into the range of possibilities associated with any given modification to the plan.

Contract strategy selection and *milestone preparation* are not applications that can effectively use the Monte Carlo model.

This technique can be applied in *design guidance* if the ranges of cost and schedule implications are required for a variety of different potential designs.

Source selection is not a common application, but Monte Carlo has been applied to examine cost and schedule ranges for different potential vendors based on their submitted costs, schedules, and WBSs.

Budget submittal is also a rare use for this technique, although Monte Carlo models will provide management with clear insight into the best-case, worst-case, and most likely cost and schedule parameters for the project.

Outputs

The subjective nature of most input data used to conduct the analysis determines the *accuracy* of output results. The more accurate that the inputs are, then the more accurate are the outputs.

The analysis does nothing to increase risk visibility at a lower *level of detail*. Values are computed by aggregating detailed information into overall project cost and schedule risk information.

The overall *utility* of this type of analysis for actually identifying risk, controlling risk, or planning risk responses is limited. However, this type of analysis can be used to display cost and schedule risks known to exist at the cost account level in an aggregate manner (the way some management executives will want to see it).

Summary

This type of analysis gathers cost and schedule uncertainty due to risk for any number of work packages into a distribution of the cost and schedule uncertainty for the entire project. It provides the project manager with the information necessary to answer the following questions:

What is the probability that the project will be complete for X dollars or less?

What is the probability that the project will be complete on or before X date?

How much budget should we assign to this project based on the risk and our desire for X percent confidence?

How much time should we allot for the project based on the risk and our desire for X percent confidence?

These are not inconsequential questions. To the contrary, they are classics of project management. They represent the body of knowledge that many managers desire at the outset of their projects.

The challenge in applying Monte Carlo is not in understanding the outputs or even the tools. Instead, the challenge stems from attempting to gather information on likely distributions of time and cost for individual work elements. There is also risk with Monte Carlo analysis that derives from the innate complexity and detail in the data outputs. That detail generates an aura of certainty, which may or may not be deserved (based on the quality of the inputs).

31
RISK FACTORS

This method is simple to implement. It consists of applying risk consideration to the individual work package budgets within the work breakdown structure (WBS). If the risk input values for the work packages are in hand, then the effort moves rather quickly. However, in many cases obtaining sound and dependable risk input values can be a challenge. Often, the input values are based on quick judgments made by project personnel. The method does not include procedures for systematic and scientific development of the needed input data. Nevertheless, the primary use of the method is to estimate the total additional project costs that might be expected due to risks associated with the individual work packages.

Technique Description

The basic concept of the risk factor method is to determine factors, or multipliers, with which to increase cost estimates of individual baseline WBS work packages to cover anticipated risk-associated cost growth. A reasonable budget above that resulting from the baseline cost estimate is the objective. The method uses a WBS based on a technical (deliverable) breakdown like that shown in Figure 31.1.

First, the baseline estimate must be developed for each cost element. Applying whatever considerations are appropriate, a risk factor is established between 1.0 (indicating no risk) and 2.0 (indicating so much risk that expected costs could be twice the baseline cost estimate values). Each baseline estimate is then multiplied by its corresponding risk factor to obtain new WBS element cost estimates. These new estimates are then finally summed to derive a budget that will account for technical or other risks.

Obtaining sound WBS element risk factors is the critical feature of this method and may be difficult to attain. Data analysts have

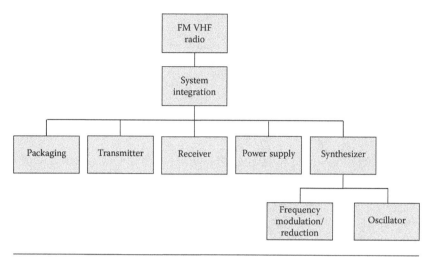

Figure 31.1   Sample technical breakdown.

scant documentation to use in substantiating such factors. Because these factors significantly affect analysis results, the inputs must be obtained from highly experienced technical experts. (In other words, the apparent simplicity of the method has not relaxed the requirement that the most experienced project personnel should take key roles in the analysis.) After preparing a baseline cost estimate using cost estimating methods, an analyst should be able to formulate a new cost estimate by expeditiously using the risk factor. The effort will depend on the difficulty an analyst has in securing the assistance of technical experts and on how detailed the WBS or cost breakdown is.

When Applicable

In surveys conducted by the Department of Defense (DOD) (as part of the original draft of this text), only a handful of respondents had used this technique. Since that time, however, different industries have adopted similar techniques to the point where risk factor calculations are now being applied to deal with security risks in some information technologies as prescribed in ISO 17799. Risk factor applications are more suitable early in the life of a project when the information required for some of the more sophisticated risk analysis techniques is unavailable. However, this technique is applicable only when single data-point estimates, broken out by the work package, are available. Moreover, the method's simplicity makes it applicable to even small, low-cost projects.

Inputs and Outputs

One of the primary inputs of a risk factor assessment is a baseline cost estimate broken out to the work package level. The second primary input is a set of risk factors for each work package. These factors usually will be the subjective judgments of experienced personnel who know the project, its current status, and potential problem areas. Using checklists or watch lists and the number of items on the lists that apply to each work package is one way of helping to judge the level of risk associated with each element of work.

Outputs of a risk factor application consist of a budget or cost estimate that is increased over the baseline budget (or estimate) by an amount required to cover risk-induced costs.

Major Steps in Applying the Technique

Obtain project cost estimates. These should be broken down to the work package level and should include sufficient detail to resolve any questions or issues about their content. Such estimates should be available from project planners. Their actual preparation is not considered to be part of applying this method.

Identify work package risk factors. Each work package should be assessed to determine the level of additional risk associated with it. That level of additional cost risk should be expressed as a percentage of the original estimate and should be added to the task costs to accommodate additional potential work resulting from risk. Knowledgeable technical and project management personnel should offer their opinions on these factors. Analysts should also review lessons learned for similar systems to gain insight on how much risk might be involved. If similar tasks have been performed in the past by the same people assigned to the current project, then risk should be lower. It is important to remember that past projects were also risky, so the original estimates may already factor in some of the risks.

Recalculate project costs. Sum the work packages *and* their risk factor budgets to derive a new project cost estimate.

Use of Results

According to the DOD survey of project offices, those offices using risk factor results found them helpful, particularly in the early development of cost estimates during requirements development.

Resource Requirements

Resource requirements for this method can vary greatly. Frequently, the same cost estimator responsible for preparing the baseline cost estimate can also develop the risk factor-adjusted estimates quickly if the appropriate experts provide the work package factors in a timely manner. However, applying the method can become more involved as more technical and other experts are used to derive the individual work package risk factors.

Reliability

The reliability of this technique can vary widely, both in fact and in the opinion of those reviewing results. Because use of the technique generally requires judgments based on limited information, the knowledge and skill of those making judgments will greatly affect the reliability of the results. However, providing documented justification for all factor values used increases reliability. A single cost analyst who is assigned risk-level factors for all WBS elements without inputs from technical and other experts would likely produce relatively low-reliability results.

Selection Criteria

As with each chapter on techniques, the risk factors technique is assessed using selection criteria relating to resource requirements, applications, and outputs for the technique. To compare risk factors with other techniques, review Table II.1.

Resource Requirements

The time required to develop activity-by-activity breakdowns of the cost estimates, coupled with the time spent in obtaining WBS activity risk factors from qualified experts, generally drives the *cost* of the technique.

The *proper facilities and equipment* for the technique consist of a personal computer loaded with project management and spreadsheet software applications.

The resource time spent in gathering data and assessing risk factors from experts drives the *time needed to implement* the technique much as it does the cost.

After data are developed, the technique has relatively high *ease of use.* The project manager must review the computations and apply them.

The project manager's *time commitment* normally consists of tracking down the correct experts to provide risk factors for each activity.

Applications

The method applies to product and service projects of virtually any size but can be used only when a cost estimate broken out by work package is already available. It can quickly provide a systematically derived estimate of required funds to cover risk-related project costs. However, the method is best applied when project personnel with experience on other projects are available to provide judgments regarding the level of risk involved with each work package.

Project status reporting is a reasonable use for this approach because it provides an estimate of the total funds required to complete the project. That figure, along with actuals to date, provides the project manager with the baseline status, current status, and potential status of the project at completion.

The results of the analysis of the technique, as described in the previous paragraph, may also drive *major planning decisions*.

Contract strategy selection and milestone preparation are not typically applications for this technique.

This technique can support *design guidance* only from the perspective of the cost implications of different design recommendations.

Source selection is not a prime application for risk factors because this technique requires a fully developed, comprehensive WBS. Normally at this preliminary stage, such information is not readily available.

The technique can support *budget submittal* only if the budget is being developed comprehensively from the bottom up in the WBS. If an exhaustive WBS is not developed for the budget, then the technique will not apply.

Outputs

The *accuracy* of this technique is a direct function of the expertise of the resources providing data for inputs. This model is the classic example of a "garbage-in/garbage-out" scenario. If the information provided is less than sound, then the outputs will have a low accuracy level. To the contrary, if the experts have extensive experience on similar efforts, then the accuracy of the method increases significantly.

The *level of detail* is low for risk factors because the technique focuses on a project-wide, rather than a task-by-task, perspective.

The *utility* of the technique is high as long as the correct goals are sought. If the project manager is looking for project-wide information and a perspective on the overall costs associated with remaining risks, then the technique is ideal. For other goals, though, it would be somewhat inappropriate.

Summary

This analysis method has been used widely to develop an estimate of the funds required to cover added costs resulting from individual risks associated with specific work packages. It is designed not to analyze potential task-by-task overruns but rather to analyze the aggregate overruns for the project, as some of the risks identified will come to pass and others will not. In the long term, however, the method balances out those risks that do become problems and those that do not in establishing a reasonable, whole-project estimate.

32

RISK RESPONSE MATRIX/
PUGH MATRIX

In risk response development, one key challenge is finding strategies that will not take longer to implement than the project itself. The risk response matrix technique addresses that concern by affording individuals and team members the opportunity to analyze and generate strategies that deal with multiple risks and cause the fewest problems in terms of other project risk.

Technique Description

The risk response base matrix or Pugh Matrix is a grid the team creates that lists risks on one axis and strategies on another. The grid is then populated by plus and minus signs (or plus and minus signs *with* weights) to reflect positive and negative influence on other risks. Ideally, the grid should include the standard risks of cost and schedule. The risks and strategies are juxtaposed as shown in Figure 32.1. For more in-depth analyses, an additional set of grids can be placed across the top of the base grid to encourage evaluation of risk strategies in the context of other strategies, thus creating a diagram not dissimilar from the famed "house of quality" used in quality function deployment (QFD). This expanded type of diagram is shown in Figure 32.2.

In the base matrix example, it is possible to see that only one strategy has been developed for the "no viable names" risk, and it is the same strategy that helps mitigate at least one copyright issue. It is also evident that writing the site in HTML code will mitigate a host of risks and may actually save time and money. Some Web designers, however, would argue that the site will tend to be unimaginative as a result (which illustrates how the matrix can help in identifying new risks based on risk strategies).

Risks associated with starting a commercial Web site	Write the entire Web site in very simple HTML code	Beta test the system, along with a major "stress test," using dozens of representatives from our biggest corporate clients	Make up a nonsense word and conduct a Web search for it to ensure no previous use	Mount the system on redundant servers around the world	Establish minimum entry criteria for the site (e.g., "Browser must be version 7.0 or later")	Meet with corporate client network staff to include them in the design
No viable names will be available, so traffic will be significantly reduced			+			
Legal challenges on copyright issues could occur, tying up the site in court			+			
Web site could generate too much traffic, causing serious downtime and server errors	+	+		+	+	
The code behind the site could be too ornate, and upgrades may not be possible	+					+
A programming language could be included that does not work well through corporate firewalls, causing a loss of business	+	+				+
Project will be over budget	+	−	+	−	+	
Project will be late	+	−		−		−

(Risk strategies)

Figure 32.1   Risk response matrix.

The addition of the roof to the base matrix illustrates how the diagram can highlight potential relationships among the strategies. In this instance, a browser at the 7.0 level can apparently handle HTML code with ease and the two should work together favorably. But the 7.0 requirement could be a hindrance for beta tests because some beta

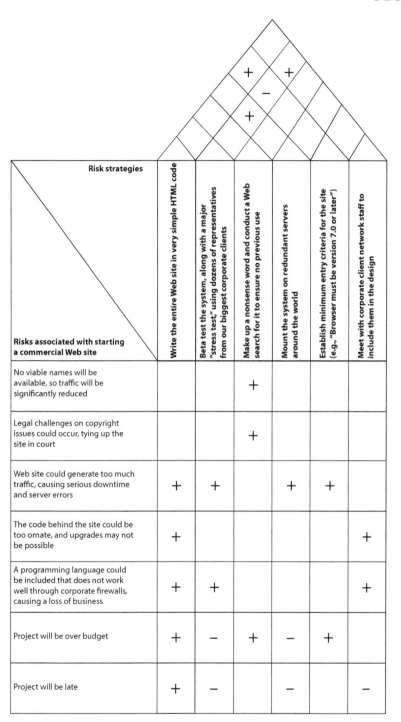

Figure 32.2   Expanded risk response matrix.

testers are apparently operating on old 5.0 or 6.0 version browsers. Thus, the matrix roof highlights potential support or conflict.

The grid is used with a limited number of risks to keep the information manageable. Ideally, these should be the top-priority risks as identified during risk qualification or quantification.

When Applicable

The grid is applied after the project team has identified and quantified risks to establish those that are the greatest concerns. It is best applied when the skills and insights of the entire team can be exercised because team members may have widely different perceptions as to what constitutes a corresponding strategy or a conflicting risk approach.

The grid should be applied whenever risk strategies are being evaluated and should be a part of any strategy assessment or major risk reassessment.

Inputs and Outputs

The inputs for the tool include the prioritized risk listing that has been whittled down to the top 5 to 10 risks. The inputs will also consist of multiple strategies for those risks, allowing team members to review them in the greater context of the project, its other risks, and other strategies. In addition, the inputs incorporate the team members' evaluations of the risk implications and risk strategies in the context of other risks and risk strategies.

The outputs are completed grids, which can then be interpreted to determine which risk strategies address the greatest number of concerns with the least impact to cost and schedule.

Major Steps in Applying the Technique

Construct the grid. Before beginning the data gathering, it is reasonable to generate a grid in which all the appropriate risk control information will be placed. The grids (like those used in Figures 32.1 and 32.2) should list both "Project will be over budget" and "Project will be late" as risk events. Some analysts feel "Project will not meet scope" is a risk event that should also be included as a standard. These standard elements are recommended for each grid because risk strategies should always be assessed for their potential role in generating schedule delays or cost overruns.

Gather the prioritized risks. Actual prioritization of the risk events should have been completed using another technique, such as expected value or a simple qualitative "high-high" sort. The top 5 or 10 risks should be listed on the left side of the grid (as depicted in Figure 32.1).

Identify multiple strategies. Ideally, multiple strategies should be developed for each risk in the list. This can be accomplished by reviewing the basic options of avoidance, acceptance, mitigation, and deflection for each risk event. The key is to expand the list of available options and establish the broadest possible range for risk control opportunities. As strategies are identified, they should be arranged in boxes along the top of the grid (as depicted in Figure 32.1).

Assess the strategies' impact on the risks. Even though a strategy may have been created primarily to resolve or deal with a single risk, each strategy should be evaluated for its own potential impact on the other risk events listed. Risk strategies frequently have unforeseen consequences (both favorable and unfavorable) when considered against the project's other risk events. To document the influence of the risks, a plus sign (+) can indicate when a risk strategy will have a positive influence on a risk event (for instance, a plus sign next to budget overrun would indicate that the strategy would likely reduce overall cost or minimize the possibility of budget overruns). A minus sign (–) can indicate when a risk strategy might have a negative influence on the risk event (for example, a minus sign next to schedule delay would indicate that the strategy will likely add to the schedule or increase the probability of delays). Some users put zeroes in sectors where the risk event has neither a negative nor positive influence. Others use circles to indicate risk strategies deemed to be optimal for the situation. If the plusses or minuses are not all of equal value, they can be numerically weighted to highlight a minor versus a major impact on the risks.

(Optional) Assess the strategies' impact on other strategies. This step is often undertaken as a matter of course rather than as a formal step in the process. However, to formalize it, some users will put the roof on the grid to illustrate possible connections among risk strategies. The process is much the same as the previous step with the difference being that the evaluation is designed to determine whether the risk strategy will make it easier or more challenging to implement other risk strategies.

Select the strategies with the greatest overall positive influence. Although this is a subjective decision, it is tempered by virtue of the tool's indications that some risk strategies have a broader span of influence than others. Thus, by determining which risk strategies in general are the most beneficial and have the least negative influence, it is possible to review options in the context of the project's overall risk environment.

Select secondary options. The obvious advantages of one set of risk management options developed using the tool may render this step moot. However, because management and team members frequently prefer to decide which are the best available options, a set of options should be identified as logical alternatives to the primary selections.

Select optimal risk management actions. With the options and information in hand, either the project manager or the team should determine which strategies have the greatest overall positive influence and should therefore be deployed on the project. Implementation should be expressed as work packages and should be incorporated into the WBS or the project plan.

Use of Results

Outputs from the matrix can be used in basic decision making or to present information to upper-level or executive management to facilitate *their* decision making. However, the information ultimately needs to be captured, reviewed, and presented to build organizational support and acceptance for the risk management options selected.

Resource Requirements

The resource requirements for the technique are somewhat limited, although those individuals with a history of creative risk intervention should be welcomed in this process. The primary resources required for this approach are participants who are willing to provide inputs and offer insight on the optimal risk approaches and options. One key physical resource requirement is a large wall on which to post flip chart pads that depict the grid so as to encourage a comprehensive perspective on which options will work in this environment and which will not.

Reliability

The approach is surprisingly reliable as it forces a level of assessment on risk response development that frequently does not occur at all. Because it adds a layer of checks on the process, the risk response matrix technique creates a more reliable process. Still, there is never an assurance that *all* possible risk responses have been reviewed inasmuch as the responses are as diverse as the participants themselves. This technique ensures that considerations have been made for the bulk of the available options.

Selection Criteria

As with each chapter on techniques, the risk response matrix technique is assessed using selection criteria relating to resource requirements, applications, and outputs for the technique. To compare the risk response matrix with other techniques, review Table II.1.

Resource Requirements

The *cost* of the technique is a function of the participants' time
commitment in the process. Although the effort is occasionally tedious, it does not consume an excessive amount of time.
Thus, the cost is relatively low.

The *proper facilities and equipment* for the technique consist of
flip charts or erasable boards adequate to create the grid and
input the data. Some project managers may opt to capture the

information after the session using a digital camera as supplemental equipment.

The resource time expended in gathering data and cataloging the information on the grid drives the *time needed to implement* the technique, much as it does the cost.

The tool has high *ease of use* as its application is primarily intuitive. However, the tedium of completing the grid sometimes disguises the minimal effort required for its application.

The project manager's *time commitment* normally consists of seeking the appropriate experts to provide inputs and evaluate the strategies across multiple risk events.

Applications

This approach can be applied to virtually any type of project but will work well only on a relatively small number of activities. One key to success is to ensure it is applied to a limited number of activities simultaneously. Thus, the tool is best applied after the top 5 to 10 risk events have been established.

The risk response matrix does not support *project status reporting*. The matrix is an ideation and decision-making tool rather than one for gathering data on past performance.

The matrix may drive *major planning decisions*. Because such decisions rely on a breadth of background and information, the insights generated using the matrix can provide a distinct tactical advantage in determining which decisions are the correct ones.

Contract strategy selection can expect modest support from the risk response matrix because diverse contract strategies can be seen as different risk management approaches and thus be loaded into the matrix. In that regard, the matrix can be most effective in helping to determine which risk responses represent the most viable options in terms of contract strategy.

The matrix does not support *milestone preparation*.

As with contract strategy selection above, the matrix supports *design guidance* if and when different designs are integrated as potential risk responses into the matrix itself.

The tool supports *source selection* well. That support is accessed when sources are identified as potential risk response strategies and are integrated into the matrix. From that perspective, risk responses can be assessed as more or less viable in terms of overall project risk mitigation.

The technique can support *budget submittal* only by virtue of the costs of individual risk responses. Because the tool helps ascertain the optimal responses, those responses can then be evaluated for potential budget impact. That can be expressed either as budget line items (for the risk responses that are incorporated into the WBS) or as a contingency (for the risk responses that may be deployed at some later date if the project conditions change or meet certain criteria).

Outputs

The *accuracy* of this technique is largely a function of the expertise of the experts providing the data for inputs. If the resources are creative and experienced in developing risk strategies, the opportunities here are virtually boundless. As the risk responses are spelled out in greater detail, the tool becomes more accurate. The more detail that is written into each risk response, then the more accurate the tool becomes. However, the tool becomes highly inaccurate if the risk responses applied here are only one or two words. In such instances, there is a distinct tendency to make the responses more inclusive (that is, to claim that the responses will solve more risks than they actually will).

The *level of detail* is high as numerous specific risks are addressed at the work package level.

The *utility* of the technique is high. The tool can be applied at virtually any point in the project as long as risk events have been identified and prioritized. The technique can be used both to discern new strategies and to present those strategies to the team or management. Moreover, if used as presented in Figure 39, the tool affords the ability to review risk responses in the context of the other responses.

Summary

This technique is the model of practicality in risk response development. It affords clear understanding of project risks, the options available to respond to those risks, and the most viable and practical of the options. That breadth of capability is rare. And because the tool is relatively intuitive, that breadth of capability is something that can readily be applied at a variety of levels within the organization.

33

PERFORMANCE TRACKING AND TECHNICAL PERFORMANCE MEASUREMENT

A U.S. government report on technical risk devoted much discussion to examining the importance of managing the technical aspects of a project. However, measuring technical risk on any effort that involves furthering the state of the art is difficult and can involve significant risk itself. Performance tracking is conducted by establishing exacting performance criteria for all aspects of the project and assessing them against the acceptable ranges around those criteria. Some concrete measurements that are available can be useful in measuring technical progress against preset goals of projects.

Technique Description

The performance-tracking technique advocates using a technical risk assessment report, which is updated periodically. The report is based on working-level data but is intended to provide an overview of current trends and status. The technique uses a set of standard technical indicators proved to be effective measures of technical performance. In addition to the standard measures, the analyst also develops project-unique technical indicators. Each indicator has clearly defined performance projections and preset alert criteria. Standard indicators are shown in Table 33.1; a sample indicator is shown in Figure 33.1.

When Applicable

This technique is most effective when objective and quantifiable criteria are established. The technique is best used to manage

Table 33.1 Standard Indicators

TECHNICAL RISK INDICATOR (TYPICAL UNIT OF MEASURE)	APPLIES TO						SOURCE			
	SYSTEM	SUBSYSTEM A	SUBSYSTEM B	SUBSYSTEM C	SUBSYSTEM D	SUBSYSTEM E	STATEMENT OF WORK	CONTRACT SPECIFICATIONS	CONTRACTOR PLANS	PREVIOUS EXPERIENCE
DESIGN										
Wait time (seconds)	×	×	×	×	×	×		×		
Size	×	×	×	×	×	×		×		
Database access	×		×	×	×	×		×		
Throughput	×							×		
Memory utilization (percentage of capacity)	×							×	×	
Design-to-cost (dollars)	×	×	×	×	×	×	×			
Design maturity (number of design deficiencies)	×	×	×	×	×	×	×		×	×
Failure activity (number of failure reports submitted)	×	×	×	×	×	×	×		×	×
Engineering changes (number of engineering change orders)	×	×	×	×	×				×	×
Drawing releases (number of drawings)	×	×	×	×	×				×	×
Engineering resource—hours	×	×	×	×	×				×	×

TEST									
Critical test network (scheduled dates for critical test events)	X	X	X	X	X			X	X
Reliability growth (mean time between failures)	X	X	X	X	X			X	X
PRODUCTION									
Transition plan (scheduled dates for critical production events)	X	X	X	X	X			X	X
Delinquent requisitions (number of delinquencies)	X	X	X	X	X			X	X
Production cost (dollars)	X	X	X	X	X	X			
Labor and material requirements (resource—hours unit and material-cost unit)	X	X	X	X	X		X		
COST									
Cost and schedule performance index (ratio of budgeted and actual costs)	X	X	X	X	X	X			
Estimate at completion (dollars)	X	X	X	X	X			X	
Contingency reserve funds (percentage remaining)	X	X	X	X	X			X	
MANAGEMENT									
Specification verification (number of specification items)	X	X	X	X	X		X		
Major project risk (ranked listing)	X	X	X	X	X				X

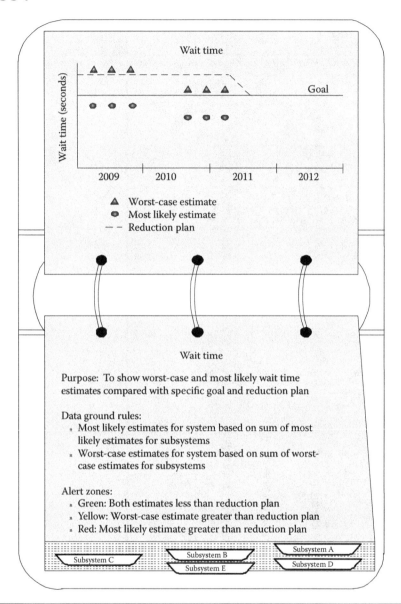

Figure 33.1   Sample indicators.

near-term requirements, but with minor modifications, it can be implemented on any type of project. It can also be used in conjunction with more elaborate probability-driven risk models to examine corresponding cost-and-schedule effects of current technical performance.

Inputs and Outputs

The technique requires that performance be tracked on a periodic basis for each technical indicator selected. This requires full cooperation from the various stakeholders in the project, including the customer and any subcontractors. It also requires that subcontractors participate in managing risk (a good benefit). The outputs can be in the form of risk management reports or briefings. The contents should include an analysis of each indicator's current performance and longer-term trends.

Major Steps in Applying the Technique

One of the first steps in adapting the technical risk assessment method to track risk performance is to choose indicators that can be applied to the development project. If the project were regarding aircraft construction, then weight and size would always be significant indicators. On the other hand, weight and size may not be regarded as important factors on a system to be installed in a building. Many standard indicators (see Table 33.1) can be used on development projects, and the utility of certain indicators will vary as the project progresses.

The selection should include indicators for the entire project, as well as indicators especially for the subsystems. The unusual aspects of a developmental project frequently require the use of special technical indicators. In the case of space systems, certain indicators are appropriate, such as the production of gases from the material in the product when exposed to a space environment. Examples of special indicators are listed in Table 33.2.

Each indicator, whether standard or special, must have ground rules established for data collection and assessment. These can be in the form of a dictionary and can describe the objective of the indicator, the reason it was chosen, the use of the indicator, and the procedure to follow when a signal is generated that indicates a problem is developing. The dictionary should have sufficient detail to inform the system operator of the indicator's meaning and the relationship of the measurement to risk.

It is advisable to explain the trends that might be expected during the life of the indicator. Expected values may take many different forms or curve functions but should include traceability to the project

Table 33.2   Sample Special Indicators

DERIVED FROM SPECIFICATION REQUIREMENTS	DERIVED FROM PROGRAM REQUIREMENTS
Performance characteristics: Speed, capacity, accuracy	Schedule: Feasibility and probability of timely accomplishment
Physical characteristics: Memory utilization, support requirements	Resources: Adequacy, distribution
Effectiveness characteristics: Reliability, safety, logistics support	Test plan: Sufficiency of planned testing
Environmental conditions: Platform, workstations	Procurement factors: Availability of multiple sources
Design and construction: Technology, packaging, materials	

goals (cost, schedule, performance, or various combinations thereof). Evaluation criteria must be set so that they will highlight situations that signal problems. Color coding (such as red, yellow, and green for high, medium, and low risk, respectively) can be used, as can percentage bands for the same type of message. These bands may vary as time progresses: that is, getting tighter as completion is nearing or getting more tolerant as time passes to indicate that a risk is disappearing. In any case, the project manager and any contractors should agree and understand the evaluation criteria chosen and their significance so as to facilitate rapid corrective action.

All this planning would be useless without a formal reporting system. This will vary in form from organization to organization and from manager to manager. It may be produced in report form for presentations to customers and management or stored as raw numerical data points. In any case, it must be in a form that both the contractor and project manager can immediately use for making critical project decisions. As in any system that requires the coordinated efforts of a matrix organization, someone must ensure that the job is done accurately and in a timely fashion and that proper decision makers are informed of risk situations.

In summary, the major steps in applying risk measurement techniques are as follows:

Select standard indicators
Select special indicators
Establish data definitions
Project expected trends

Set the evaluation criteria
Plan the reporting system
Assign responsibilities

Ensure that the job is done accurately and meets deadlines

Use of Results

Technical risk assessment reports furnish information needed to start any action to correct potential problems. Each indicator should be first examined separately and then again in related groups of indicators. In using the results, analysts must simultaneously consider the factors of cost, schedule, and technical risks.

Resource Requirements

This technique requires personnel with knowledge and skills in highly specialized technical areas. The data received are derived from many functional groups and must be analyzed by people who have skills within the various functional areas. This does not mean that each functional risk assessment area requires a full-time person. It does mean, however, that each functional area may need to contribute expertise.

Reliability

To have a reliable technical risk assessment, all major participants must understand the importance of the assessment and must be actively involved in establishing and implementing the system. Each team member should participate in the initial assessment of the project's technical risk and help select indicators to be used in tracking the risk. These same people should also provide updates for each reporting period. Raising problems early allows the manager to take action to preclude failure or at least to temper risk.

Supplemental Information

Performance tracking is not new. It has existed in one form or another for many years but has recently surged in popularity and use. Many variations on the theme are presented in this discussion. Control is one of the most critical elements in risk management, and performance tracking is one of the most effective control techniques. Another variation of the method is fully integrated performance measurement. This is a capability being developed to integrate technical, schedule, and cost performance. It also provides earned value performance measurement capability to project managers who are not receiving formal performance data from their contractors or team. The major steps are described in the following sections.

Technical Performance

Identify specific technical parameters (based on the project's objectives, plans, and specifications) and their value for performance, producibility, quality assurance, reliability, maintainability, supportability, and so on. A few examples (for an aircraft) are shown in Table 33.3.

Relate each technical parameter to specific WBS elements whenever practical. Many will relate only to the total system level, but quite a few will be derived from the specifications, which should match the WBS. In Table 33.3, for example, the topic of facility square footage under producibility could be aligned with either an existing WBS activity (such as "Lease construction hangar") or under a separate analysis activity designed exclusively for performance tracking (such as "Evaluate hangar size"). A typical parameter might be "Hangar size is not to exceed 45,000 square feet."

Define specific methods for calculating, measuring, or observing the value of each technical parameter. For example, it is important to clarify the parameters of how calculations will be derived: "Hangar size evaluations shall include all building square footage used in the actual construction of the aircraft, including all storage areas and housing facilities that are adjacent to the facility."

Assign a specific individual or organization the responsibility for managing each technical parameter and the progress toward achieving the goal value. Returning to the example of the hangar, a single team member from the maintenance team might

Table 33.3 Fully Integrated Performance Measurement—Typical Technical Parameters

PERFORMANCE	PRODUCIBILITY
Speed (kn)	Capital ($)
Weight (lb)	Human resources (number of people)
Range (NM)	Facilities (sq ft)
Power (kW)	Material ($)
Turn rate (deg/sec)	Equipment (machinery required)
Takeoff distance (ft)	Schedule (time)
Climb rate (ft/sec)	Risk (1.0–2.0)
Accuracy (ft)	
RADAR CROSS SECTION (SQ FT)	
QUALITY ASSURANCE	RELIABILITY
Scrap, rework, and repair (% of labor) Yield (% of first-time inspection successes)	Mean time between failures (MT BF) (hr/days)
Supplier rating (%)	Mean time to repair (MTTR) (hr/days)
Quality costs ($)	Probability of component/assembly failure (0–1.0)
Customer satisfaction (0–1.0)	Life-cycle analysis ($)
Software lines of code (LOC) in violation per 1000 LOC	Design-to-cost ($)
SUPPORTABILITY	MAINTAINABILITY
Parts inventory ($)	Standardization (%)
Costs ($)	Modularity (%)
Resources (human, equipment, facilities)	Update ability (0–1.0)
Modularity (%)	Special equipment ($)
Operational availability (%)	Frequency (how often, how long)
MT BF(hr/days)	Costs ($)
MTTR(hr/days)	

be assigned ongoing responsibility to account for any space utilization modifications that occur as the project progresses.

Schedule Performance

Identify or create specific schedule events where the calculation or observation is to be made.

Determine values or conditions to be achieved at each milestone. In addition, set a tolerance or alarm value to represent a threshold for corrective action.

Identify or create a specific schedule event where the goal is to be achieved.

Identify whether calculation or observation will be used to assess the event at various points in time.

Plotting the technical performance parameter value against time creates a visual portrayal of the relationship between technical performance and schedule (see Figure 33.2 and Table 33.4).

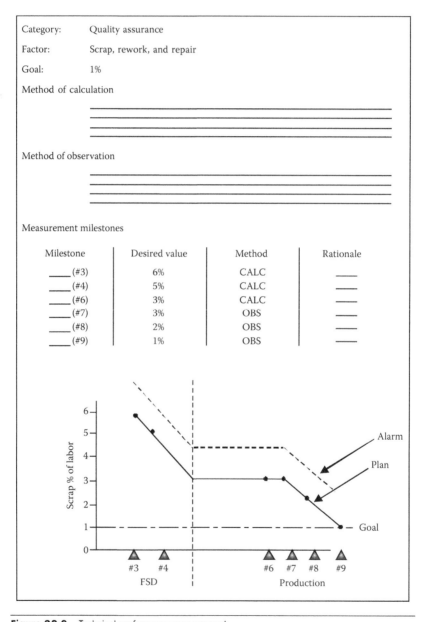

Figure 33.2 Technical performance management.

Cost Performance

Assign budgets to each technical performance parameter. These budgets may be real and may add up to contractual values, or they may be hypothetical units created just to determine relative weights. These budgets can be assigned in many different ways; the only requirements are rationality, traceability, and consistency.

Distribute the assigned budgets to each of the measurement milestones based on the engineering judgment of the percentage of the total value associated with each milestone.

Use conventional earned value techniques to measure accomplishment (such as 50-50 milestones).

Apply the schedule performance index to appropriate activities in the resource-loaded network to determine the cost impact of the technical and schedule performance.

A quick example may help clarify the technique. As shown in Table 33.4, Performance Parameter 1 has a numeric goal. A method for calculating progress against the goal has been derived. At Specific Milestone 1, progress against the goal is calculated (CALC). By Specific Milestone 3, progress against the goal can be observed (OBS); and by Specific Milestone 5, the goal should be attained (GOAL).

Selection Criteria

As with each chapter on techniques, performance tracking is assessed using selection criteria relating to resource requirements, applications, and outputs for the technique. To compare performance tracking with other techniques, review Table II.1.

Resource Requirements

The *cost* of the performance-tracking technique is limited if the systems are already in place and they are maintained on an ongoing basis. Setting up the initial indicators is somewhat time-consuming and should be done with exacting care.

The *proper facilities and equipment* are limited because little more than a spreadsheet is required to track the data and maintain accurate project records.

Table 33.4 Technical Performance Schedule Milestones

PARAMETER	SPEC OR GOAL	DEVELOPMENT PROJECT SPECIFIC MILESTONES					PRODUCTION PROJECT SPECIFIC MILESTONES					
		1	2	3	4	5	6	7	8	9	10	OPS
PERFORMANCE												
Parameter 1	V_{GOAL}	V_{CALC}			V_{OBS}	V_{GOAL}						
Parameter 2	V_{GOAL}		V_{CALC}	V_{OBS}	V_{GOAL}							
Parameter 3	V_{GOAL}			V_{CALC}		V_{OBS}		V_{OBS}	V_{GOAL}			
QUALITY ASSURANCE												
SCRAP	1_{GOAL}			6_{CALC}	5_{CALC}		3_{CALC}	3_{OBS}	2_{OBS}	1_{OBS}		
Factor 2	V_{GOAL}					V_{CALC}			V_{OBS}		V_{GOAL}	
Factor 3	V_{GOAL}		V_{CALC}		V_{CALC}	V_{CALC}	V_{OBS}	V_{GOAL}				
—												
—												
RELIABILITY												
Parameter 1	V_{GOAL}	V_{CALC}	V_{CALC}	V_{CALC}	V_{OBS}	V_{OBS}	V_{OBS}	V_{GOAL}				
Parameter 2	V_{GOAL}											

MAINTAINABILITY
Condition 1 — C_{GOAL} C_1 C_1 C_2 C_3 C_{GOAL}
Condition 2 — C_{GOAL} C_2 C_3 C_{GOAL}

—
—

SUPPORTABILITY
Condition 1 — C_{GOAL} C_1 C_2 C_3 C_{GOAL}
—

PRODUCIBILITY
Parameter 1 — V_{GOAL} V_{CALC} V_{OBS} V_{GOAL}
Parameter 2 — V_{GOAL} V_{CALC} V_{OBS} V_{OBS} V_{GOAL}

If the entire team and the project manager commit to performance tracking from the beginning of the project, their *time needed to implement* will be minimal on an individual basis. Collectively, however, the time appears more significant. If the project manager decides to implement performance tracking at midproject, then significant initiative with extensive time commitments will be required.

The *ease of use* of the technique is a function of the clarity of the instruction that the project manager provides for the effort. Although performance tracking is not overly complex, it does require clear direction for the uninitiated.

The project manager's *time commitment* for the effort primarily stems from ensuring total involvement (including all team members and contractors) in the process.

Applications

This technique can be used in most categories in Table II.1. Because the technique focuses on monitoring progress after an item is assigned, using it in the resource allocation process is of little value.

Project status reporting is a key asset of this technique. Although there are schedule-tracking tools (like earned value) and cost-tracking tools (like budgets and interim reports), performance tracking affords the project manager a means to quantify and report on quality and requirements achieved. No other tools go to quite this level of depth in establishing specific values for the activities as they relate to the requirements.

The results of performance tracking can drive *major planning decisions* because the information derived from the technique points to areas of organizational expertise and weakness. Because most organizations strive to find projects and approaches that take advantage of their strengths, performance tracking is an excellent technique for identifying what those strengths may be.

Contract strategy selection both supports and is supported by performance tracking. The strategy to support performance tracking will incorporate the vendor's or subcontractor's detailed reporting to mirror the systems that the host organization deploys. Performance tracking supports contract strategy selection by building, over time, a historic database that includes information on how the organization has performed against specific types of activities and, therefore, in relation to specific types of subcontractors and vendors.

In *milestone preparation*, performance tracking allows for a completely different type of milestone. Rather than identifying milestones for a percentage of schedule achieved or a percentage of costs spent, performance tracking allows for milestones developed against degrees of anticipated customer satisfaction achieved, based on performance to date. It can be used to establish triggers and thresholds for risk, which can then be converted into project milestones.

Design guidance is supported in much the same fashion as major planning decisions. Performance tracking identifies strengths, thereby allowing the project manager to endorse designs that work with the organization's high-skill areas.

Performance tracking may drive *source selection*, particularly if there is an established database of performance-tracking numbers. Performance tracking identifies responsibility for tasks that are at a designated level of quality, as well as for those that are not high quality. This affords the project manager a quantitative measure to apply in assessing past performance of vendors.

Performance tracking supports *budget submittal* primarily as an element of the budget's cost. Project managers need to account for the costs associated with performance tracking. But the development of performance-tracking data gives the project manager a much more detailed analysis of each work package and what it will take to achieve quality with it. As such, a budget submitted after an initial performance-tracking review may be far more accurate than one developed without using the technique.

Outputs

In general, the outputs of the technique are very good. If appropriate indicators are selected, then a quantified measure for each potential problem area is graphically presented. This information is extremely useful for project management as well as management communication.

- The indicators selected, the measures used to assess those indicators, and the personnel responsible for tracking the performance in the context of those indicators primarily drive the *accuracy* of the technique.

- Most project managers would consider the *level of detail* associated with performance tracking to be extensive. Because the technique requires a thoughtful, painstaking review of each work package to determine its contributions to quality outputs, the level of detail is often much higher than is normally developed in a project without performance tracking.

- The main *utility* of the technique is in tracking project quality and providing management communication both internally and to the customer. By tracking all the various aspects of the project and the deliverables, the project manager can, on short notice, develop comprehensive analyses of the organization's ability to provide the deliverables as promised to the customer.

Summary

The performance-tracking technique challenges the project team to meet preordained success criteria for each element of the project. No single significant component is overlooked, and team members clearly understand what is expected of them. In many organizations, that is a significant shift from an attitude that pushes team members toward an overall satisfactory deliverable to the customer. Performance tracking propels the organization toward higher levels of quality.

34

RISK REVIEWS AND AUDITS

Although risk reviews and audits come in a variety of forms and formats, there are sufficient common elements to discuss them as a whole. The key for any quality risk review is to acknowledge that it is a comprehensive examination rather than a review of a single risk event in isolation. The objective of a risk review is to reevaluate the risk environment, the risk events, and their relative probability and impact. A risk audit is a more exhaustive assessment that involves a task-by-task, risk-by-risk analysis, as well as an examination of the process efficacy as a whole.

Technique Description

For both risk reviews and risk audits, the technique most often involves conducting a meeting with team members and any external risk stakeholders (such as vendors and subcontractors). The session is focused exclusively on the risks, with an emphasis on the elements and perspectives that have changed.

When Applicable

Risk reviews are conducted when change is planned, when change occurs, and at regular intervals. The changes need not be dramatic but rather only sufficient to alter the climate in which the risks occur. As for the regular intervals, they should be appropriate to the project's schedule and scope. A project of several years in duration may be host to quarterly risk reviews, whereas a project of two months may have a single midterm review or weekly reviews, depending upon the organization's investment in the project and the complexity of the project. A risk audit entails a more exhaustive review, normally conducted either at a predetermined milestone or when a major problem prompts a dramatic shift in the potential for project success. The audit frequently focuses on the success or failure of the risk response strategies.

Inputs and Outputs

Inputs and outputs are largely the same as for the risk process as a whole. The inputs include the risk management plan, the WBS, the risk event listing, and earlier assessments of the events for probability and impact. Outputs are updates to risk documentation, including any changes to the risk events, probabilities, impacts, response strategies, or environment. The output for an audit may also include updates to the risk management plan.

Major Steps in Applying the Technique

The steps in applying risk reviews and audits are largely the risk management process in miniature. A good risk review will include risk re-identification, requalification, re-quantification, and a reassessment of responses.

- *Identify the risks.* In a risk review or audit, risk identification includes both the basic practice of identifying risks using the WBS or idea-generation techniques, as well as the identification of risks based on project documentation and experience to date. An audit will also include an evaluation of the effectiveness of the original process for risk identification.
- *Qualify the risks.* Establish the probability and impact for each risk event identified, based on any organizational rating scheme (see Chapter 25). This should include both new risks identified as well as those risks identified in previous reviews or during the original risk identification process. Again, the audit will include an evaluation of the effectiveness of the qualitative terms established for the process.
- *Quantify the risks.* To establish contingency funds for any newly identified serious risks, the risks identified as the most significant (during risk requalification) should be evaluated for their potential financial impact and their relative probability of occurrence. If there is any question as to the validity of the initial quantification, it should also be reflected in a risk audit.

Reassess responses. This is the most comprehensive step in a risk audit. It involves examining each risk response identified to date and establishing the level of success, the potential for future success, and any repercussions associated with implementing the strategy. In Chapter 3, "The Risk Management Structure," the discussion on watch lists points to how project management software tools can be applied to store data on basic risk analyses and approaches. If those tables are expanded, then they can be applied here as well, using additional text columns to record response strategies, outcomes, and follow-up requirements:

WBS #	Task Name	Text 12	Text 13	Text 14	Text 15	Text 16

Renamed, the fields take on a different look and now support the risk audit:

WBS #	Task Name	Risk Event	Risk Response	Response Owner	Outcome	Follow-up Required

On the other hand, in a risk review, the reassessment may be little more than an examination of the risk responses applied to date and an update on implementation plans for the near term for the remaining strategies.

Communicate updates. No risk review or audit is complete until the findings have been communicated across the organization to those who need the information and can apply it in the project context. Without communicating newly identified risks, shifting priorities, and changed strategies, a risk audit becomes nothing more than an administrative exercise. It takes on life only when those responsible for implementation are aware of what has been planned, and how the risk management approach has changed, if at all.

Use of Results

The results are used in the day-to-day management of risks on the project. They are also used to establish any newly needed contingency funding and to clarify strategy for handling risk in the near term.

Resource Requirements

A proper risk audit should involve those who have been responsible for risk management on the project to date, as well as the project manager and any team members who will be taking on new responsibilities in the near term. The last group is doubly important because they frequently have the lowest awareness of project risk and may be facing the most significant (and yet invisible) risks due to their new roles in the project. When team members do not know what to look for, it frequently remains hidden.

Reliability

The reliability of these practices relates directly to the reliability of risk management as a process. Because they are little more than a microcosm of the risk process, they reflect on the reliability of risk management as a course of action. The reliability of the audits and reviews will be high if—and only if—they are applied consistently. As with any effective process, consistency is essential. If the reviews and audits are conducted at regular intervals and carried out consistently as change occurs or is planned, then their reliability will be high. If, however, they are conducted on an ad hoc basis, then there will be a far lower level of reliability.

Selection Criteria

As with each chapter on techniques, risk reviews and audits are assessed using selection criteria relating to resource requirements, applications, and outputs for the technique. To compare risk reviews and audits with other techniques, review Table II.1 in Part II.

Resource Requirements

The *cost* of risk reviews and audits ties to the levels of risk associated with the project and with the thoroughness of the initial work done in establishing risk events, their priority, and the responses. The more documentation and history that are generated in the first cycle through the process, then the more costly the review will be. Even so, the most exhaustive risk reviews and audits will rarely take more than a couple of days' time, except for those projects spanning multiple years.

Proper facilities and equipment for a risk review generally include a location where large volumes of documentation can be spread out for analysis and/or where there is a personal computer projection display to allow for group data sharing. Otherwise, very little equipment is required.

As described for cost, the *time needed to implement* the technique is a function of the magnitude of the risk assessment and response effort. Generally, a matter of days, at most, should be required for a risk review or audit.

Risk reviews have relatively high *ease of use*; but because they follow a consistent practice, they are sometimes perceived as administratively onerous. That perception is ill-founded, particularly in organizations where data are well maintained and where processes are pursued consistently.

The project manager's *time commitment* for the risk review is the time required to assemble relevant project data and conduct the audit itself. As stated before, the time commitment should be minimal.

Applications

Risk reviews and audits provide strong support for *project status reporting* as the reviews serve primarily a status function. Audits (because of their comprehensive analyses of risk strategies and their applications to date) provide even more valuable insight into project work to date, changes in the environment, and efficacy of the overall risk approach.

Major planning decisions receive support during risk reviews because the reviews provide guidance on which planning decisions in the project have been effective and which risk strategies are bearing fruit. A reassessment of the strategies will facilitate any decision making required at midproject.

Because risk reviews and audits are generally conducted at midproject, their support of *contract strategy selection* is extremely low. However, audits serve a valuable role in helping to identify strategies that may be more appropriate for future projects of a similar nature.

Risk reviews do not support *milestone preparation*.

Risk audits and reviews can support *design guidance*, particularly as they apply to shifts in approach at midproject. Because risk reviews are intended to highlight new areas of risk and new strategies, a thorough risk review may support any changes in design.

Although *source selection* relies heavily on risk analysis, risk reviews offer support only on those midterm decisions for sources or vendors that may be brought in to address a need not initially considered at project inception.

As a project progresses, budgets often need to be reconsidered; consequently, risk reviews provide strong support for *budget submittal*. By establishing any new needs for contingency funding or to finance new risk strategies, there is a strong correlation between risk reviews and any midterm budget assessment.

Outputs

The *accuracy* of the technique is high, as it is built on a much greater data foundation than the original risk assessments and because the process is more familiar to participants at midproject than it normally is early in the project.

The *level of detail* associated with the technique is directly related to the level of detail originally generated for the risk analysis. The more detailed the original risk analysis is, then the more extensive the risk review will ultimately be.

Utility on this method is high because it is a brief reiteration of the risk management process in toto.

Summary

Risk reviews and audits serve a valuable function in forcing organizations to look at risk in light of new information, changes in the environment, and the passage of time. Believing that project risk will remain static throughout the project life cycle is a foolhardy assumption. Risk changes are virtually constant. Vigilance is essential. Consistency affords the project manager and the team the ability to justify the reviews. To conduct only a single risk analysis at the beginning of the project is analogous to putting oil in a car once, only when the vehicle is purchased. Conditions change and risks change. A fresh perspective is sometimes essential.

35

OTHER COMMON TECHNIQUES

Cost Performance Reports Analysis

Cost performance reports (CPRs) have become useful in uncovering areas in which technical problems are causing variances. In these reports, team members explain cost and schedule variances using narrative to indicate the specific problem causing the variance. Many of the variances reported can signal risk situations as they are developing, such as late vendor or subcontractor deliveries. Continuing these types of schedule slips can put an entire project schedule at risk. Normally, project managers are limited in what they can do to alleviate these situations except when the sponsoring organization is causing the delays. In such cases, high-level coordination with the sponsoring organization can sometimes alleviate problems. However, this does not always work. For example, tight control over a highly specialized, highly technical subcontractor may not be very effective and the risk of inaccurate specialty work may add risk to risks in other areas of the project.

Just as cost variance may drive risk, risk can also drive cost variances. Cost growth must be considered a significant risk item. The CPRs are designed to display cost growth as a variance and then to discuss that variance in terms of cause, effect, and corrective actions that might alleviate the situation.

If the project is using CPRs as cost reporting tools, then they should also be used for risk assessment and analysis. The discussion of variances in that report can contain data vital to risk identification, qualification, quantification, and response development. The reports may also present new and previously undiscovered risks. These risks should then be investigated to ascertain their effects on the project.

Independent Technical Assessment

An independent technical assessment is nothing more than a formal technical review that an expert (or experts) in the field conducts to determine the project's potential for achieving specific objectives. An independent technical assessment requires personnel other than those subordinate to the project manager and, therefore, will always require the approval of some higher level of authority. The timing of these reviews is crucial. If problems are found, then there must be time to correct them before any critical milestone reviews. This technique has been cited for substantially reducing project risk, especially risk associated with multi-organizational involvement.

Technique Description

A team of experts from outside the project office reviews a number of specified aspects of the project. The team usually consists of senior personnel who can make timely evaluations of project activities and progress based on their extensive experience. Team size can vary with the size of the project and the number of issues the team is tasked to review. The entire process is usually limited to several weeks of near-full-time effort on a multiyear project. On a smaller effort or a short-term project, however, the assessment may last only a day or two. The final product is a briefing to the sponsor or manager authorizing the review, as well as a written report.

When Applicable

This technique can be used to support design reviews. It can also be used to address perceptions of a troubled project. A good time for an independent technical assessment is when a project is (or is perceived to be) in trouble. If the trouble is real, then this technique will give the project manager added credibility and will quiet critics. When possible, such reviews should be scheduled to cause minimum disruption of milestone activities. An independent technical assessment is usually more appropriate during system development than during actual implementation or production.

Inputs and Outputs

Inputs will vary widely depending on the issues to be addressed and the team members' expertise. Team members will obtain necessary information through project team briefings, reviews of project documentation, interviews, and visits to project facilities. The expertise and experience that team members bring with them are important inputs. The most common outputs are briefings to the sponsor or manager. As appropriate, other stakeholders may also be brought into the briefing. The briefing must address each of several criteria or issues defined at the outset of the review. It should also include recommendations for follow-up action.

Major Steps in Applying the Technique

The following procedure is common to most independent technical assessments:

Upper management (with control over the expert resources required) calls for the review.

The project manager and upper management specify issues to be addressed.

The project manager and upper management form the review team.

The team gathers the required information about project objectives, status, resources, and activities.

The team analyzes the information gathered.

The team and the project manager present their results to the authority requesting the review and to other appropriate stakeholders.

Use of Results

Independent technical assessments are useful for design, contracting, strategy, planning, and implementation coordination. When review results are favorable, project risk is reduced immediately. An associated benefit is the ability to meet pending milestone reviews.

Resource Requirements

Two types of resources are required to carry out an independent technical assessment. First, as many as 10 experts may be needed to form the review team. (Team size will depend largely on the expertise required and the magnitude of the project.) The team should include experienced personnel from the middle-management level or higher. These people should anticipate having to commit roughly half their time for the duration of the assessment.

In addition to team resource requirements, the project manager must arrange a number of informational briefings and interviews to provide the review team with the required information quickly. If review team members are from off-site locations, then the project manager may have substantial administrative tasks in dealing with the needs of out-of-town guests.

Reliability

Even though the reliability of an independent technical assessment is usually high, it depends somewhat on the quality of team members in terms of their recognized level of expertise. Although team independence is essential, cooperation between the team and the project manager is nevertheless also a requisite trait. The project manager must provide all required information, and the review team must present a balanced picture rather than focusing on the most negative areas. The major disadvantage of an independent technical assessment is that it can disrupt other project activities. This is especially true if it uncovers deficiencies and there is not enough time for corrective actions before an important milestone. Therefore, the review schedule is an important consideration.

Selection Criteria

The selection criteria for this technique are all rather positive. Although independent technical assessments do not place great demands on any single resource during the project, they do require some of the project manager's time to support the individual or team. Many organizations require project managers to submit periodic jeopardy reports that mirror much of the information that independent technical assessments generate. The technique has applications across the project life cycle and provides other key pieces of data that can readily be incorporated into the historic project database that every organization should maintain. Outputs may be marginally less accurate than other techniques because they reflect an individual or group perspective. But the level of detail and utility of the technique is without peer: it is easy to understand, requires little training, and provides valuable real-time information.

Independent Cost Estimates

Independent cost estimates must be developed one or more times for many projects, depending on the level of control that the sponsoring organization demands. Historically, it has been the perception that project managers drive these estimates because they naturally tend to be optimistic regarding the risks and costs of the project (particularly in the early stages) due to their commitment to achieving project goals. As a result, independent cost estimates have become popular in an effort to provide decision makers with data reflecting a neutral viewpoint. The premise is that because cost estimators are outside the influence of the project, they should develop estimates that more accurately portray the challenges, risks, and costs associated with developing and implementing projects.

An independent cost estimate basically entails the same procedures, methodologies, and techniques that would be used to develop any major project cost estimate. Ideally, an independent estimate should select methodologies and techniques different from those that underlie the original cost estimate. In addition, an independent cost estimate should incorporate a detailed comparison of the two approaches and explain the differences.

The key aspect of the independent cost estimate technique is that it is developed in organizational channels separate from the project. This helps it serve as an analytical tool to validate or cross-check estimates the project manager develops. This second opinion helps avoid the risk that some significant costs have been overlooked or that the project manager's sense of advocacy has resulted in low estimates that could jeopardize the success of the project.

To the extent that a technical staff detached from the project team advise and support those preparing independent cost estimates, some independent assessment of technical risks may also be accomplished while preparing the cost estimate. Because technical and cost aspects are inextricably woven, an independent perspective on the technical perspectives of the project may ultimately lead to a revision of the independent cost estimate as well.

The selection criterion for independent cost estimates is that it is resource intensive; thus, management may not approve it for any but the most significant projects. The applications for the technique are almost exclusive to the beginning of the project or major design decision points. Outputs from the technique vary widely in value because the organization may or may not be equipped to handle the information this technique provides.

Glossary

Acceptance: The risk response strategy of acknowledgment and lack of a proactive response. Passive risk acceptance involves taking no action and tolerating any potential outcomes. Active risk acceptance involves either setting aside contingency funds or establishing contingency plans (contingent responses) that will be applied only if the risk event actually comes to pass. *See also* avoidance, mitigation, *and* transference.

Activity: A component of project work that may or may not be subdivided into other elements (such as tasks). *See also* task.

Activity duration: The planned time associated with accomplishing a specific element of project work (based on work and resource allocations).

Activity-on-arrow: *See* arrow diagramming method.

Activity-on-node: *See* precedence diagramming method.

Actual cost: Cost incurred in the execution of a project and/or its tasks as evidence by generally accepted accounting principles.

Analogy-based estimating: Estimating practice that draws on elements, components or aspects of one project (and the costs associated therewith) in determining the cost of similar elements, components or aspects in a project under consideration.

Analogy comparisons: Risk identification tool that draws on elements, components or aspects of one project (and the risks that were associated therewith) in determining whether similar elements, components or aspects of a project under consideration may or may not drive similar risk events. *See also* Lessons learned.

Appetite: The degree to which an organization or individual feels compelled to exert influence over risk events.

Arrow: The activity component of the arrow diagramming method (ADM). In ADM, the arrow represents the work to be performed, initiated from a circle (representing the beginning of the activity) and terminated into a circle (representing the end milestone of the activity, which may also be the start milestone of the next activity in sequence).

Arrow diagramming method (ADM): Network diagramming practice using arrows to represent activities graphically, with arrows initiated from a circle (representing the beginning milestone of the activity) and terminated into a circle (representing the end milestone of the activity, which may also be the start milestone of the next activity in sequence). Employing only finish-to-start relationships, the diagram progresses from left to right, illustrating all dependencies among the project activities.

Assumption: A belief (not yet validated) held regarding any aspect of a project or project performance. Assumptions are applied for making decisions in an environment where information is deficient.

Assumptions analysis: A review of project assumptions either to validate them or to determine whether a project (or project organization can withstand the impact if the assumptions prove invalid.

Attitude: The degree to which an individual will act on risk appetites (either in accordance or in conflict with the appetites).

Audit: A formal, methodologically driven review of any aspect of a project. Often modified by a specific adjective (such as in schedule audit, earned value audit, financial audit, and so forth), audits focus on ensuring a comprehensive review of the practices under consideration.

Avoidance: The risk response strategy that creates an environment where the organization and/or the project is no longer potentially exposed to the threat in question. This can be accomplished by eliminating the causes, changing approaches, or stopping projects altogether. *See also* acceptance, mitigation, *and* transference.

Bar chart: *See* Gantt chart.

Baseline: The approved, accepted project plan that serves as the metric against which project performance will be evaluated through the life of the project. It is often modified by an adjective (such as in schedule baseline, cost baseline, requirements baseline) to define the nature of the baseline in question.

Brainstorming: Idea-generation technique that involves presenting a premise to a group and allowing and encouraging all members of that group to provide their insights in a free-form fashion without criticism or commentary. The technique is designed to allow participants to build on the ideas of others and to generate a large volume of information in a relatively short span of time. Frequently applied as a risk identification technique.

Breakdown: Logical decomposition of components into subcomponents. In scope management, work is decomposed into its component elements (as in the work breakdown structure). In risk management, risk categories are decomposed into their specific risk areas and risk events (as in the risk breakdown structure).

Budget: Scheduled time and/or funds committed to a project by management. Normally established by the baseline (plus any contingency), the budget represents the anticipated expenditure of time and/or funds by the organization for a project.

Business risk: Risk with the possibility of loss or gain

Cause-and-effect diagram: *See* Ishikawa diagram

Chance: Possibility or probability of a given outcome in a situation that is not certain. *See also* probability.

Checklist: Risk identification support technique that uses a list of specific actions, behaviors, environmental considerations, or other factors to highlight risks that have been identified with sufficient frequency in the past that they are considered endemic within the organization or the project environment.

Closeout phase: The final phase in a generic project life cycle in which project commitments are fulfilled, documented, and archived for historical purposes.

Concept phase: The ideation phase in a generic project life cycle in which the project is conceived, initiated and accepted.

Confidence interval: The range of parameters (such as cost, schedule, and performance) between which a given likelihood of incidence exists.

Confidence level: Normally expressed as a percentage, the confidence level expressed the degree to which there is a (most always quantifiable) belief that a given parameter r set of parameters can be achieved. At the mean of a normal distribution, there is normally a 50 percent confidence level that that value can be achieved.

Contingency: Financial allowance, schedule allowance or specific action established to be applied only if a risk event actually comes to fruition. *See also* contingency reserve *and* contingency plan.

Contingency allowance: *See* contingency reserve

Contingency plan (or Contingent response): Specific action or actions established to be applied if a risk event comes to fruition. Although the plan is developed prior to the risk event's occurrence, contingency plans differ from the mitigation strategy in that contingency plans require no resource actions until or unless the risk comes to pass.

Contingency reserves: Financial or schedule allowance established to be applied when risk events cause harm to the cost, schedule, or requirements. Some organizations include this value in the performance measurement baseline (PMB), while others include it in the budget baseline, but not in the PMB.

Contract: The culmination of an offer and acceptance between two or more parties, obligating the parties to specific performance.

Contract work breakdown structure (CWBS): A decomposition of a project product into its components that are prepared in direct response to customer requirements. The CWBS serves as a reporting structure for the contractor to the customer. *See also* work breakdown structure.

Control

1. The process of taking action to report problems, correct them, and prevent future concerns based on comparative analysis between planned performance and actual outcomes.
2. As a risk response strategy, control is another name for mitigation (the effort to minimize the probability and/or impact of a given risk event).

Cost baseline: The authorized budget for a project, allocated across a timeline to allow for monitoring of planned performance.

Cost estimate: The forecast cost for a project or project element, normally expressed in a range.

Cost estimating: The process of generating forecast costs for projects or project elements.

Cost estimating relationship (CER): A mathematically driven cost forecasting method based on the observation that costs of systems correlate with design or performance variables.

Cost performance report (CPR): Project progress report delineating costs planned, costs incurred and work accomplished. Such reports may also include references to schedule progress.

Cost risk

1. Risk events related to failure to achieve cost and budget targets.
2. Overall evaluation of possible financial loss or gain associated with a project.

Crawford slip method (CSM): Idea-generation technique that involves establishing a clear premise, collecting participant responses (on paper slips), and then repeating the process 10 times to extract all information available.

Critical path: In network diagramming, the path through the network with the least or zero float. The critical path represents both the shortest possible duration for the project as planned and the single longest path through the network. *See also* critical path method.

Critical path method (CPM): Network review process that involves establishing the earliest and latest possible start and finish dates for tasks to determine the available amount of float on the project and to discern which path will ultimately be the primary driver for the finish date of the project. The early schedule is determined by starting from the project start date and adding the duration of activities through the end of the schedule. The late schedule is determined by starting from the end of the project and subtracting the duration of activities through the beginning of the schedule. Tasks that have the same early and late dates are deemed "critical."

Critical risk: Any risk that may endanger the project or the project organization as a whole

Cumulative density function (CDF): The area under a probability density function up to a given point and the probability of an occurrence within that area.

Decision analysis: An assessment of decision alternatives, their outcomes, and the probability of those outcomes and the alternatives that may surface while waiting for those outcomes to occur.

Decision making: Analyzing alternatives to determine a course of action and then taking that action.

Decision tree: Diagram to graphically represent the decision analysis process, including separate branches for each decision to be made and for each respective event that may result from that decision. The diagram highlights the events, their probabilities, costs and outcomes.

Deflection: Transferring risk from one party to another through insurance, warranties, guarantees, or contractual arrangements.

Delphi technique: An idea-generation or clarification technique designed to take advantage of experts' insights through iterative written questioning and followed by data sharing and clarification.

Dependency: A precedence relationship between two activities in a network diagram that illustrates the logical connection between those activities. *See also* logical relationship.

Development phase: In a generic project life cycle, the phase during which project plans are generated in full and the project performance measurement baseline is fully established and integrated.

Documentation review: Risk identification and review technique whereby project documents are analyzed and parsed in-depth to generate ideas on risks that may be associated with the documents' content or intent.

Duration: The interval (in working time) for performance of a task, activity, or project as expressed in units of time (such as workdays, weeks, or months).

Earned value (EV): A project assessment technique that involves comparing the performance measurement baseline of time and cost with actual task performance and costs incurred.

Effort: The resource consumption level required to perform a task, activity or project (expressed as effort-hours, effort-days, effort-months, and so forth). For example, 10 resources working on an activity for an hour would represent 10 effort-hours consumed.

Estimate: The forecast for any aspect of project performance (such as cost, schedule, materials consumption, and so forth), normally expressed in a range.

Estimating relationships: Any mathematically driven forecasting method based on the observation that performance aspects of systems correlate with design or performance variables.

Expected monetary value (EMV): In quantitative risk assessments, the value of probability times impact for a given threat or opportunity. For example, a $40 opportunity with a 10 percent chance of occurrence has an EMV of $4.

Expert interviews: One-on-one exchanges with individuals having significant project and/or technical expertise to determine potential risk events, assess risks, determine risk strategies, or assess strategy efficacy.

Expert judgment: Insights shared by individuals with significant project and/or technical expertise relating to specific requests for information.

Feasibility: Viability of a given idea, approach or strategy; the likelihood and/or potential efficacy of a solution or effort.

Finish-to-finish (FF): In precedence diagramming method (PDM), the relationship between activities where the finish of an activity (i) serves to establish the finish of its successor (j). Described by the phrase: "Task i must finish and then (lag) days later, task j may finish." *See also* logical relationship.

Fishbone diagram: *See* Ishikawa diagram.

Float: The amount of time that an activity may be delayed without having an impact on either the next activity in sequence (free float) or on the project finish date as a whole (total, path, or network float).

Flow diagram: Also known as a flowchart, a graphic display of the relationships among activities to illustrate the process associated with those activities.

Gantt chart: A time-scaled bar chart of project activity with tasks listed on the left and horizontal bars representing their duration and timing on the right. Named for creator Henry Gantt.

General and administrative expense (G&A): Expense associated with management, administration, and facilities costs incurred by an organization. G&A is normally incurred by projects as a percentage of other project costs, either material or human resource.

Graphical evaluation and review technique (GERT): Probabilistic conditional diagramming technique that allows for network analysis of project activities, while acknowledging that some activities may have to be repeated in the performance of the project and other activities may be obviated by project realities.

Histogram: Vertical bar chart frequently used to illustrate resource allocation over time.

Impact: The severity associated with a given threat or opportunity; an assessment of the level of influence that a risk may have.

Impact analysis: Quantitative or qualitative evaluation of the severity associated with a given threat or opportunity; an assessment of the level of influence that a risk may have and how that may influence project or task outcomes.

Implementation phase: In a generic project life cycle, the phase during which the majority of the actual work in producing deliverables is performed.

Independence (statistical independence): The state of two unrelated risk events where the occurrence of one has absolutely no influence over the probability of the occurrence of the other.

Independent cost estimate

1. A forecast cost developed using alternative sources and/or techniques to validate an existing cost estimate.
2. A forecast cost developed outside the normal project management organization or structure

Independent technical assessment

1. An evaluation of project capabilities, performance, or approach conducted by individuals (experts) outside the normal project management organization or structure.
2. An evaluation used to validate project capabilities, performance, or approach using alternative sources and/or techniques.

Inputs: Information or deliverables that serve as the foundation, guidance, or source material for a process, tool, or technique that will convert them for other uses.

Insurable risk: Also known as "pure risk," this term applies to any risk that has the opportunity only for loss. In business language, these are risks that an organization cannot manage independently, and as such, they must be managed through external means.

Ishikawa diagram: Also known as a "cause-and-effect diagram" or a "fishbone diagram," this graphical representation is highlighted by a specific risk event (or "effect"), which is then analyzed into progressively greater levels of detail to determine the causes, the causes of the causes, the causes of those causes, and so on, until a root cause (or root causes) has been discovered. The initial breakdown of an Ishikawa diagram frequently begins by analyzing causes in four categories: human, method, materials, and machine. Named after its creator, Kaoru Ishikawa.

Lessons learned: Documentation capturing specific project experiences and the ways in which managers and team members worked to deal with and resolve those experiences. Lessons learned are documented in such a way that the behaviors associated with resolution of the first experience become repeatable throughout the organization.

Level of effort: The amount of resource time and commitment required to accomplish a given task or component of a task. May be expressed in resource hours, days, weeks, or months. May also refer to general work (overhead) not readily captured under specific task headings.

Life cycle: Conceptually, the entirety of a project or system expressed in documentation or graphics from beginning to end. In a project, the life cycle will include phases such as concept, development, implementation, and termination. In a system, the life cycle will include phases such as ideation, creation, acceptance, operations and maintenance, and decommissioning.

Life-cycle costs: The totality of costs associated with a project or system life cycle

Logical relationship: In precedence diagramming, the relationship between any two tasks. The four logical relationships are finish-start, finish-finish, start-start, and start-finish. The relationships fill in the blanks in the statement (where i is the preceding activity and j is i's successor): "Task i must _____ and then (the lag value) days later, task j may_____."

Management reserve: Funds that management has set aside (or allocated) to resolve risks that the project manager could not (or should not) have anticipated and that are outside the purview of the project and its plans (unknown unknowns).

Mean: The average of a set of numbers.

Median: From a sample of numbers, the value for which an equal number of the sample set is both above and below that value. The midpoint of the samples.

Metrics: Any established numeric values used to evaluate or assess any characteristic(s) of a project, task, resource, or deliverable.

Milestone: An activity of zero duration, used to mark or represent a significant event or achievement in a project.

Mitigation: Risk response strategy designed to proactively minimize either or both the probability or impact of a risk event on the project (or organization) as a whole.

Mode: The peak of a probability curve. The high point that represents the juncture at which the likelihood of a given risk moves from increasing to decreasing

Model: A representation of a concept, often applying mathematical values, to provide an alternative context for interpretation and to provide a consistent standard.

Modified Churchman–Ackoff method: A process of prioritizing risk events according to their probability of occurrence.

Monte Carlo analysis: A simulation-drive, iterative statistical analysis of possible project outcomes that generates a curve to reflect the likelihood of given time and cost parameters based on the outcomes of the multiple iterations.

Most likely time: In a PERT analysis, the time (work duration) believed to have the greatest probability of occurrence.

Network: A graphic representation of a project's tasks and their dependencies, arranged in sequential fashion from left to right.

Network analysis: Using a graphic representation of a project's tasks and their dependencies, a review of the earliest possible start and finish times and the latest possible start and finish times for the activities involved. May be conducted using the arrow diagramming method or precedence diagramming method.

Network-based scheduling: Project scheduling practice where task and project timing is established based on activities and their interdependencies.

Network diagram: Graphic display of a project's activities and their dependencies, arranged in sequential fashion from left to right. If tasks are displayed on lines between nodes, then the diagram is built using the arrow diagramming method. If tasks are displayed on nodes connected by dependencies, then the diagram is built using the precedence diagramming method.

Node: Junction point in an activity-on-arrow network diagram or activity in a precedence diagram (connected by dependencies).

Nominal group technique (NGT): Idea-generation technique where participants are asked to document as many responses to a given question as possible on a sheet of paper within an allotted period of time. Next, the responses are aggregated, and participants are asked to prioritize or rank the responses. The rankings are then evaluated, and all items generated by all participants are ranked as a whole.

Odds: Likelihood of occurrence, normally expressed as a ratio. A risk with equal likelihood of occurring or not as 1:1 odds (the classic 50:50 chance). The odds of throwing a given value on a die are 5:1 because five sides do not have the value sought, whereas one side does.

Opportunity

1. The positive aspect of risk. An uncertain event, that if it occurs, will work to the benefit of the organization or project in question.
2. The known potential, positive rationale for pursuing a given approach or project.

Optimistic time: In the Program Evaluation and Review Technique (PERT) process, the quickest reasonable time (working duration) in which a task can be completed.

Outputs: Information or deliverables generated by a process, tool, or technique

Parametric cost estimating: Forecasting practice based on historical data that have been analyzed and converted to formulae that can be used to predict the outcomes of future projects or aspects of projects (for example, dollars per square foot of construction).

Performance: Work toward achieving a specific objective and the efficacy thereof.

Performance tracking: Assessment of work toward achieving a specific objective and the efficacy thereof, specifically using tracking metrics and tools such as time, cost, earned value, or technical performance measurement.

PERT: *See* Program Evaluation and Review Technique.

Pessimistic time: In the Program Evaluation and Review Technique (PERT) process, the longest reasonable time (working duration) in which it is believed a task will be achieved.

Plan evaluation: A risk identification practice that involves parsing through the elements of a plan to identify areas of potential risk (based on missing information and/or particularly challenging plan elements.

Planning meetings: Group sessions used to establish future approaches to work, risk management, or any aspect of project performance.

PMBOK® Guide: The popular name and trademark for *A Guide to the Project Management Body of Knowledge,* authored by the Project Management Institute, Inc.

PMI®: The Project Management Institute, Inc. of Newtown Square, PA, USA.

PMI-RMP®: The Risk Management Professional certification issued by the Project Management Institute, Inc.

PMP®: The Project Management Professional certification granted by the Project Management Institute, Inc.

Precedence diagramming method (PDM): Network analysis technique where tasks are established on nodes that are connected by dependencies. Dependency relationships may include finish-to-start, start-to-start, finish-to-finish, and start-to-finish relationships. Lines between the nodes reflect the sequence and nature of the relationships. *See also* activity-on-node diagramming.

Probability: Mathematical expression of the possibility or likelihood of occurrence, normally expressed as a percentage.

Probability density function (PDF): A means of expressing the range within a population between two points or values as a probability of occurrence between those values.

Program Evaluation and Review Technique (PERT): Network analysis technique that applies a mathematical weighted average to all durations ((Optimistic + (4*Most Likely) + Pessimistic)/6) to establish the durations of the individual tasks within the network. Standard deviations for the individual tasks can also be determined applying this technique with a different formula ((Optimistic—Pessimistic)/6). Moreover, for a path in the network, the standard deviation for the path as a whole can be determined using the square root of the sum of the squares of the standard deviations of the individual tasks on that path.

Programmatic risk: Risk involved in obtaining and using applicable resources and activities that may be outside the project manager's control, but can affect the project's duration.

Project: Any unique, time-constrained undertaking or venture to produce a planned outcome that requires the integration and application of resources.

Project Management Body of Knowledge (PMBOK): A compendium of best practice in project management. Colloquially known as the *PMBOK® Guide*, it normally refers to the document *A Guide to the Project Management Body of Knowledge* published by the Project Management Institute, Inc.

Project Management Institute, Inc. (PMI): PMI is the international nonprofit association representing the project management profession and serves as the primary certifying body for project managers and project risk managers.

Project Management Professional (PMP): The prevailing certification for project managers who have both met the professional requirements and passed the certification exam offered by PMI.

Project manager: Individual responsible and accountable for performance on projects and production of project deliverables (whether service, process, or tangible deliverables). Responsible for integrating, planning, executing, controlling and closing out projects.

Project risk

1. The cumulative risk on a project as a whole, often expressed in terms of dollars, ranges of potential outputs, or other metric terms

2. Any threat or opportunity associated with a project, consisting of a specific event, its likelihood of occurrence, and the impact if it should occur.

Project risk management: The effort to plan for, identify, qualify, quantify, respond to, and control project risk.

Project stakeholder: Any individual or entity that directly influences or is influenced by a project and its success or failure

Project templates: Forms, formats and protocols designed to render processes consistent in the project environment. Risk lists, forms, and registers are common examples of project templates.

Pugh matrix: *See* risk response matrix

Qualitative risk assessment: Determination of project risk probability, impact, urgency, frequency, detectability, and/or contingency using relative, nonnumeric values (such as high, medium, and low).

Quality risk: Risk related directly to the capability of the project outputs to perform as per the requirements.

Quantitative risk assessment: Determination of project risk probability, impact, urgency, frequency, detectability, and/or contingency using numeric values.

Range: The complete extent of all possibilities for a given set of values.

Rating scheme: *See* risk rating scheme

Regression analysis: Determination of the values of constants in a mathematical expression that gives results that are closest to the observed values associated with values of the data used in the expression. Regression analysis is a process by which the relationship between paired variables can be described mathematically using the tendency of jointly correlated random variables to approach their mean.

Request for proposals (RFP): A contract bid document used in solicitations for goods and services of a complex nature. Frequently involves some negotiation and assumes that cost will not be the sole deciding factor in bid evaluations.

Reserve: Money or time set aside to deal with project risks either proactively or reactively. *See also* management reserve *and* contingency reserve.

Risk: *See* project risk

Risk allowance: Time or money set aside to deal with project uncertainty. *See also* contingency reserve *and* management reserve.

Risk analysis: Qualitative or quantitative evaluations of the potential impact and probability of project risk events. *See also* risk assessment.

Risk assessment

1. Individual or organizational evaluation of project risks to determine whether they exceed project or organizational thresholds.
2. Identification and analysis of risk events, to determine their nature, likelihood of occurrence, and the qualitative or quantitative impact they may have on the project. Also called risk evaluation.

Risk avoidance: *See* avoidance

Risk breakdown structure (RBS): A decomposition of project risks and risk categories into their component risks; used to identify common sources of risk and areas of potential concern within the project and the organization. *See also* sources of risk.

Risk budget: Money and time set aside to deal with risks of all types. The sum of management reserve and contingency reserve.

Risk database: Repository for storing risk information on a project. *See also* risk register.

Risk deflection: *See* deflection.

Risk description: Written summary of a risk event, normally couched as the event that may happen and the implications and impacts it may cause.

Risk drivers

1. Technical, programmatic and supportability facets of risk.
2. Those elements in a culture, environment, or project that cause risk events to happen.

Risk evaluation: *See* risk assessment.

Risk event: A specific discrete occurrence that may affect a project to its benefit or detriment. *See also* project risk.

Risk exposure

1. The probability of a risk event's occurrence multiplied by its impact
2. The amount of risk that can be withstood, based on historical information.

Risk factor

1. Area of concern related to its propensity for causing risk events.
2. The event, probability, or impact of a given risk.

Risk handling: *See* project risk management *and* risk response control

Risk identification: Detecting, recognizing, and categorizing risk events associated with a given project.

Risk indicators

1. Cost and schedule facets of risk.
2. *See also* risk triggers

Risk management: *See* project risk management.

Risk management plan: Clear strategy and design for practices and protocols to be followed in identifying, qualifying, quantifying, and responding to risks. The road map for how project risk management will be implemented consistently by all project parties. Includes procedures for a wide range of practices from documentation to management escalation to reserve application.

Risk management planning: Efforts at the project or organizational level to establish and maintain consistent risk practices and protocols.

Risk management professional (PMI-RMP) certification: The prevailing risk certification for project managers who have both met the professional requirements and passed the certification exam offered by PMI.

Risk management strategy: Clearly stated visions of organizational goals and missions relating to risk management, including a general perspective on roles and responsibilities.

Risk mitigation: *See* mitigation

Risk modeling: Risk identification and portfolio risk assessment technique that involves creating a set of questions that, when answered candidly, will provide a metric value as to the overall risk and opportunity associated with the project.

Risk monitoring and control: Process of establishing current risk state, interpreting acceptable levels of risk, and taking corrective action to keep projects within organizational and project tolerances.

Risk planning: Establishing and implementing processes, protocols, and procedures to deal with risk in a consistent and focused fashion.

Risk probability: The determination of the chance, odds or likelihood of a specific risk event occurring, normally expressed as a percentage

Risk qualification: Risk assessment and prioritization that applies nonquantitative techniques.

Risk quantification: Risk assessment and prioritization that applies numerically valued techniques.

Risk rating scheme: System for stratifying and clarifying risk probability and impact by creating terms and terminology that allow for consistent interpretation of those respective values.

Risk response control: Process of communicating current risk responses, interpreting and implementing those responses, and (as required) taking corrective action to maintain projects within organizational and project tolerances.

Risk response development: The establishment of steps or practices to optimize opportunities and minimize threats using a variety of strategies, including acceptance, avoidance, mitigation, and transfer for threats; exploitation, sharing, enhancement, and acceptance for opportunities.

Risk response matrix: A tool that cross-references risk events and the strategies that can be applied to respond to them to identify those strategies that have the greatest potential influence across the body of significant risk events. A form of Pugh matrix: Risk review: A reevaluation of the risks, environmental factors, organizational process assets, risk events, and the relative probability and impact to affirm that the risk process is functioning and that risk thresholds have not been exceeded. *See also* audit.

Risk symptom: An indicator of the existence of or imminent occurrence of a given risk event that serves as an immediate precursor to the occurrence of the risk at full impact (or an indicator that it is occurring but is in its early stages). *See also* risk trigger

Risk trigger: An indicator of the imminent occurrence of a given risk event that serves as an immediate precursor to the occurrence of the risk. Often used to initiate specific actions, behaviors, or responses.

Schedule: The timing plan for a project and its activities. May be displayed as a milestone chart (featuring specific project achievements), as a Gantt chart (featuring time-scaled horizontal bars), or as a network diagram (featuring dependency relationships among activities).

Schedule risk: Events or conditions that may have a negative influence on the project's timing.

Schedule simulation: One aspect of a Monte Carlo analysis where iterative reviews of the project schedules (based on individual distributions of potential individual task outcomes) produce a curve of possible outcomes for the timing of the project.

Scope: The extent of a project. What a project shall include, incorporate, and deliver.

Simulation: A Monte Carlo analysis where iterative reviews of project schedules and costs (based on individual distributions of potential individual task outcomes) produce a curve of possible outcomes for the timing and final cost of the project and/or its phases.

Skew: The unevenness of a probability density function. The skew applies to the area under the function where the largest percentage of the population lies.

Slack: *See* float.

Sources of risk: Environmental and organizational factors that engender and create a climate where risk events are more likely to occur.

Stakeholder: *See* project stakeholder

Standard deviation

1. Square root of a variance. In a normal distribution, one standard deviation accounts for roughly 68 percent of the population. Two standard deviations account for 95 percent of the population, whereas three standard deviations account for 99.7 percent of the population in the distribution.

2. In the Program Evaluation and Review Technique (PERT), a standard deviation for a task is the optimistic duration minus the pessimistic duration with the remainder divided by 6. The standard deviation for a path is determined by using the value of the square root of the sum of the squared values of the task standard deviations.

Start-to-finish: In the precedence diagramming method (PDM), the relationship between activities where the start of an activity (i) serves to establish the finish of its successor (j). Described by the phrase: "Task i must start and then (lag) days later, task j may finish." *See also* logical relationship.

Start-to-start: In the precedence diagramming method (PDM), the relationship between activities where the start of an activity (i) serves to establish the start of its successor (j). Described by the phrase: "Task i must start and then (lag) days later, task j may start." *See also* logical relationship.

Statement of work (SOW): Narrative outline of the agreements on performance between the buyer and seller. Often a component of the contract or memoranda of understanding, it details performance, deliverables, and specific management practices.

Strategy: Clearly stated visions of organizational goals, missions, and performance standards, including a general perspective on roles and responsibilities for carrying out those goals.

Strengths, weaknesses, opportunities, and threats (SWOT) analysis: A high-level project assessment technique that examines organizational capabilities (strengths and weaknesses) and how the project, in process or if realized, will have positive and negative influences (opportunities and threats) on the organization. The emphasis in a SWOT analysis is identification of how the opportunities may offset organizational weaknesses and how threats may be offset by organizational strengths (or jeopardized by organizational weaknesses).

Supportability risk: Risks associated with fielding and maintaining systems that are being developed or have been developed and are being deployed.

SWOT analysis: *See* strengths, weaknesses, opportunities, and threats (SWOT) analysis

Task: Clearly delineated work element.

Technical performance measurement (TPM): Risk measurement technique conducted by establishing exacting project performance criteria and assessing them against the acceptable ranges around those criteria.

Technical risk: Risk directly associated with the technology, task performance, or design of the deliverables or services produced by the project.

Templates: Formally crafted guidelines designed to capture, archive, and disseminate information.

Transference: Risk response strategy to shift responsibility, ownership, and/or accountability from the performing organization to a third party. Often accomplished using warranties, guarantees, and/or contract provisions.

Uncertainty: Inability to ascertain the probability of potential risk events

Value analysis: Evaluation approach (from the buyer's perspective) as to whether a given tactic, strategy, deliverable, or output is worth the relative investment. Determining whether the buyer is receiving the optimal deliverable(s) at the most effective cost.

Value engineering: Evaluation approach (from the seller's perspective) as to whether a given tactic, strategy, deliverable, or output is worth the relative investment. Determining whether the seller is generating the optimal deliverable(s) at the most effective cost.

Variance: Difference between actual (realized) and projected (anticipated) performance in terms of cost, schedule, or requirements.

Venture evaluation and review technique (VERT): A probabilistic network diagramming approach that accounts for cost, schedule, and resource considerations.

WBS dictionary

1. A single, in-depth work package description, detailing background information regarding project performance, expectations, and process steps required to carry out a work package.
2. The aggregation of WBS dictionaries for all work packages in a project.

Work breakdown structure (WBS): Decomposition of a project into its component parts using a logical hierarchy. Breaking down the project by any logical groupings, including deliverables, phases, or task performance areas.

Work package: The lowest level of a work breakdown structure, and the project manager's level of control. The level of the WBS where work is assigned, resources allocated, and control is exerted.

Workaround: Impromptu response to threats. Developed in ad hoc fashion as a risk trigger, symptom, or risk event occurs.

Appendix A: Contractor Risk Management

Organizational Responsibilities

In putting work out for bid, the purchasing agency must accept the fact that risk management is a key part of a procurement strategy. Thus, it is best for the organization to establish a formal plan of risk assessment and response very early in each major project or program. This plan considers contractor and internal organizational risks. Assessment and analysis of each significant element of project risk should continue throughout the purchasing or procurement cycle. The procurement strategy ought to be designed to lower risks to acceptable levels. The internal purchasing or contracting agency should include requirements in the requests for proposals (RFPs) for risk management on the part of the contractors. If the process is followed well, then contractors must stipulate their approach to identifying and managing risks inherent in the project.

Good procurement strategies incorporate demands that contractors will provide their own risk management plans and risk assessment reports to bolster internal efforts. Similarly, in an ideal world, all RFPs would include a clear request for identifying project risks and trade-offs and an understanding of who bears those risks.

Sample statements (DSMC 1990) that could be used in RFPs follow.

Engineering/Design

The offeror shall describe the engineering/technical tasks to be accomplished during the project that contribute to risk reduction. The discussion shall contain the following item:

A discussion of major technical risk items associated with the offeror's proposed concept, including payoffs that will potentially result from the proposed approach, as well as problem areas. The approach to determining the technical risks involved in your project and your approach to reducing such risks to acceptable levels shall be described. Key development issues and the proposed solution approach shall be identified. The discussion shall present the criteria to be used to evaluate critical decision points and information requirements, and the process to be used to develop, evaluate, and implement fallback positions as required.

Reliability and Maintainability (Quality)

Describe your approach to determining the technical risk involved in your reliability and maintainability (quality) programs and your approach to reducing such risks to acceptable levels. This discussion shall present the criteria you plan to use in determining the criticality of technologies; the techniques used to evaluate critical decision points and information requirements; and the process used to develop, evaluate, and implement fallback positions as required.

Quality in Design

Identify quality in design risks, and factor these risks into design trade-off studies.

Producibility

Describe the approach to determine the technical risk involved with your capacity to produce and the method to reduce such risks to acceptable levels. This discussion shall present the criteria you plan to use in determining the criticality of technologies; the techniques used to evaluate critical decision points and information requirements; and the process used to develop, evaluate, and implement fallback positions as required.

Manufacturing Research/Technology

Provide an assessment of the likelihood that the design concept can be produced using existing technology while meeting quality, cost, and schedule requirements. Include an evaluation of the capability to follow through on the design concept, including requirements for critical process capabilities and special facilities development. Also include tests and demonstrations required for new materials and alternative approaches, anticipating implementation risks, potential cost and schedule impacts, and surge capabilities.

Project Control System

Describe your risk management approach. Discuss how information from functional areas will be integrated into the risk management process.

Planning

Describe the initial planning accomplished in the following areas: risk identification, risk resolution, risk control implementation, fallback position identification, resource requirements, critical materials, and critical processes. Also identify risks associated with any long lead-time requirements, management systems, organizational requirements, staffing, and scheduling.

Quality Assurance

Describe any quality assurance risks you foresee for this project and the actions planned to reduce those risks.

Evaluation Summary

The overall evaluation of each proposal may include on-site inspections and results of preaward surveys to provide information to the contracting authority. This information may include offeror's current and future capability to perform all aspects of the project. Risk assessment associated with the major areas of the project will be accomplished. In assessing risk, an independent judgment of the probability of success, the impact of failure, and the alternatives available to meet the requirements will be considered.

Contractor Responsibilities

The contractor must be made aware through the language in the contract that the information contained in its response will be used for risk analysis. The contractor should be responsible for making a thorough assessment of risks in its proposal. The contractor should include sufficient information to convince the purchasing authority that the contractor recognizes and has quantified the risk inherent in the project. The proposal should identify areas in which actions by the organization can support risk reduction. These areas can include items such as long lead-time funding and the need for approval of priority status for materials.

In proposing a risk management system, the contractor should highlight how it can use existing internal systems to provide information on risk. The contractor should also focus on how it can include risk management in its normal management practices and in its regular communication with the organization.

Appendix B: An Abbreviated List of Risk Sources

An exhaustive list of risk sources would be as lengthy as the dictionary (or longer). As such, the sources listed in Table B.1 represent only a small percentage of *possible* sources. However, this list of risk sources includes risks that are most common and prevalent in the community that created it. This list was generated for a bureaucratic organization focusing on field deployment of large-scale hardware and software systems and was engaged in intense activity on short notice. This may or may not describe your organizational environment. However, this background information should provide some perspective on why these sources were selected above all others.

Risk sources are where risks originate. Risk sources are not categories, although treating them as categories could help identify and define other risks, or facilitate development of the risk breakdown structure. Categories sort risks to aid in identification. Sources generate risks.

Table B.1 Possible Risk Sources

RISK	COST	PROJECT	SCHEDULE	TECHNICAL	COMMENTS
Capacity				×	The lack of facilities and tools to produce at the desired rate (rate tooling) could prevent production flow from reaching the desired level.
Concept, failure to apply logistics support analysis (LSA) during concept exploration				×	Failure to participate in the definition of system concepts could produce a system design in follow-on phases that does not meet supportability objectives and requires excessive or unattainable operation and support (O&S) costs, as well as labor, to meet the readiness objectives.
Concurrency	×		×		Concurrent development or preparation for production could cause deviations. Concurrency often results in discovery of problems at a time when a cost premium must be paid to resolve problems and keep the project on or near the original schedule.
Configuration control of vendor products				×	Organizations do not control the configuration of items procured from the marketplace, which presents potential risks in both initial design and availability of spares.
Contracting, inadequate provision for support	×				In terms of impact and the probability of its occurrence, the major risk area in integrated logistics support (ILS) contracting is the failure to contract properly for data, materials, and services.
Contractor, communication by		×			Failure of the subcontractors' and contractors' personnel to keep prime contractor and project management organization informed of problems and potential problems in a timely manner. Communication problems may also occur if management fails to fully communicate direction to all involved in the project in a timely manner.
Contractor, lack of financial strength of	×		×		If any contractors have not been able to adequately finance project requirements, the required work may be delayed or curtailed.
Contractor, production readiness of			×		A contractor may fail to be adequately prepared for production.

					Description
Contractor, subcontractors and control of			X		A prime contractor may not maintain adequate control of subcontractor quantity, schedule, and cost performance.
Contractor, underbidding by		X		X	A contractor may underbid or buy in to get contracts and may fail to provide the desired products and services on schedule and within budget.
Coordination, inadequate			X	X	Organizations often fail to coordinate purchases with other departments or divisions, which minimizes available logistics support and the economies of scale that would otherwise be available.
Data, inadequate planning for utilization of	X				Collecting data without detailed planning for its use may lead to a mismatch of data collection information requirements and failure to accomplish the intended purpose of the assessment.
Data, incomplete or inaccessible	X	X			Without sufficient data available from each test and used properly for planning subsequent tests, it is not possible to evaluate the adequacy of the system to meet all readiness requirements. Without accurate failure rates, system and component reliability cannot be determined. Lacking the necessary data, system design and ILS progress cannot be established, problems cannot be identified, and additional testing may be required.
Design, delayed definition of logistics criteria		X			Delayed decisions on reliability and supportability requirements could result in suboptimum support. After the design is committed, the options become limited.
Design, impact of engineering changes				X	A high number of design changes made during development could overwhelm ILS planning and create an inability to reflect ILS and O&S cost considerations fully in engineering change decisions.
Design, invalid application of component reliability and maintainability (R&M) data			X		Design and manufacture determines the mean life and failure rate of components when viewed in isolation. The consequences of improperly computed material replacement rates are invalid labor requirements, incorrect supply support stockage lists, and invalid repair level analyses.

continued

Table B.1 (continued) Possible Risk Sources

RISK	COST	PROJECT	SCHEDULE	TECHNICAL	COMMENTS
Design, lack of life-cycle cost (LCC) impact on design and logistics support process	X			X	LCC is most effective when it is integrated into the engineering and management process that makes design and logistics engineering choices. This integration must start at project initiation. Failure to implement LCC throughout may result in costly reworking, test failures, contract termination costs, and increased O&S costs.
Design, unrealistic R&M requirements	X		X		Unrealistic R&M requirements could lead to increased design and development costs incurred as a result of excessive design iterations.
Design stability	X		X		There may be lack of design stability during the production phase.
Engineering, late establishment of readiness and supportability objectives	X		X	X	The system engineering process is a key factor in identifying and attaining realistic readiness and supportability objectives. If a well-organized process is not started at the project inception and continued throughout the development phases, then the project risks are increased design, development, and O&S costs; schedule delays; and degraded readiness factors.
Engineering, site survey results		X	X		Historical or archeological site survey findings could delay site construction and cause significant deployment problems.
Environmental impact	X		X		Natural disasters (such as fires, floods, storms, earthquakes) may occur.
Equipment, common support	X		X		Common support equipment may not be available to operate and maintain the system.
Failure to structure or tailor LSA requirements	X		X	X	Failure to establish an LSA plan specifically designed to meet the needs of the material system could result in excessive costs, the performance of unwanted analysis while failing to complete needed studies, and the development of excessive documentation while overlooking critical information needs.
Familiarization		X			Contractor personnel may be unfamiliar with the systems or equipment or may lack experience producing similar systems or equipment.
Familiarization, tolerance levels		X			Difficulties in achieving closer than usual tolerance levels may occur.

	C1	C2	C3	C4	Description
Fault detection	X				A failure to obtain designed performance may be detected.
Funding, advanced buy authorization limitations				X	Long lead-time requirements may create problems if there is insufficient advanced-buy funding to meet the needs of the project.
Funding, constraints on				X	Lack of timely receipt of project funds may cause delays.
Funding, long-term		X		X	The requirement to execute a project over a period of time with funds provided through a fiscal-year-to-fiscal-year agreement may result in constraints.
Inflation				X	Levels of inflation significantly higher than originally forecast may increase costs.
Integration/interface			X		New and unique requirements (such as adaptability, compatibility, interface standard, and interpretability) may delay the project.
Joint partner project decision		X			Problems and delays resulting from reduced joint partner participation or other user decisions could disrupt the project.
Labor disputes		X		X	Labor difficulties (such as strikes, lockouts, slowdowns) could increase costs and delay schedules.
Legal disputes		X		X	Award and performance disputes and related legal actions could delay a project.
Legislation		X		X	Higher taxes, new labor laws affecting pay and benefits, social security increases, and so on, could increase costs.
Maintainability	X				Failure to achieve maintainability using a design that is compatible with established maintenance procedures may force changes in the maintenance approach.
Material properties				X	Material property requirements beyond those usually expected may increase costs.
Modeling validity			X		Inaccuracies in models used to develop mathematical and physical predictions may disrupt the project.
Objectives and strategies	X		X		Changes in objectives and strategies may disrupt the project.
Operating environment	X				Performing in an unusually harsh environment could increase technical difficulties.
Operating policies			X		Changes in operating policies may affect system or system support requirements.

continued

Table B.1 (continued) Possible Risk Sources

RISK	COST	PROJECT	SCHEDULE	TECHNICAL	COMMENTS
Personnel, available skills of		X			The shortage of personnel with technical, management, and other skills needed to carry out internal and contractor activities may disrupt the project.
Personnel, downsizing and streamlining of	X			X	Initiatives on downsizing and streamlining could impose restrictions on the project manager as well as the designer early in the definition of requirements. Although intended to decrease cost and improve efficiency, casual application of such guidance could result in a loss of standardization, attendant cost increases, and loss of documented lessons-learned experience.
Personnel, forced placement of		X			If the project has several inadequate personnel and managers, either internally or under key contractors, seriously counterproductive events could occur.
Personnel, security clearances of			X		Any delays in obtaining required personnel security clearances could delay the schedule.
Physical properties	X				Different-than-expected dynamics, stress, thermal, or vibration requirements could increase costs.
Planning, delayed facilities			X		Failure to perform timely facility planning could result in substantial deployment delays.
Planning, delayed postproduction support				X	Continued support of the material system by the industrial base existing in the post-production time frame might not be economically feasible.
Planning, updating deployment		X		X	Unreported and uncorrected deployment problems could generate a serious flaw in an updated deployment plan.
Policies, new		X			Added workload or time requirements brought about by new direction or policy may disrupt the project.
Priority			X		Problems resulting from changing the priority assigned to the project and thereby timely access to testing facilities, funds, materials, and so on, could delay the schedule.

			Description
Project stretchout	×		Direction to slip the project schedule from the original plan may disrupt the project.
Radiation properties		×	Increased radiation stress resistance requirements could cause technical difficulties.
Reliability	×	×	Failure to forecast system reliability properly may affect predicted reliability growth.
Scarce resources	×	×	Shortages of critical materials, components, or parts may disrupt the project.
Scheduling, accelerated acquisition	×	×	Lead times for delivery of nondevelopmental items could be extremely short, particularly for in-stock items. This poses a substantial risk of deployment with incomplete or inadequate logistic support and attendant degraded readiness.
Scheduling, accelerated projects	×	×	An accelerated system development project may be required to overcome a critical deficiency in an existing capability. This "streamlining" could pose the risk of delaying design maturation with frequent configuration changes occurring in late development.
Scheduling, accelerated projects		×	Compressed schedules increase the demand for critical assets during the time of normal asset shortages, which could create unrecoverable delays.
Scheduling, decision delay	×		Disruption of the project schedule may result from delays in obtaining higher-level approval to award contracts, proceed to the next phase, and so on.
Scheduling, excessive lead times	×		Lead times for critical components or services that are longer than expected may delay the schedule.
Scheduling, slippage	×		Failure to understand how slippage in one functional element affects other elements and milestone events could ultimately delay the entire project.
Service roles and mission changes	×	×	Problems may cause deviations from the project resulting from changing service roles and missions that significantly alter the planned use of the system.
Software design	×		Unique software test requirements and unsatisfactory software test results could result in changes in the basic project.

continued

Table B.1   (continued) Possible Risk Sources

RISK	COST	PROJECT	SCHEDULE	TECHNICAL	COMMENTS
Software language			×		A new computer language or one unfamiliar to those responsible for planning and writing software could cause schedule delays.
State-of-the-art advances, lack of supporting		×			Advances from other projects that might not be as expected could significantly affect the current project.
State-of-the-art advances, major		×		×	Problems resulting from greater-than-anticipated advances in techniques and development (such as complexity/difficulty in meeting requirements, percent proven technology, lack of work on similar projects, special resources required, operating environment, theoretical analysis required, and degree of difference from existing technology) could disrupt the project.
State-of-the-art field failures				×	Field failures of state-of-the-art equipment types that were assumed to be ready for incorporation into the project could cause technical difficulties.
Survivability		×			New requirements for nuclear hardening, chemical survivability, and so on, might require revised planning to meet original or new goals.
Testing, extrapolation requirements				×	The need for extensive extrapolation using field test results could hamper the assessment of the project under actual deployment conditions.
Testing, facility compatibility			×		Not having suitable test facilities available during the required time frame could cause schedule delays.
Testing, incomplete or delayed support package for			×		Without an adequate test support package on-site and ready to support the scheduled test, it might be possible to start testing, but the chances of continuing on schedule would be low.
Testing, inconsistencies				×	Inconsistent field test results could cause increased technical risk and require retesting.

				Description
Testing, safety	X			Problems could result from requirements that testing is nondestructive or that it does not interfere with other activities.
Testing, security requirements		X		The testing of classified equipment could cause scheduling concerns associated with clearances, data transfer, and public interest.
Testing, unrealistic scenarios for			X	A subtle risk, particularly during development testing, and one that can have a lasting effect on the viability of a project, is testing to an unrealistic scenario. A realistic approach does not necessarily mean that stresses put on the system under test must duplicate those of actual service, because in most cases this is impractical. It does mean, however, that the test is planned to simulate conditions as closely as possible, with differences carefully documented.
Testing, weather		X		Weather-related occurrences could cause testing delays.
Threat changes		X		Possible changes could require alterations in schedule and performance objectives.
Uniquely harsh requirement	X			Existing design technology that differs significantly from that required for success of the new system could cause technical difficulties.
Vendor base		X	X	A shortage of qualified vendors can affect adequate price competition and a satisfactory supply quantity base.

Appendix C: Basic Probability Concepts

This appendix serves as a very basic introduction to probability and statistical concepts that may be useful for risk analysis. It is by no means all-inclusive but rather may be thought of as a primer. The appendix contains three sections. The first section is an introduction to probability, centering on definitions and simple examples. The second section provides a summary of descriptive statistics, including a look at statistical confidence and confidence intervals, and explains probability density functions (PDFs) and cumulative density functions (CDFs) defining distributions that are relevant to risk analysis, such as the normal, uniform, and triangular. The third section discusses statistical independence, which is the prerequisite for the concept of expected value. Decision tree analysis is illustrated to show the merit of the expected value approach.

Probability

Probability is a concept used by many people every day. As an example, the weather forecaster predicts a 30 percent probability of rain. This means that, in the long run, rain is expected 30 days out of 100 when conditions are the same as they are at the time the forecast is made. For risk analysis, a statement might be made to the effect that the developmental stage of weapons system A has a 10 percent probability of a schedule (time) overrun. This is equivalent to saying that

10 percent of all developmental stages of weapons systems similar to A have had a schedule overrun in the past.

More formal definitions of probability follow.

The quality or condition of being probable; likelihood.

A probable situation, condition, or event.

The likelihood that a given event will occur: *little probability of rain tonight.*

Statistics. A number expressing the likelihood that a specific event will occur, expressed as the ratio of the number of actual occurrences to the number of possible occurrences. (*The American Heritage Dictionary of the English Language* 2000)

"In practical situations, probability is used as a vehicle in drawing inferences about unknown population characteristics. Additionally,… probability concepts can be used to give us an indication of how good these inferences are." (Pfaffenberger and Patterson 1987)

Many individuals think of probability in relation to gambling and games of chance, such as card playing and dice throwing. They measure the probability of an event in terms of the odds against the event's happening. For example, throwing a pair of dice (illustrating the inverse relationship between probability and the odds against an event) results in 1 of 36 possible outcomes, which are illustrated in Figure C.1.

The probability of throwing a 10 is 3/36 or 0.083. That is, 3 out of the 36 possible outcomes result in a 10. The odds of not throwing a 10 are 33/36 or 0.917.

Probability is a key quantitative measure associated with many risk assessment techniques. The above examples are simplistic but show how easy it is to comprehend probability concepts.

Descriptive Statistics, Confidence, and Distributions

Any group of numbers, such as a sample composed of quantitative evaluations, may be described with the following basic statistical parameters:

Mean
Median

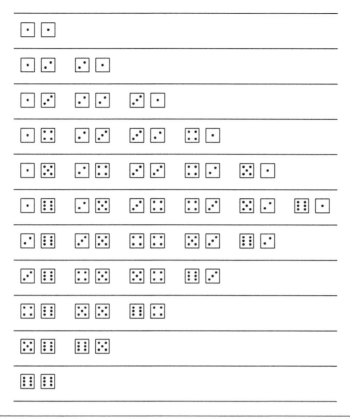

Figure C.1 Results of variance in throwing dice.

Range
Mode
Variance and standard deviation

These parameters enable the statistician to determine what level of confidence (or assurance) may be accorded to predictive statements about the entire population of numbers. The parameters also help determine where the sample lies in a possible statistical distribution. Conversely, a statistical distribution may be described by such parameters. A statistical distribution is basically just a way to describe which numbers will appear more often (or with a high probability) and which numbers will appear less often (or with a low probability). The following paragraphs define the parameters in some detail and then discuss confidence levels, PDFs and CDFs, and the other relevant distributions applied in risk analysis.

For illustrative purposes, let the following numbers represent exam scores for an introductory statistics course:

75	60	100	65	80	45
25	45	60	90	60	40
50	70	55	10	95	70
85	20	70	65	90	90
65	80	70	55	70	

Let X_i represent these numbers, where i is indexed from 1 to 29. So $X_1 = 75$, $X_2 = 25$, $X_3 = 50,...$, $X_{28} = 70$, $X_{29} = 90$. The mean of these numbers is nothing more than the arithmetic average. The mean is computed as follows, where n is the number of exam scores:

$$Mean = \frac{\sum_{i=1}^{n} X_i}{n} = \frac{1{,}885}{29} = 63.96$$

The *mode,* the score that occurs more often than any other score, is 70. The mode occurred five times (more often than any other score).

The *median* is the middle score if the scores are ranked top to bottom. Because there are 29 scores altogether, the median is the fifteenth score, which is a 65. The *variance* and *standard deviation* of a group of numbers are attempts to describe the dispersion or scattering of the numbers around the mean. The variance is computed using the following formula:

$$Variance = \frac{\sum_{i=1}^{n} X^2 - \dfrac{\left(\sum_{i=1}^{n} X_i\right)^2}{n}}{n - 1}$$

For this example, the variance is as follows:

$$\frac{132{,}275 - \dfrac{1{,}855^2}{29}}{28} = 486.4$$

The *standard deviation* is the square root of the variance. The standard deviation has a more intuitive appeal than does the variance because the standard deviation is the mathematical average variation of a value from the mean. For this example, the standard deviation is:

$$\sqrt{486.4} = 22.05$$

The *range* is the high score minus the low score. For this example, the range is $100 - 10 = 90$.

Many times when examining data, a *level of confidence* or *confidence interval* is used to indicate what certainty or faith is to be put in the sample being taken as representative of the entire population. Far and away, the most common measure is the confidence interval for the mean. A statement such as the following can be made about a particular sample mean:

The 95 percent confidence interval for the mean is 56 to 72.

Statistically, this statement means that of all the possible samples of this size taken from this population, 95 percent of the samples will have a mean between 56 and 72. It does not mean that 95 percent of all possible values that are sampled will fall between 56 and 72, which is the common, though faulty, interpretation of the statement.

Confidence intervals are determined by adding and subtracting some calculated value from the mean of the sample. Usually, but not always, this value is based on the standard deviation of the sample. As an example, if the population from which a sample is taken is determined to be normally distributed, and this was assumed in previous statements (this determination may be made based on the relative values of the mean, variance and standard deviation, mode, median, range, and other factors), then a 95 percent confidence interval for the population is calculated in this manner where $\overline{X}$ is the sample mean and σ is the standard deviation:

$$\overline{X} \pm 1.96\,\sigma$$

A 95 percent confidence interval for the mean is calculated in this manner:

$$\overline{X} + 1.96\frac{\sigma}{\sqrt{n}}$$

where $\sigma/\sqrt{n}$ is commonly referred to as the standard error.

How is the population determined to be normal (or normally distributed) in the first place? Similar groups of numbers have similar relationships between their respective parameters. These similarities help determine which distribution describes the entire population. Typical distributions for problems associated with risk are normal, uniform, triangular, and beta. (Discussion of the beta distribution is beyond the scope of this appendix. If further information on the beta distribution is needed, any of several statistics and operations research books can supply the information.)

For the normal distribution, 68.3 percent of all possible values lie within one standard deviation of the mean, 95.4 percent lie within two standard deviations, and 99.7 percent lie within three standard deviations. This is shown in the probability density function. The PDF gives the probability that certain values will occur. Figure C.2 illustrates a PDF for the exam scores example, assuming that the scores are from a normal distribution.

The normal distribution is, by strict definition, a continuous distribution. However, it is implied in Figure C.2 that fractional exam scores are possible—and of course it is not realistic in this example. A discussion of the differences between discrete and continuous distribution is beyond the scope of this appendix, and because the example is meant to be used only for illustrative purposes, this finer point of statistics will be ignored. It is also implied in Figure C.2

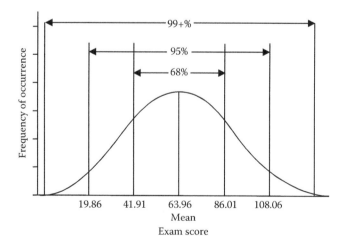

Figure C.2 PDF of a normal distribution.

that extra credit is given because scores exceeding 100 are possible, and this could certainly be within the realm of the example. The most important distinction of the normal distribution PDF is the bell shape of the curve. This shape is the most definitive characteristic of any PDF.

The cumulative density function is the arithmetic summation of the PDF. In other words, the CDF gives the probability value (or any value less than the value) that will occur. The shape of the various distribution CDFs are distinctive, and the CDF is merely another way of illustrating the distribution. Figure C.3 illustrates a typical CDF for normally distributed values, in this case the exam scores example.

The uniform distribution is used to describe a set of values where every value has an equal probability of occurrence. Returning once again to the exam scores example, one might hypothesize that all possible scores (1 through 100+) have an equal probability of occurrence: 0.01. The PDF for this is illustrated in Figure C.4. Figure C.5 illustrates the uniform CDF.

The triangular distribution is used often in risk analysis situations to describe the most optimistic, most likely, and most pessimistic durations of some event or activity. The PDF of the triangular distribution, illustrated in Figure C.6, is not necessarily symmetric. Indeed, often the triangular distribution is purposely asymmetric or skewed to the right to reflect the possibility of very long time durations. These long durations are less likely to occur but do happen

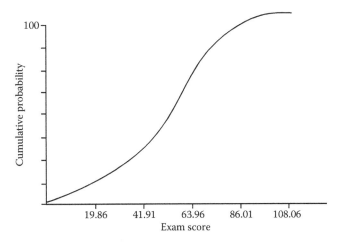

Figure C.3 CDF of a normal distribution.

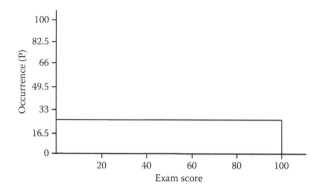

Figure C.4   PDF of a uniform distribution.

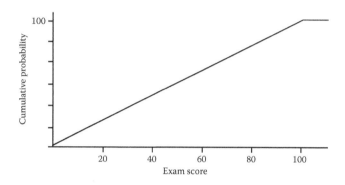

Figure C.5   CDF of a uniform distribution.

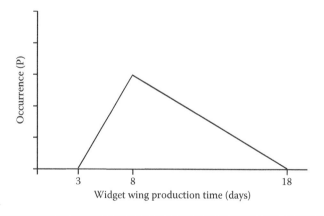

Figure C.6   PDF of a triangular distribution.

occasionally. Figure C.6 shows that the most likely production time for a widget wing is 8 days. Clearly, the average is skewed to the right and is very close to 9.3 days. Hence, the triangular distribution, when skewed, has a mode and mean that are clearly different. Contrast this to the normal distribution, where the mode and mean are the same (as is the median).

Independence, Expected Value, and Decision Tree Analysis

Statistical independence is an important concept on which many methodologies are based. Most discussions of statistical independence begin with a tutorial on conditional probability, sample space, and event relationships. Rather than discuss these concepts, a more practical definition of statistical independence is presented: Two events are said to be independent if the occurrence of one is not related to the occurrence of the other. If events are occurring at random, then they are independent; if events are not occurring at random, then they are not independent. A set or group of possible events are said to be mutually exclusive and collectively exhaustive if they are all independent and the sum of their probabilities of occurrence is 1.0. This is the basic notion behind value.

To illustrate expected value, suppose that a simple game of chance can be played for $1. The bettor pays $1 and has a chance to win $50 or $2 or no money at all. The dollar amounts and probabilities are shown in Table C.1.

The bettor would like to know, before actually paying $1, what the expected winnings are. The expected value of winnings is the sum of the winning amounts multiplied by their respective probability of occurrence:

$$(\$50)\,(0.01) + (\$2)\,(0.10) + (\$0)\,(0.89) = \$0.50 + \$0.20 + \$0 = \$0.70$$

Table C.1 Expected Values Example

AMOUNT VALUE	PROBABILITY OF WINNING	EXPECTED VALUE
$50	0.01	$0.50
2	0.10	0.20
0	0.89	0.00
Totals	1.00	$0.70

Because the bettor can expect winnings on the average of only $0.70 but pays $1 to play the game, the net profit is a negative $0.30.

This is a very realistic example of gambling and risk. Most individuals, when forced to face this logic, would choose not to play. However, many would play. They are willing to accept the risk of losing $1 to take a chance at winning $50. These individuals are risk prone. The individuals who follow the basic logic of this example and do not play are risk averse.

The notion of expected value is a prerequisite for discussing decision tree analysis, which attempts to break down a series of events into smaller, simpler, and more manageable segments. Many similarities exist between decision tree analysis and more complicated forms of management and risk analysis, such as the Program Evaluation and Review Technique (PERT) and the critical path method (CPM). All three forms of analysis presume that a sequence of events can be broken down into smaller and smaller segments that more accurately represent reality.

Decision tree analysis helps the analyst break down a problem into various sectors or branches to simplify potential decision making. As an example, suppose a widget is being manufactured as follows: Either machine A or machine B can be used for the first step (of a two-step

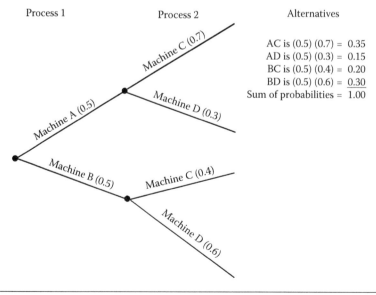

Figure C.7   Decision tree analysis.

manufacturing process) with equal probability of 0.5. Either machine C or D can be used for the second step. Machine C is used 70 percent of the time if the widget was first processed with machine A and 40 percent of the time if the widget was first processed with machine B. The rest of the time, machine D is used for the second step. Decision tree analysis can help compute the probability of the widgets being produced by these various combinations (AC, AD, BC, BD). Figure C.7 illustrates the decision tree and the expected probability for each manufacturing process alternative.

Note that each alternative's probability is merely the product of the individual processes making up that alternative because the individual processes are independent of each other. Note also that the sum of the probabilities for all of the four processing alternatives is 1.

Appendix D: Quantifying Expert Judgment

All risk assessment techniques or models share a common requirement: acquiring expert judgment as inputs. Inherent in judgment is a degree of uncertainty. When acquiring quantifiable expressions of judgment, the axioms of probability must not be violated:

The probabilities of all possible events must sum to 1.

The probability of any event, $P(A)$, must be a number greater than or equal to 0 and less than or equal to 1 ($0 \leq P(A) \leq 1$).

The probability of joint events is the product of the probability that one event occurs and the probability that another event occurs, given that the first event has occurred, ($P(A) \times P(B1|2A)$). Under these circumstances, the events are termed dependent.

When the probability of joint events occurring is simply the product of the probabilities of each $P(A) \times P(B)$, the events are said to be independent. That is, the two events have nothing in common or can occur simultaneously.

The challenge for the analyst is to obtain expert judgment, which is qualitative by nature, in the areas of cost, schedule, and technical performance. Next, the analyst must convert that judgment into a quantitative form so that the results can be depicted in the form of a probability density function (PDF), which serve as inputs to the various risk models. (This is necessary only when a quantitative model has been selected.)

A PDF is a smooth line or curve, as shown in Figure D.1. The PDF of a random variable, x, is a listing of the various values of x with a corresponding probability associated with each value of x. In the example shown in Figure D.1, x would be a cost, schedule, or performance value. Note that the total area under the curve equals 1.

In Figure D.1, the random variable x might represent a hardware system cost, where the probability of the system costing $10,000 is 0.13.

Several methods can be used to convert qualitative judgment into quantitative probability distributions. The remainder of this appendix focuses on a few of the most popular, practical, and accurate techniques for doing so, chosen because they are relatively simple and easy to master. This factor is of paramount importance because, in most cases, the analyst performing this task will have neither the time nor the knowledge of the advanced probability concepts required to perform more complex techniques. Those interested in more exotic, complex techniques are referred to "Sources of Additional Information" at the end of this appendix.

The following techniques are discussed in this appendix: diagrammatic, direct, betting, and modified Churchman–Ackoff.

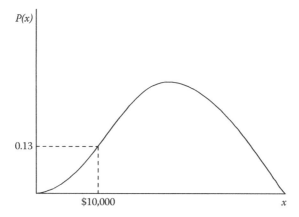

Figure D.1   Probability density function.

Description of Techniques

Diagrammatic

Many analysts prefer the diagrammatic method as a way of capturing and representing an expert's judgment. This method describes an expert's uncertainty by presenting the expert with a range of PDF diagrams and having the expert select the shape of the PDF that most accurately reflects the schedule, cost, or technical parameter in question. Using this method, the analyst can ascertain whether the PDF is symmetric or skewed, the degree of variability, and so on. For example, if the expert believes that there is a great amount of risk associated with completing an activity within a certain period of time, a PDF skewed to the right may be selected. Likewise, activities with little risk may be skewed to the left. If the expert believes that each value over a given range is equally likely to occur, then a uniform distribution may be most appropriate. The analyst and the expert, working together, can select the PDF that most accurately reflects the schedule, cost, or technical item in question.

The diagrammatic method of obtaining PDFs is applicable when the expert has a sound understanding of probability concepts and can merge that understanding with his or her understanding of the parameters in question. In this way, the expert can accurately identify the appropriate PDFs.

Direct

The direct method is used to obtain subjective probability distributions by asking the expert to assign probabilities to a given range of values. This method of obtaining PDFs is applicable (1) when questions can be phrased to the respondents in such a way that no confusion is likely to exist in the respondents' minds and (2) when the results will not violate the axioms of probability. The direct method is applicable when time or resource constraints do not allow for more complex, resource-intensive methods.

By applying the direct method, the analyst defines a relevant range and discrete intervals for the parameters for constructing the PDF. For example, the analyst might define the relevant time duration for a project activity (test of a piece of equipment) to be between 0 and 27 days. The analyst then breaks down this relevant range into intervals, say of 4 days. The resulting formulation would be as follows:

0–3 days	16–19 days
4–7 days	20–23 days
8–11 days	24–27 days
12–15 days	

Given these intervals over the relevant range, the analyst then queries the expert to assign relative probabilities to each range. From this, the form of the PDF could be identified. It is imperative that the axioms of probability not be violated.

In addition to the application already described, the analyst could request that the expert provides a lowest possible value, a most likely value, and a highest possible value. The analyst then makes an assumption about the form of the density function. That is, is the PDF normal, uniform, triangular, or beta?

Betting

One method of phrasing questions to experts in order to obtain probabilities for ranges of values (cost and schedule) states the problem in terms of betting. A form of this method helps the expert (assessor) assess probabilities of events that are in accordance with his or her judgment (Winkler 1967). The assumption with this method is that the judgment of the expert may be fully represented by a probability distribution, $f(x)$, of a random variable, x. This method offers the expert a series of bets.

Under ideal circumstances, the bets are actual, not hypothetical. That is, in each case the winner of the bet is determined and the amount of money involved actually changes hands. (This is not feasible, however, because betting is illegal.) In each case, the expert must choose between two bets (the expert may not refrain from betting). The expert must choose between a bet with a fixed probability of winning *(q)* and of losing (1–*q*), and a bet dependent on whether some event (a particular project activity duration range or cost range) occurs *(E)*. The bet can be depicted as follows:

Bet 1a	• Win \$A if event E occurs.
	• Lose \$B if event E does not occur.
Bet 1b	• Win \$A with probability of q.
	• Lose \$B with probability of $1-q$.

The expected values of bets 1a and 1b to the expert are respectively $Ap + Bp = B$ and $Aq + Bq = B$, where p is the probability of the occurrence of event E. The following inferences may be drawn from the expert's decision: if bet 1a is chosen, $Ap + Bp - B \geq Aq + Bq - B$, so $p \geq q$; likewise, if 1b is selected, $p \leq q$.

By repeating the procedure, varying the value of q, the probability of event E can be ascertained. It is the point at which the expert is indifferent to both bets 1a and 1b that $p = q$. The degree of precision depends on the number of bets and the incremental changes of the value of q. To avoid the problem of a large number of bets to obtain p is to assess the probabilities by using direct interrogation and then using the betting situation as a check on the assumed probabilities.

To complete a PDF, the analyst repeats this procedure over a relevant range of interval values. The analyst then plots the points at the center of the range for each event and smooths in a curve so that the area under it equals 1, as in Figure D.2. The analyst must ensure that all relevant axioms of probability are maintained.

When questioned one way, many people are likely to make probability statements that are inconsistent with what they will say when

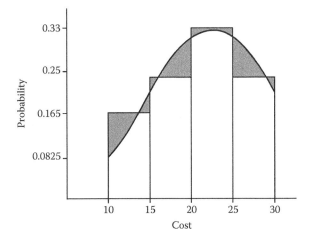

Figure D.2   Fitting a curve to expert judgment.

questioned in another equivalent way, especially when they are asked for direct assignment of probabilities. As the number of events increases, so does the difficulty of assigning direct probabilities. When this is a problem, the betting method is most appropriate.

To apply the betting technique, select one interval for the relevant range to demonstrate how this method can be used to obtain probability estimates and, hence, PDFs. The bet is established as follows:

Bet 1a	• Win $10,000 if cost is between $15,100 and $20,000.
	• Lose $5,000 if cost is not between $15,100 and $20,000.
Bet 1b	• Win $10,000 with probability of q.
	• Lose $5,000 with probability of $1-q$.

The value of q is established initially, and the expert is asked which of the two bets he or she would take.

The value of q is then varied systematically (either increased or decreased). The point at which the expert is indifferent between the two bets (with the associated q value) provides the probability of the cost being between $15,100 and $20,000. This process is repeated for each interval, and the results create the PDF associated with the cost of that particular project event.

Modified Churchman–Ackoff

Another way to ascertain PDFs for cost, schedule, or performance parameters is the modified Churchman–Ackoff method (Churchman–Ackoff 1951). This technique was developed as a way to order events in terms of likelihood. The technique was modified so that after the event likelihoods were ordered, relative probabilities could be assigned to the events and, finally, PDFs could be developed. For relevancy, events are defined as range values for cost, schedule, or performance (activity durations) relating to the outcome of a specific activity in a project.

The modified Churchman–Ackoff technique is most appropriate when there is one expert and that expert has a thorough understanding of the relative ranking of cost and schedule ranges and a limited understanding of probability concepts. The remainder of this section is extracted and modified from the *Compendium on Risk Analysis Techniques* (Atzinger 1972). Note that although the mathematical calculations appear to make this a precise technique, it is still an approximation of an expert's judgment and should not be interpreted to be more exact than other similar techniques.

The first step in applying the modified Churchman–Ackoff technique is to define the relevant range of values. That is, the end points along a range of values with 0 probability of occurrence must be specified. These values can be any low and high values the expert specifies as having 0 probability of occurrence. Next, ranges of individual values within the relevant range must be determined. These ranges of values, which will form the set of comparative values for this technique, are specified by the following approach:

Step 1 Start with the low value in the relevant range.

Step 2 Progress upward on the scale of values until the expert is able to state a simple preference regarding the relative probabilities of occurrence of the two characteristic values. If the expert is able to voice a belief that one value has either a greater or lesser chance of occurring than the other of the two values, then it is inferred that the expert is able to discriminate between the two values.

Step 3 Using the higher of the two previously specified scale values as a new basis, repeat Step 2 to determine the next value on the scale.

Step 4 Repeat Steps 2 and 3 until the high end-point value of the range of parameter values is approached.

Using this procedure for the duration required to test a piece of equipment successfully may yield the results shown in Table D.1.

Table D.1 Characteristic Values for Equipment Test Durations

VALUE	DURATION (DAYS)
O_1	0–3
O_2	4–7
O_3	8–11
O_4	12–15
O_5	16–19
O_6	20–23
O_7	24–27

The descending order of probability of occurrence can be determined by applying the following paired comparison method. Ask the expert to compare, one at a time, the first interval value (O_1) of the set to each of the other values $(O_2, O_3,$ and so on), stating a preference for that value in each group of two values that he or she believes has the greater chance of occurring (denoting a greater probability of occurrence by >, an equal chance by =, and a lesser chance by <). The following hypothetical preference relationships could result for a set of seven values: $O_1 < O_2, O_1 < O_3, O_1 < O_4, O_1 < O_5, O_1 < O_6, O_1 < O_7.$

Next, ask the expert to compare, one at a time, the second interval value (O_2) of the set to each of the other interval values succeeding it in the set (that is, $O_3, O_4,$ and so on). The following preference relationships might result: $O_2 < O_3, O_2 < O_4, O_2 < O_5, O_2 > O_6, O_2 > O_7.$ Continue this process until all values have been compared.

Now total the number of times a given value was preferred over other values. The results for this procedure are listed in Table D.2.

List the values in descending order of simple ordinal probability preference and change the symbols for each value from O_i to X_j as shown in Table D.3.

Arbitrarily assign a rating of 100 points to the characteristic value with the highest subjective probability (that is, X_1). Then, as in the first step, question the expert regarding the relative chance of occurrence of each of the other values on the ordinal scale in Table D.3 with respect to the value at the top of the scale. Assigning X_1 a rating of 100 points, the expert is first interrogated as to his or her feeling of the relative chance of occurrence of the second highest scale value (X_2), with respect to X_1. Does it have a 25, 60, 70, or 80 percent chance? Or even as much chance of realization as X_1 has?

Table D.2 Summary of Preference Relationships

VALUE	TIMES
O_4	6
O_3	5
O_5	4
O_2	3
O_6	2
O_1	0
O_7	0

Table D.3   Transformation

CHARACTERISTIC	VALUE (DAYS)	REFERENCE RANK	NEW SYMBOL
12–15	O_4	1	X_1
8–11	O_3	2	X_2
11–19	O_5	3	X_3
4–7	O_2	4	X_4
20–23	O_6	5	X_5
0–3	O_1	6	X_6
24–27	O_7	7	X_7

The relative probability rating, based on 100 points, then will be posted for X_2.

Next, question the expert about the relative chance of occurrence of the next highest scale (X_3), first with respect to the most preferred value (X_1) and then with respect to the second most preferred scale value (X_2). The resulting numerical ratings should occur. For example, if the expert decides that X_2 has 80 percent as much chance of occurring as does X_1, and that X_3 has 50 percent as much chance as X_1 and 62.5 percent as much chance as X_2, the ratings would be $X_1 = 100$ points, $X_2 = 80$ points, and $X_3 = 50$ points.

This process continues for each successively lower interval value on the ordinal scale as shown in Table D.3. Determine the relative number of points to be accorded each value with respect to the top scale and with respect to all other values down the scale that are above the characteristic value in question.

If there are minor disparities between relative probability ratings for a given value, then the average of all such ratings for that characteristic value might be computed. For example, X_4 might be determined to be 30 percent as probable as X_1, 25 percent as probable as X_2, and 50 percent as probable as X_3. The three absolute ratings for X_4 are thus inferred to be 30, 20, and 25 points, respectively. The average of these ratings is 25. However, before averaging such figures, it might be beneficial to have the expert reevaluate the relative ratings for X_4 with respect to X_1, X_2, and X_3.

As a result of this process, the relative probability values shown in Table D.4 might be attained.

Finally, the scale of relative probability values can be converted directly into a scale of actual probability density values by having

Table D.4 Relative Probability Ratings

VALUE	PROBABILITY POINTS
RX_1	100
RX_2	80
RX_3	50
RX_4	25
RX_5	10
RX_6	0
RX_7	0

$P(X_1)$ equal the actual subjective probability or occurrence of the highest value. Then $P(X_2)$ is defined as

$$\frac{RX_2}{RX_1}\left[P(X_1)\right]$$

Similarly, for $i = 2, 3, \ldots 7$, $P(X_i)$ is defined as

$$\frac{RX_i}{RX_1}[P(X_1)]$$

Assuming that the independent characteristic values evaluated represent all possible values attainable by the component characteristic, the respective probabilities must total 1 (that is, $P(X_1) + P(X_2) + P(X_3) + P(X_4) + P(X_5) + P(X_6) + P(X_7) = 1$). Substituting the expressions for $P(X_i)$, $i = 2, \ldots 7$, it follows that

$$P(X_1) + \frac{RX_2}{RX_1}[P(X_1)] + \frac{RX_3}{RX_1}[P(X_1)] + \frac{RX_4}{RX_1}[P(X_1)]$$
$$+ \frac{RX_5}{RX_1}[P(X_1)] + \frac{RX_6}{RX_1}[P(X_1)] + \frac{RX_7}{RX_1}[P(X_1)] = 1$$

Solving this equation for $P(X_1)$, the remaining $P(X_i)$, $i = 2, \ldots 7$ can be determined using the relationship

$$P(X_1) + \frac{RX_i}{RX_1}[P(X_1)]$$

As an illustration, consider the relative probability ratings in Table D.4. Using the values, the preceding equation is given by

Table D.5 Probability Density

COMPONENT CHARACTERISTIC VALUE	PROBABILITY
X_1	0.377
X_2	0.301
X_3	0.189
X_4	0.095
X_5	0.038
X_6	0.000
X_7	0.000
Total	1.000

$$P(X_1) + \frac{80}{100}P(X_1) + \frac{50}{100}P(X_1)$$
$$+ \frac{25}{100}P(X_1) + \frac{10}{100}P(X_1) = 1$$

Solving this equation, $P(X_1) = 0.377$.

This value can be used to determine the remaining probabilities as follows:

$$P(X_2) = \frac{RX_2}{RX_1}P(X_1) = 0.80(0.377) = 0.301$$

$$P(X_3) = \frac{RX_3}{RX_1}P(X_1) = 0.50(0.377) = 0.189$$

$$P(X_4) = \frac{RX_4}{RX_1}P(X_1) = 0.25(0.377) = 0.095$$

$$P(X_5) = \frac{RX_5}{RX_1}P(X_1) = 0.10(0.377) = 0.038$$

$$P(X_6) = \frac{RX_6}{RX_1}P(X_1) = 0(0.377) = 0$$

$$P(X_7) = \frac{RX_7}{RX_1}P(X_1) = 0(0.377) = 0$$

The resulting probability density appears in Table D.5.

Sources of Additional Information

Atzinger, E.M. *Compendium on Risk Analysis Techniques.* AD 746245, LD 28463. Aberdeen Proving Ground, Md.: DARCOM Material Systems Analysis Activity, 1972.

Brown, R.V., A.S.S. Kahr, and C. Peterson. *Decision Analysis for the Manager.* New York: Holt, Rinehart & Winston, 1974.

Churchman, C.W., and R.L. Ackoff. Methods of inquiry: An introduction to philosophy and scientific method. *Philosophy and Phenomenological Research* 12;1951:149–150.

DeGroot, M.H. *Optimal Statistical Decisions.* New York: McGraw-Hill, 1970.

Singleton, W.T., and J. Hovden. *Risk and Decision.* New York: John Wiley & Sons Ltd., 1987.

Winkler, R.L. Probabilistic prediction: Some experimental results. *Journal of the American Statistical Association* 66;1971:675–685.

Winkler, R.L. The quantification of judgment: Some methodological suggestions. *Journal of the American Statistical Association* 62;1967:1105–1120.

Appendix E: Special Notes on Software Risk

Although the techniques and processes discussed in *Risk Management: Concepts and Guidance* apply to software, they do not address some of the peculiarities that are a part of software development. Software has a tendency to change dramatically during the development cycle when compared with hardware. This appendix suggests some useful actions in managing software development efforts.

One of the most effective risk management (handling) techniques for software is establishing a formal software quality assurance program early in the development cycle. The program should establish a team of experts whose charter is to look at issues that will ensure a reliable product in a reasonable time and at a reasonable cost. Some of the questions the team must answer include the following:

Is independent verification and validation warranted?
Is the development environment (tool sets, compiler) adequate?
Is the higher-order language selection appropriate?
Are the requirements clearly stated?
Will rapid prototyping be used?
Will Agile development be applied?
Has the software approach been baselined?

Has the testing philosophy been established?
Has the development philosophy been established?

Addressing these issues early in the development cycle will help avoid surprises. The basic process for risk management—plan, assess, analyze, and handle—still applies to software. Tables E.1 to E.5, which are extracts from government pamphlets (AFSC 1985, 1987), may prove useful in quantifying software risk.

Table E.1 Quantification of Probability and Impact of Technical Drivers

	MAGNITUDE		
TECHNICAL DRIVERS	LOW (0.0–0.3)	MEDIUM (0.4–0.5)	HIGH (0.6–1.0)
REQUIREMENTS			
Complexity	Simple or easily allocatable	Moderate, can be allocated	Significant or difficult to allocate
Size	Small or easily broken down into work units	Medium or can be broken down into work units	Large or cannot be broken down into work loads
Stability	Little or no change to established baseline	Some change in baseline expected	Rapidly changing or no baseline
Reliability and maintainability	Allocatable to hardware and software components	Requirements can be defined	Can be addressed only at the total system level
CONSTRAINTS			
Computer resources	Mature, growth capacity within design, flexible	Available, some growth capacity	New development, no growth capacity, inflexible
Personnel	Available, in place, experienced, stable	Available, but not in place, some experience	High turnover, little or no experience, not available
Standards	Appropriately tailored for application	Some tailoring, all not reviewed for applicability	No tailoring, none applied to the contract
Buyer-furnished equipment and property	Meets requirements, available	May meet requirements, uncertain availability	Not compatible with system requirements, unavailable
Environment	Little or no effect on design	Some effect on design	Major effect on design

continued

Table E.1 (continued) Quantification of Probability and Impact of Technical Drivers

	MAGNITUDE		
	LOW (0.0–0.3)	MEDIUM (0.4–0.5)	HIGH (0.6–1.0)
TECHNICAL DRIVERS			
TECHNOLOGY			
Language	Mature, approved high-order language used	Approved or nonapproved high-order language	Significant use of assembly language
Hardware	Mature, available	Some development or available	Total new development
Tools	Documented, validated, in place	Available, validated, some development	Unvalidated, proprietary, major development
Data rights	Fully compatible with support and follow-on	Minor incompatibilities support and follow-on	Incompatible with support and follow-on
Experience	Greater than 3 to 5 years	Less than 3 to 5 years	Little or none
DEVELOPMENTAL APPROACH			
Prototypes and reuse	Used, documented sufficiently for use	Some use and documentation	No use and/or no documentation
Documentation	Correct and available	Some deficiencies, available	Nonexistent
Environment	In place, validated, experience with use	Minor modifications, tools available	Major development effort
Management approach	Existing product and process controls	Product and process controls need enhancement	Weak or nonexistent
Integration	Internal and external controls in place	Internal or external controls not in place	Weak or nonexistent
Impact	Minimal-to-small reduction in technical performance	Some reduction in technical performance	Significant degradation to non-achievement of technical performance

Table E.2 Quantification of Probability and Impact of Operational Drivers

OPERATIONAL DRIVERS	LOW (0.0–0.3)	MAGNITUDE MEDIUM (0.4–0.5)	HIGH (0.6–1.0)
USER PERSPECTIVE			
Requirements	Compatible with user environment	Some incompatibilities	Major incompatibilities with operations concepts
Stability	Little or no change	Some controlled change	Uncontrolled change
Test environment	Representative of the user environment	Some aspects are not representative	Major disconnects with user environment
Test results	Test errors/failures are correctable	Some errors/failures are not correctable before implementation	Major corrections necessary
Quantification	Primarily objective	Some subjectivity	Primarily subjective
TECHNICAL PERFORMANCE			
Usability	User friendly	Mildly unfriendly	User unfriendly
Reliability	Predictable performance	Some aspects unpredictable	Unpredictable
Flexibility	Adaptable with threat	Some aspects not adaptable	Critical functions not adaptable
Supportability	Timely incorporation	Response times inconsistent with need	Unresponsive
Integrity	Responsive to update	Hidden linkages, controlled access	Insecure
PERFORMANCE ENVELOPE			
Adequacy	Full compatibility	Some limitations	Inadequate
Expandability	Easily expanded	Can be expanded	No expansion
Enhancements	Timely incorporation	Some lag	Major delays
Threat	Responsive to change	Cannot respond to some changes	Unresponsive
Impact	Full mission capability	Some limitations on mission performance	Severe performance limitations

Table E.3 Quantification of Probability and Impact of Support Drivers

SUPPORT DRIVERS	LOW (0.0–0.3)	MAGNITUDE MEDIUM (0.4–0.5)	HIGH (0.6–1.0)
DESIGN			
Complexity	Structurally maintainable	Certain aspects difficult	Extremely difficult to maintain
Documentation	Adequate	Some deficiencies	Inadequate
Completeness	Few additional support requirements	Some support requirements	Extensive support requirements
Configuration management	Sufficient, in place	Some shortfalls	Insufficient
Stability	Little or no change	Moderate, controlled change	Rapid or uncontrolled change
RESPONSIBILITIES			
Management	Defined, assigned responsibilities	Some roles and mission issues	Undefined or unassigned
Configuration management	Single-point control	Defined control points	Multiple control points
Technical management	Consistent with operational needs	Some inconsistencies	Major inconsistencies
Change implementation	Responsive to user needs	Acceptable delays	Nonresponsive to user needs

TOOLS AND MANAGEMENT

Facilities	In place, little change	In place, some modification	Nonexistent or extensive change
Software tools	Delivered, certified, sufficient	Some resolvable concerns	Not delivered, certified, or sufficient
Computer hardware	Compatible with operations system	Minor incompatibilities	Major incompatibilities
Production	Sufficient for distributed units	Some capacity questions	Insufficient
Distribution	Controlled, responsive	Minor response concerns	Uncontrolled or nonresponsive

SUPPORTABILITY

Changes	Within projections	Slight deviations	Major deviations
Operational interfaces	Defined, controlled	Some hidden linkages	Extensive linkages
Personnel	In place, sufficient experience	Minor discipline mixed concerns	Significant concerns
Release cycle	Responsive to user requirements	Minor incompatibilities	Nonresponsive to user needs
Procedures	In place, adequate	Some concerns	Nonexistent or inadequate
Impact	Responsive software support	Minor delays in software modifications	Nonresponsive or unsupportable software

Table E.4 Quantification of Probability and Impact of Cost Drivers

COST DRIVERS	MAGNITUDE		
	LOW (0.0–0.3)	MEDIUM (0.4–0.5)	HIGH (0.6–1.0)
REQUIREMENTS			
Size	Small, noncomplex, or easily broken down	Medium, moderate complexity, can be broken down	Large, highly complex, or cannot be broken down
Resource constraints	Little or no hardware-imposed constraints	Some hardware-imposed constraints	Significant hardware-imposed constraints
Application	Non-real-time, little system interdependency	Embedded, some system interdependency	Real-time, embedded, strong interdependency
Technology	Mature, existent, in-house experience	Existent, some in-house experience	New or new application, little experience
Requirements stability	Little or no change to established baseline	Some change in baseline expected	Rapidly changing or no baseline
PERSONNEL			
Availability	In place, little turnover expected	Available, some turnover expected	High turnover, not available
Mix	Good mix of software disciplines	Some disciplines inappropriately represented	Some disciplines not represented
Experience	High experience ratio	Average experience ratio	Low experience ratio
Management engineering	Strong management approach	Good personnel management approach	Weak personnel management approach

REUSABLE SOFTWARE			
Availability	Compatible with need dates	Delivery dates in question	Incompatible with need dates
Modifications	Little or no change	Some changes	Extensive changes
Language	Compatible with system requirements	Partial compatibility with requirements	Incompatible with system requirements
Rights	Compatible with competition requirements	Partial compatibility some competition	Incompatible with concept, non-competitive
Certification	Verified performance, application compatible	Some application-compatible, some competition	Unverified, little test data available
TOOLS AND ENVIRONMENT			
Facilities	Existent, little or no modification	Existent, some modification	Nonexistent, extensive changes
Availability	In place, meets need dates	Some compatibility with need dates	Nonexistent, does not meet need dates
Rights	Compatible with development plans	Partial compatibility with development plans	Incompatible with development plans
Configuration management	Fully controlled	Some controls	No controls
Impact	Sufficient financial resources	Some shortage of financial resources, possible overrun	Significant financial shortages, budget overrun likely

Table E.5 Quantification of Probability and Impact of Schedule Drivers

SCHEDULE DRIVERS	MAGNITUDE		
	LOW (0.0–0.3)	MEDIUM (0.4–0.5)	HIGH (0.6–1.0)
RESOURCES			
Personnel	Good discipline mix in place	Some disciplines not available	Questionable mix and/or availability
Facilities	Existent, little or no modification	Existent, some modification	Nonexistent, extensive changes
Financial	Sufficient budget allocated	Some questionable allocations	Budget allocation in doubt
NEED DATES			
Threat	Verified projections	Some unstable aspects	Rapidly changing
Economic	Stable commitments	Some uncertain commitments	Unstable, fluctuating commitments
Political	Little projected sensitivity	Some limited sensitivity	Extreme sensitivity
Buyer-furnished equipment and property	Available, certified	Certification or delivery questions	No application evidence
Tools	In place, available	Some deliveries in question	Little or none
TECHNOLOGY			
Availability	In place	Baselined, some unknowns	Unknown, no baseline
Maturity	Application verified	Controllable change projected	Rapid or uncontrolled change
Experience	Extensive application	Some dependency on new technology	Incompatible with existing technology
REQUIREMENTS			
Definition	Known, baselined	Baselined, some unknowns	Unknown, no baseline
Stability	Little or no change projected	Controllable change projected	Rapid or uncontrollable change
Complexity	Compatible with existing technology	Some dependency on new technology	Incompatible with existing technology
Impact	Realistic achievable schedule	Possible slippage in implementation	Unachievable Implementation

Index